CiTY·SMaRT™
GUIDEBOOK

Austin

by Eleanor S. Morris,
Paris Permenter,
and John Bigley

John Muir Publications
Santa Fe, New Mexico

Acknowledgments
Many thanks to Gwen Spain, director of public relations/advertising, and the entire staff of the Austin Convention and Visitors Bureau for their assistance.

ABOUT THE AUTHOR
Eleanor S. Morris is a freelance travel journalist and photographer based in Austin. She has been widely published in national newspapers and magazines and is the author of *Recommended Country Inns of the Southwest* (Globe Pequot Press), *Country Roads of Texas*, *Country Towns of Texas*, and *Texas Fairs and Festivals* (Country Roads Press) among others. She is a member of ASJA (American Society of Journalists and Authors) and SATW (Society of American Travel Writers).

Paris Permenter and John Bigley are a husband-wife team of freelance travel writers and photographers based in Austin. Widely published in magazines and newspapers, the pair have authored numerous guidebooks including *Caribbean for Lovers* (Prima Publishing), *Texas Getaways for Two* (Two Lane Press), *Day Trips from San Antonio and Austin* (Globe Pequot Press), *Gourmet Getaways* (Callawind Publications), and *Texas Barbecue* (Two Lane Press), named Best Regional Book by Mid-America Publishers Association. Both Paris and John are members of the American Society of Journalists and Authors and the Society of American Travel Writers.

John Muir Publications, P. O. Box 613, Santa Fe, New Mexico 87504

Copyright © 1997 by John Muir Publications
Cover and maps © 1997 by John Muir Publications
All rights reserved.

Printed in the United States of America.
First edition. First printing August 1997.

ISBN 1-56261-365-0
ISSN 1093-3220

Editors: Dianna Delling, Marybeth Griffin, Krista Lyons-Gould
Graphics Editor: Tom Gaukel
Production: Marie J. T. Vigil, Nikki Rooker
Design: Janine Lehmann
Cover Design: Suzanne Rush
Typesetter: Kathleen Sparkes, White Hart Designs, Albuquerque, NM USA
Map Production: Julie Felton
Printer: Publishers Press
Front Cover Photo: © 1993 Robert Baumgardner
Large Back Cover Photo: © Jean Higgins/Unicorn Stock Photos
Small Back Cover Photo: Austin Convention and Visitors Bureau

Distributed to the book trade by
Publishers Group West
Emeryville, California

While every effort has been made to provide accurate, up-to-date information, the author and publisher accept no responsibility for loss, injury, or inconvenience sustained by any person using this book.

CONTENTS

How to Use This Book

1 Welcome to Austin   1
City History 2 • Austin Timeline 4 • The People of Austin 6 • Business and Economy 7 • Homes 8 • Schools 8 • Taxes 9 • Calendar of Events 10 • Austin Weather 11 • Cost of Living 13 • Dressing in the City 13

2 Getting Around Austin   15
City Layout 15 • Public Transportation 17 • Driving in Austin 20 • Biking in Austin 21 • Airports 22 • Train Services 25 • Bus Services 25

3 Where to Stay   26
Downtown Austin 27 • North Austin 31 • Northwest Austin 38 • Southwest Austin 41 • South Austin 41 • East Austin 47

4 Where to Eat   50
Downtown Austin 52 • North Austin 61 • Northwest Austin 64 • Southwest Austin 69 • South Austin 70 • East Austin 74

5 Sights and Attractions, Public Art, and City Tours   77
Sights and Attractions 77 • Public Art 95 • City Tours 99

6 Kids' Stuff   100
Animals and the Great Outdoors 100 • Museums 105 • Puppets and Theater 110 • Libraries 111 • Stores Kids Love 112 • Fun and Games 114

7 Museums and Galleries   116
Art Museums 116 • Science and History Museums 120 • Galleries 124

8 Parks, Gardens, and Recreation Areas   129
Parks and Recreation Areas 129 • Greenbelts 136 • Gardens 139

9 Shopping   141
Shopping Districts 141 • Other Notable Stores 151 • Major Department Stores 152 • Major Shopping Malls 153 • Factory Outlet Centers 154

10 Sports and Recreation   155
Biking 155 • Boating 156 • Bowling 158 • Camping/Backpacking 159 • Canoeing 159 • Day Hikes 159 • Disc Golf 161 • Fishing 161 • Fitness Clubs 163 • Golf 163 • Horseback Riding 165 • Jogging 166 • Rock Climbing 166 • Sailing 166 • Scuba Diving 167 • Skating–Ice 167 • Skating–Roller and In-line 167 • Skiing/Jet Skiing 168 • Swimming 168 • Tennis 169 • Professional Sports 169 • University Sports 170

11 The Performing Arts — 171
Theater 171 • Classical Music and Opera 176 • Dance 179 • Concert Venues 180 • Buying Tickets 182

12 Nightlife — 183
Dance Clubs 185 • Music Clubs 185 • Pubs and Bars 195 • Comedy Clubs 197 • Concert Venues 197 • Movie Houses of Note 198

13 Day Trips from Austin — 199
Fredericksburg 199 • LBJ Ranch 201 • Longhorn State Cavern 202 • Lost Pines of Texas 203 • New Braunfels 204

Appendix: City-Smart Basics — 206
Important Phone Numbers 206 • Hospitals 206 • Visitor Information 206 • City Tours 206 • Car Rental 206 • Babysitting/Daycare 206 • Disabled Access Information 207 • Multicultural Resources 207 • Booksellers 207

Index — 208

MAP CONTENTS

Austin Zones vi

2 Getting Around Austin
- The 'Dillo Bus 18
- Robert Mueller Airport Map 23

3 Where to Stay
- Downtown Austin 28
- North Austin 33
- Northwest Austin 40
- Southwest Austin 42
- South Austin 44
- East Austin 48

4 Where to Eat
- Downtown Austin 53
- North Austin 60
- Northwest Austin 65
- Southwest Austin 68
- South Austin 71
- East Austin 75

5 Sights and Attractions
- Downtown Austin 79
- North Austin 84
- Northwest Austin 87
- Southwest Austin 89
- South Austin 91
- East Austin 94

6 Kids' Stuff
- Downtown Austin 101
- North Austin 104
- Northwest Austin 106
- Southwest Austin 109
- South Austin 113

7 Museums and Galleries
- Downtown Austin 118
- North Austin 122
- Greater Austin 125

8 Parks, Gardens, and Recreation Areas
- Southwest Austin 131
- South Austin 134
- Greater Austin 137

9 Shopping
- North Austin 143
- Greater Austin 149

10 Sports and Recreation
- Greater Austin 157

11 The Performing Arts
- Greater Austin 173

12 Nightlife
- Downtown Austin 184
- North Austin 188
- South Austin 191
- Greater Austin 194

13 Day Trips from Austin
- Day Trips 200

HOW TO USE THIS BOOK

Whether you're a visitor, a new resident, or an Austin native, you'll find *City-Smart Guidebook: Austin* indispensable. Authors Eleanor S. Morris, Paris Permenter, and John Bigley bring you an insider's view of the best Austin has to offer.

This book presents the city in six geographic zones. The zone divisions are listed at the bottom of this page and are shown on the map on the following page. Look for a zone designation in each listing and use it to help you locate the listing on one of the zone-specific maps included in each chapter.

Example:

GOVERNOR'S MANSION
1010 Colorado St., Austin
512/463-5516   DA

Zone Abbreviation = DA
The location of the Governor's Mansion will be shown on the Downtown Austin map unless otherwise noted.

Austin Zones

DA—Downtown Austin
The area bounded by Martin Luther King Jr. Boulevard on the north, Mo-Pac Boulevard on the west, Town Lake on the south, and I-35 on the east. Includes the state capitol area.

NA—North Austin
The area north of downtown, between I-35 and Mo-Pac Boulevard. Includes the University of Austin–Texas campus.

NWA—Northwest Austin
The area northwest of downtown, bounded by the Colorado River on the south and Mo-Pac Boulevard on the east.

SWA—Southwest Austin
The area southwest of downtown, bounded by Mo-Pac Boulevard on the east and the Colorado River on the north.

SA—South Austin
The area south of Town Lake, bounded by I-35 on the east and Mo-Pac Boulevard on the west.

EA—East Austin
The area east of I-35, including the Robert Mueller Municipal Airport.

GREATER AUSTIN ZONES

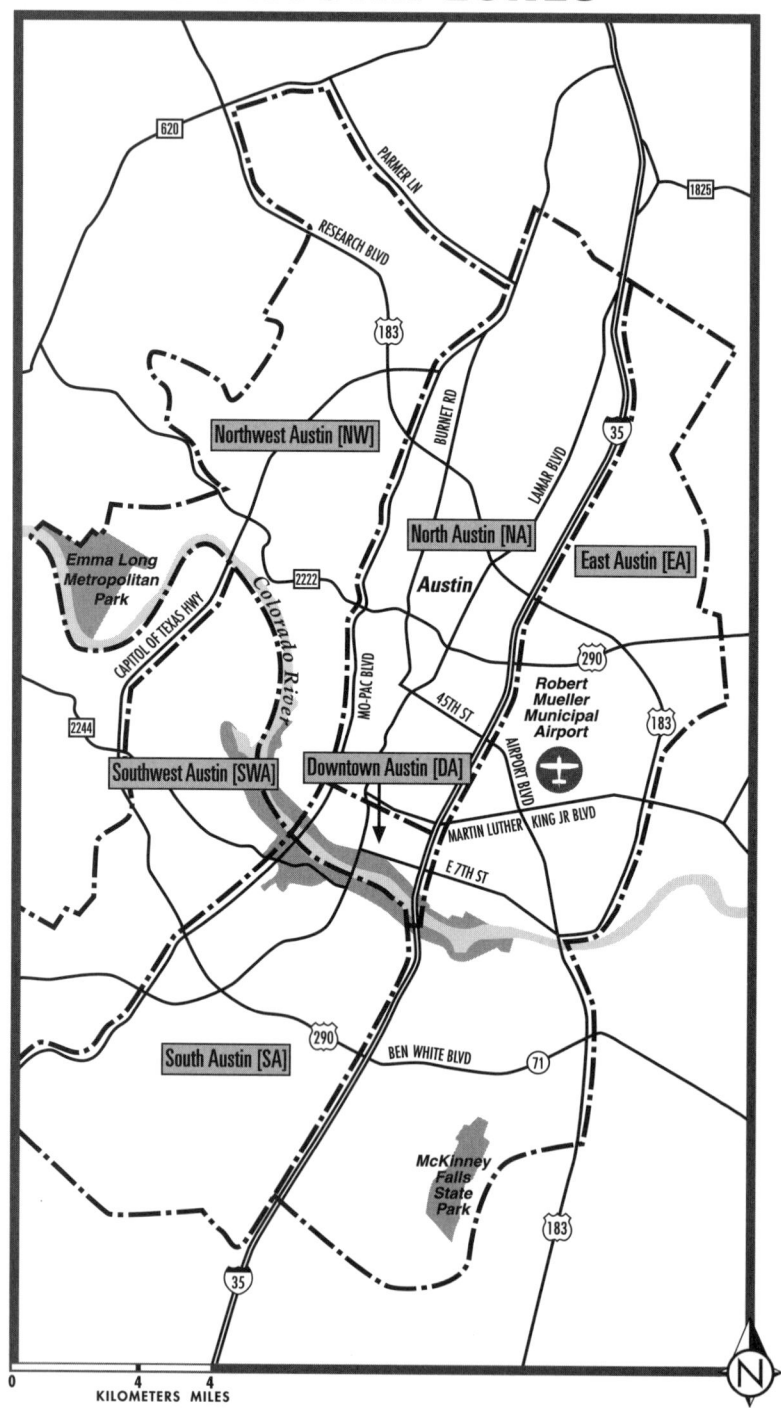

1
WELCOME TO AUSTIN

Austin is a multilayered, multifaceted city, and its residents enjoy a high quality of life that combines both progress and an appreciation for relaxed living. These are the values admired by Austin's visitors and so fiercely protected by the folks who live here. An open-minded, down-home kind of place that not only tolerates, but likes, respects, and welcomes people who are different, Austin is a city where folks consider greeting strangers in passing as just plain good manners.

High hills and wide horizons may explain Austin's openness to difference, or maybe it's the city's highly educated residents who promote and respect cultural diversity. Whatever the reason, Austin is a magnet for creative souls and a community everyone loves to love. The capital of Texas and the seat of Travis County, Austin has an estimated population of 548,000 inhabitants within the city and 1.3 million in the metropolitan area. The population grew by nearly 30 percent between 1980 and 1990.

Austin is a beautiful lake city with wooded hills, broad streets, and period architecture, but it's also a bustling metropolis and high tech haven. The city is known both nationally and internationally for its top-notch research and development in the rapidly expanding microelectronics industry. High tech whiz kids barely out of college come to Austin to begin Fortune 500 computer and computer game companies.

Austin is also a city with a rich intellectual climate. In the midst of town there is a major research university, The University of Texas, as well as three other universities. One of them, Huston-Tillotson College, is the oldest African American university in the nation. Per capita Austin has one of the most educated populations in the country.

Sixth highest in the nation for its large number of artists and musicians, Austin is a place where hopefuls follow legends like Willie Nelson, who put Austin on the map as a major music venue when he moved here in 1970. Here they might get a start in one of the 100 live-music clubs featuring local, national, and international talent every night. This artistically inclined city also offers symphony, opera, theater, museums, galleries, and exotic street markets.

City History

Austin is the capital of Texas, but it didn't begin as such, and it didn't capture the title without a struggle. Originally it was a small village called Waterloo, settled by Jacob Harrell in 1835 along the mouths of Waller, Shoal, and Barton Creeks, which drained into the Colorado River. Several other settlers joined Harrell, building log cabins and erecting a stockade for protection against Indians. The Republic of Texas declared its independence from Mexico in 1836. When Mirabeau B. Lamar, vice president of the Republic, came to Waterloo on a buffalo hunt, he was so impressed with the beauty of the area that he decided to make it the Republic's capital. Without delay, he renamed the city Austin, after Texas colonizer Stephen F. Austin.

After hastily renaming the city, Lamar had to battle for several years with Sam Houston, president of the Republic, who insisted that the capital be either Houston (the city named for himself) or the original site of Washington-on-the-Brazos to the east. Houston got his way until 1844, when new president Anson Jones changed the capital back to Austin. When Texas joined the United States a year later, Austin managed to

---

O. Henry

The humorist O.Henry (writer William Sydney Porter) was one of Austin's earliest famous citizens. According to O. Henry, the unlikely group of Stephen F. Austin, Daniel Boone, Davy Crockett, and Ponce de Leon, while navigating the Colorado River by canal boat, stopped at the foot of what is now Congress Avenue, and here's what happened:

"Suddenly an idea struck Stephen F. Austin. He was too generous a man to conceal it:

"'Boys, let's start a town site here and call it Austin.'

"'Just as you say,' they replied, and they laid out Austin. It has been laid out ever since."

Town Lake Trail and the Austin skyline

remain as the capital. The issue was permanently settled when it passed two statewide voter referendums, one in 1850 and another in 1852.

During the years of the Republic, various diplomats lived in the city, and today the old French Legation is still maintained as a historic site. The governor's mansion, built in 1853, is adjacent to the capitol's large grounds and is a showplace of southern colonial architecture.

Austin flourished from the beginning, growing from 856 citizens in 1840 (when the first capitol was a one-story frame building that had to be protected from Indians by an 8-foot stockade) to 3,494 citizens in 1860. Large-scale growth began with the arrival of the railroad in 1871. A new capitol, built in 1853, was gutted by fire and the present building was built in 1888.

In 1938 the Lower Colorado River Authority began constructing a series of dams along the Texas length of the Colorado River, forming the beautiful chain of Highland Lakes and giving Austin two refreshing bodies of water, Town Lake and Lake Austin. Town Lake flows west to east through the city, dividing it into north and south sections. A leafy hike and bike trail lines both banks of the river within walking distance of downtown's tall office buildings. Lake Austin is on the west side of town, and both lakes provide cool green oases for outdoor recreational pleasures.

The business district, lying on both sides of the river, is bisected by Congress Avenue, which runs from south of the river to the north, ending at the spacious lawns and wide avenues of the capitol complex. The pink granite structure, constructed of fossilized native stone from Hill Country quarries, boasts a dome 7 feet higher than that of the United States Capitol in Washington, D.C. Beyond the capitol rises the 27-story bell tower of the University of Texas, founded in 1881. The university is

Austin Timeline

1835	Jacob Harrell settles along Waller, Shoal, and Barton Creeks and calls the settlement Waterloo.
1838	Mirabeau B. Lamar, Vice President of the Republic of Texas, comes to Waterloo to hunt buffalo.
1839	France recognizes the Republic and sends Alphonse DuBois de Saligny to Austin as chargé d'affaires.
1839–44	Lamar struggles with President Sam Houston to establish Austin as the capital of the Republic.
1841	French Legation is built.
1844	New president Anson Jones declares Austin the capital of the Republic.
1845	The Republic of Texas joins the United States of America; Austin remains as capital of the new state of Texas.
1850	A voter referendum ensures Austin's status as state capital.
1851	Texas State Cemetery is founded.
1852	A second referendum ensures Austin's status as state capital.
1857	General land office is built (Austin's oldest surviving office building).
1860	Population has grown from 856 to 3,494 citizens.
1861	City residents vote against secession from the Union.
1869	First Congress Avenue Bridge, a pontoon bridge, is built.
1871	The railroads arrive.
1873	First library is founded.
1875	Second Congress Avenue Bridge is completed.
1876	Huston-Tillotson College, a black institution, is founded.
1880	Austin citizens vote to establish a public school system.
1881	The University of Texas is founded.
1883	Construction is begun on present capitol building.
1885	St. Edward's University is founded.
1886	The Driskill Hotel is built.
1888	The Capitol opens for business.

St. Edward's University is built.	1889
Elisabet Ney, Texas' first eminent sculptor, builds her Hyde Park studio.	1892
Colorado River is dammed to generate electricity for street cars and Moonlight Towers.	1893
O. Henry (Sidney Porter) publishes humorous weekly *The Rolling Stone*.	1894
City streets are paved with brick—Congress Avenue is the first.	1905
Present Congress Avenue Bridge is completed.	1910
The Paramount Theater is constructed.	1915
Austin's first airport is constructed on the south side of the city.	1918
City charter is written.	1924
Construction of seven dams along the Colorado River creates, among others, Town Lake.	1930
Year of the Great Flood.	1935
Tom Miller Dam is completed.	1940
Emma Long is the first woman elected to the City Council.	1948
Austin's first television station, Lyndon and Lady Bird Johnson's KTBC-TV, takes to the air.	1952
High tech and real estate boom begins.	1960
Charles Whitman opens fire from the University of Texas' bell tower, killing 14 people and wounding 31.	1966
Tracor Electronics Company arrives in Austin.	1967
Willie Nelson moves from Nashville to initiate the Austin music scene.	1970
Willie Nelson's first Fourth of July picnic, now an Austin tradition, attracts more than 40,000 people.	1973
Treaty Oak is poisoned.	1989
The Austin Convention Center, a $69.4-million building, is dedicated.	1992
Capitol is rededicated after a six-year, $187-million restoration and expansion.	1995

the home of the Lyndon B. Johnson Library, the largest presidential library in the country. The enormous main campus is located just north of downtown, making Austin a noted educational center.

The People of Austin

Austin's population is as diverse as its history. Having flown under six different flags, the Lone Star State boasts residents with ethnic backgrounds ranging from Mexican to German to Alsatian. In fact, the Institute of Texan Cultures in San Antonio considers Texas to have more than 30 ethnic groups, many of which are represented in the city of Austin.

The influence of Texas' southern neighbor is strongly felt in Austin, where many citizens trace their ancestry to Hispanic roots. It's not uncommon to hear Spanish spoken anywhere in the city. The city celebrates Mexican holidays such as Cinco de Mayo, the May 5th victory over French troops by the small Mexican army, with as much exuberance as it bestows upon other festive days.

It's also not uncommon to see members of Austin's diverse population side by side throughout the city. For example, you might see a three-piece-suited lobbyist next to a person who's obviously a frequent visitor to one of the city's many tattoo and body-piercing parlors. All of Austin's population comes together at the many coffeehouses, Tex-Mex restaurants, and local bars, to partake of the food, music, and fun.

A sense of good-naturedness permeates Austin, from its nightlife to its festivals to its outdoor recreation. Maybe it's the college population, which tops 50,000 students. Maybe it's the live music industry, which has made this city a haven for fans and performers alike. Or maybe it's just the geography: Austin is situated on a downtown lake and perched at the edge of a rambling Hill Country lake that offers everything from windsurfing to nude sunbathing.

Sure, the city is home to both high-tech industry and countless state officials, but residents will use any excuse to toss off the ties and formal attire. They don elaborate costumes for an annual party in Pease Park to celebrate, believe it or not, the birthday of Eeyore, pal of Winnie the Pooh. And those costumes are just a dress rehearsal for the Halloween party that takes place on 6th Street, attracting as many as 70,000 merrymakers.

At night, the clubs are the place to be. But during the daylight hours

TRIVIA

Texas' own statue of liberty, the Goddess of Liberty—$1^1/_2$ tons of zinc and iron—stood atop the capitol dome from 1888 to 1985. She was eventually removed because of damage from exposure to the elements, and in 1986 was replaced by an aluminum replica.

 For more business information, check out the Business Information Center (BIC) at the Central Library at 800 Guadalupe. The collection includes business newspapers and journals, business directories, city guides, economic trends and forecasting, on-line database searching, and statistics.

Austin shows off her beauty at places like the shores of Town Lake, the clear waters of Barton Springs swimming hole, or the manicured lawn of the capitol. Regardless of political interest, many Austinites who work downtown like to sneak off to the capitol grounds for a picnic lunch. Sitting out on the rolling lawn under tall oaks, feeding squirrels, and watching the flurry of legislative comings and goings provides one of the best shows in town.

In the late afternoon hours, locals grab their sneakers and head to Zilker Park or Town Lake's shores for a jog or just a leisurely walk. When the sun sets on summer days, attention turns to Congress Avenue Bridge, location of the country's largest urban colony of Mexican free-tailed bats. The bats make their nightly exodus after sunset to feed on insects in the Hill Country and the Austin area.

Business and Economy

Austin's diverse economy revolves around state government, research, development, and high technology. Over 300 of its 800 manufacturers are considered high tech, thanks in a large part to a booming microchip industry. Sixty-five percent of the manufacturing work force is employed by high-tech industry, with a large number of workers employed by service-based high-tech businesses such as those engaged in computer programming and software design.

Littlefield Fountain on the University of Texas Campus

Many high-tech companies have relocated to Austin from Silicon Valley in search of a lower cost of living. South Korea's Samsung Electronics is moving to Austin; it will be the manufacturer's first installation outside of South Korea. Other semiconductor giants in Austin include Motorola and Advanced Micro Devices, both of which recently completed billion-dollar chip factories. The high-tech sector in Austin also includes IBM, with over 1,600 employees, and Dell

WELCOME TO AUSTIN

TRIVIA

Sixty percent of Austin's population uses computers, making it the most computer literate city in the nation.

The high-tech industry has been responsible for focusing a great deal of national attention on Austin. In 1995 Austin ranked 7th in Fortune magazine's "Best Cities for Business" list. It was the smallest city on the list.

Computer, a leader in the field of personal computers, employing over 5,000 workers.

Outside the high-tech field, the Texas Employment Commission reports that nearly 135,000 employees work for the government (the leading employer) and 131,000 persons are employed in service industries. Other top employers include financial institutions and insurance companies, construction businesses, and transportation services.

Austin's 1995 per capita income was $19,737—a growth of 4.5 percent over the previous year.

Homes

Austin's booming economy has resulted in a tight real estate market. Higher home prices, higher rent prices, and a shortage of low-cost housing have taken some of the gleam off Austin's real estate appeal, although relocators, especially from the West Coast, find that prices are still favorable.

In 1995, the average price of a new home was $150,000, compared with $115,000 for an existing home. The median price of an existing home was $92,000.

Rental prices vary by neighborhood, but the average price of a two-bedroom, one bath apartment is $650 per month.

Schools

Austin is often touted as the most highly educated community in the United States among cities with a population of more than 250,000. More than

TRIVIA

Austin (Austin's Congress Avenue Bridge, to be exact) is home to the largest urban colony of Mexican free-tailed bats in the United States.

35 percent of the adults boast 16 or more years of education; nearly half completed high school and/or some college. One in nine adults is currently enrolled in an Austin-area college or university.

Much of that education stems from the University of Texas at Austin, which enrolls over 48,000 students. The third largest state learning institution in the nation, the University of Texas at Austin, or U.T. as it's more commonly known, includes top programs in liberal arts, engineering, business, and natural sciences. The campus includes the sixth-largest academic library in the country.

Other higher education campuses include Austin Community College, St. Edward's University, Huston-Tillotson College, and Concordia Lutheran College.

There are more than 15 school districts in the Austin area, although most of the city is covered by the Austin Independent School District with nearly 100 campuses and over 73,000 students. District offices are located at the Carruth Administration Center, 1111 West Sixth Street, Austin, TX 78703-5399 (512/414-1700). On the western edge of the city, Eanes Independent School District in Westlake Hills operates four elementary schools, two middle schools, and one high school. For information, write S. Don Rogers Administration Building, 601 Camp Craft Road, Austin, TX 78746-6511, or call 512/329-3600. Enrollment at Eanes is just under 7,000 students.

> **TRIVIA**
>
> Austin's first lots were sold at auction on August 1, 1839. Bidding began at $120. Congress Avenue, at 120 feet wide, was claimed to be the widest street in the country. But as it quickly became lined with log cabins and plank houses, it could hardly be considered an elegant thoroughfare.

Taxes

Texas has no corporate or personal income tax on either a state or local level. Sales tax in Austin is 8 percent, divided at 6$\frac{1}{4}$ percent for state sales tax, 1 percent to the City of Austin, and $\frac{3}{4}$ percent for the local transit authority.

Ad valorem property tax per $100 valuation is:
```
       $ .5446   City of Austin
         .5186   Travis County
        1.2832   Austin ISD
         .0476   Austin Community College
       $2.3940   TOTAL
```

Calendar of Events

January
Red-Eye Regatta, Town Lake

February
Carnival Brasileiro, City Coliseum

March
Austin/Travis County Livestock Show & Rodeo, Heritage Exposition Center; Capitol 10,000, a run through Austin streets; Jerry Jeff Walker's Birthday Celebration, Paramount Theater; Kite Festival, Zilker Park; SXSW Music and Media Conference, 25 city venues

April
Austin Nature Center Safari, Austin Nature Center; Canterbury Faire, Waterloo Park; Eeyore's Birthday Party, Pease Park; Highland Lakes Bluebonnet Trail, Highland Lakes; Texas Hill Country Wine and Food Festival, Four Seasons Hotel; Wildflower Days Festival, National Wildflower Research Center

May
Cinco de Mayo, Fiesta Gardens; Fiesta Laguna Gloria, Shores of Lake Austin; Flora Rama, Zilker Botanical Gardens; O. Henry Pun-Off, O. Henry

---

State-of-the-Art Convention Center

The Austin Convention Center has gained national attention since its completion in 1992. "The convention center has been recognized as one of the most technologically advanced in the nation," explains Gwen Spain, Director of Public Relations/Advertising for the Austin Convention & Visitors Bureau. "It's already 'plugged in' if your group needs any Internet capabilities. It's pre-wired for any high-tech needs which saves the time and money of bringing someone in to get that done." The facility offers the latest in technological aids for any type of meetings: ISDN, fiber-optics, in-house simulcast services, satellite links, plug and play access to the Internet, and more. The 400,000-square-foot facility includes 126,000 square feet of column-free exhibit space, a 24,000-square-foot ballroom, and 29 meeting rooms for groups of 10 to 500 delegates.

Museum; Lone Star State Festival, East 6th Street

June
Ballet in the Park, Zilker Hillside Theater; Clarksville-West End Jazz and Arts Festival, West End; Hyde Park Historic Homes Tour, Hyde Park; Juneteenth Freedom Festival, Fiesta Garden

July
Annual Summer Musicals, Zilker Hillside Theater; Austin Symphony Fourth of July Concert, Town Lake; Bastille Day Celebration, French Legation;Freedom Festival and Fireworks, Zilker Park; Governor's Cup Sailing Regatta, Lake Travis

Texas state capitol building

August
Aqua Fest, Auditorium Shores; World's Largest Hot Sauce Festival, Farmer's Market

September
Diez y Seis de Septiembre, Fiesta Gardens; Lone Star State Festival, East 6th Street; Zilker Park Fall Jazz Festival, Zilker Park

October
Fall Regatta on Town Lake; Great Tastes of Austin, Auditorium Shores; Halloween on 6th Street; Pioneer Farm Fall Festival, Pioneer Farm

November
Día de los Muertos, Congress Avenue; Victorian Christmas, East 6th Street

December
Armadillo Christmas Bazaar, Austin Music Hall; Christmas at the French Legation, French Legation; Pioneer Farm Christmas Candlelight Tour, Pioneer Farm; West End Christmas Walk, West End; Wild Ideas: A Holiday Shopping Event, National Wildflower Research Center; Zilker Park Tree Lighting and Trail of Lights, Zilker Park

Austin Weather

Austin's location on the Colorado River where it crosses the Balcones Escarpment, gives it a mild climate with an average annual temperature of 70

Austin Weather

	Ave. Temps (°F)	Humidity (percent)	Ave. Days of Rain
January	50	59	8
February	53	65	8
March	60	53	7
April	75	55	7
May	75	59	9
June	82	54	6
July	85	47	5
August	85	49	5
September	79	57	7
October	70	53	6
November	59	58	7
December	52	60	7

Source: City of Austin/National Weather Service.

degrees Fahrenheit. City elevations vary from 400 to 1,000 feet above sea level, and the climate is humid subtropical, with hot summers. Although the daytime temperatures are hot, summer nights are usually more pleasant with average minimums in the lower 70s. The city enjoys an average of 300 days of sunshine each year.

Winters are mild, with below-freezing temperatures rarely occurring more than 25 days each year. Although rather strong winds, and sharp drops in temperature (which Austinites call "a cold norther from Canada") sometimes occur during the winter months during cold fronts, these are of short duration, rarely lasting more than a day or two.

The average annual rainfall is 27.86 inches, with the heaviest occurring in spring, though this is usually in the form of steady but light rain. Rainy days from April through September usually result from thundershowers, with large amounts falling in short periods of time. Snow is rare and is insignificant as a

Statue of Stephen Austin at the Elisabet Ney Museum

source of moisture; if it does fall it generally melts rapidly when it touches the ground.

Prevailing winds are southerly throughout the year. When northerly winds, accompanying colder air masses in winter, move over the Gulf of Mexico, they soon shift to southerly. Damaging hailstorms and destructive winds are infrequent; dissipating tropical storms affecting the city with strong winds and heavy rains are rare.

Cost of Living

The ACCRA Cost of Living Index measures the differences between regions by the cost of consumer goods and services and then compares the city to an "average" ranking of 100. Austin ranked 100.9 overall for the third quarter of 1995. Groceries ranked 87.1, housing 100.2, utilities 117.6, transportation 105.1, and health care 106.7. On the same scale, Atlanta ranked 99.7 overall, Boston, 139.2; Dallas, 100.4; Los Angeles, 117.9; Phoenix, 100.8; Salt Lake City 95.6; and San Francisco, 174.2.

Typical costs of everyday items and services include:

5-mile taxi ride	$9
Hotel, double room	$80
Average dinner	$10–$15
Movie admission	$6
Daily paper	50 cents
Gallon of gasoline	$1.20
Monthly bus pass	$10
Club cover charge	$3–$5

TRIVIA Seventeen of Austin's Moonlight Towers, installed in 1895 to illuminate downtown, are still standing. At 165 feet they are the city's tallest street lights.

Dressing in the City

What to wear? Fashionwise, Austin is exceedingly informal, just about anything goes so long as you won't be cited for indecent exposure. Visitors can hardly go wrong! The city is a mix of junior students, college students, ex-hippies who hate to dress up, style-conscious yuppies who love a casual-chic look, and traditionalists who won't go out without a coat and tie. At any event or eating establishment all of the above will be represented; there are few places in Austin where you'd feel uncomfortably dressed.

Jeans, shorts, T-shirts, camp shirts, sandals, and sneakers are legion

Congress Avenue, looking toward the capitol

depending upon the weather, not the time of year. Most restaurants really expect you to leave your dress-up clothes at home. (The few exceptions are noted in the restaurant section.) You wear what suits you—that's part of what being in a laid-back town means. Just don't get so laid back that you ignore the health code—shirts and shoes must be worn at all times in eating establishments.

Weatherwise, in spring, summer, and fall, cottons, shorts, short sleeves, and cool dresses are suitable. Wintertime might necessitate a sweater or a light jacket; there are only a few days, during the coldest months when a heavy coat might be a good idea. An umbrella is useful for the few rainy days.

2
GETTING AROUND AUSTIN

City Layout

It doesn't take long to orient yourself to the many sections of Austin. You can usually tell east from west because land to the east is flat and land to the west is hilly. The beautiful Hill Country begins to rise on the west side of town, and there are scenic drives with curves and panoramic views well within the city. The river (Town Lake) divides the city into north and south sides quite neatly; anything north of the river is North Austin, anything south of the river is South Austin.

Austin is located at the heart of the Lone Star State and surrounded by three major Texas cities. Houston is a three-hour drive east; the Dallas/Fort Worth Metroplex is a little more than a three-hour drive north; and historic San Antonio is little more than one hour south. Both the Dallas/Fort Worth Metroplex and San Antonio are reached via I-35, which goes right through Austin from the Texas/Mexico border all the way up to Canada. Houston can be reached by either U.S. 290 East, or Highway 71 East to I-10.

Major Highways

The city is laid out at a slightly northeast/southwest slant, with three main north and south arteries. I-35, the first, has elevated express lanes above the downtown area. MoPac Expressway (Loop 1), the second, takes its name from the Missouri-Pacific railroad tracks bisecting the expressway; trains still run on tracks between the northbound and the southbound lanes. The third main north/south highway, U.S. 183, is known north of the city as Research Boulevard and to the south as Ed Bluestein Boulevard. U.S. 183 makes a northwest/southeast circle

Walking the Historic Districts

If you're an ambitious stroller, pick up a brochure on historic Austin at the Convention and Visitors Bureau; they've divided the city into five historic areas for easy touring. The Historic Capitol touring area includes the capitol, downtown, 6th Street, and a ten-block walk through the Congress Avenue National Register District. The Historic University touring area includes both the University of Texas campus and the Hyde Park neighborhood, which is adjacent to the north side of U.T.'s campus. Other tours are the Clarksville neighborhood (and Tom Miller Dam, but you'd need to drive to the dam) and the Historic Barton Springs touring area, which provides a hearty walk around Zilker Park and the springs (there's a train ride around the park if you don't want to walk). East of I-35 both the French Legation and the state cemetery make for interesting visits.

around Austin, crossing both I-35 and MoPac to intersect with RR 620 in far northwest Austin, and U.S. 90/Highway 71 in southeast Austin.

On the north side of town, FM 2222 runs east and west, winding west into the hills from I-35 and meeting with RR 620 in far northwest Austin. East of the interstate it blends into U.S. 290. Coming from the east, U.S. 290 meets I-35 and follows it south until it connects with Highway 71. Then together they both head west and out of the city, diverging at the "Y" in Oak Hill. Ben White Boulevard on the south side runs east and west, as do both William Cannon Boulevard and Slaughter Lane. Other principal thoroughfares are Lamar Boulevard and Congress Avenue, both running north and south.

Loop 360 (Capital of Texas Highway) circles around the western half of the city from MoPac north to merge with U.S. 90 and Highway 71 (Ben White Boulevard) on the south. Ongoing improvements include elevated lanes and flyways for access onto MoPac and I-35.

Congress Avenue is the dividing line for addresses east and west. The river (Town Lake) is the dividing line for addresses north and south. Travis County includes all of Austin and the small communities of Jollyville to the north, Rollingwood and Westlake Hills to the southwest, and Sunset Valley to the south.

Public Transportation

Bus Service

Capitol Metro
512/474-1200
512/385 5872 TDD
512/478-9647 services for mobility impaired

Austin's clean-air Capitol Metro city buses (they burn natural gas) serve passengers on 48 routes downtown and around town. The transit system is not only easy to use, it's a bargain at 50 cents per trip. Special services are offered for the mobility impaired, and the fare is 60 cents.

Capital Metro's downtown information center is at 106 East 8th Street (just east of Congress Avenue) on the ground floor of the Bremond Building. There you can purchase tickets and passes, take photos for identification cards, find or return lost items, and pick up service information. The center operates for walk-in customers from 7:30 a.m. to 5:30 p.m. Monday through Friday.

'Dillo Express
512/474-1200

To get around only the downtown area, take the green 'Dillo Express—it's "free for the taking." The 'Dillo provides free circular service to downtown and the restaurants and clubs on 6th Street, to ACC (Austin Community College) Campus, UT (University of Texas) Campus, and State Office Buildings

---

The Congress Avenue Bridge

People who lived north or south of Town Lake had a transportation problem until the first bridge was built across the river in 1869. Unfortunately, it was a pontoon bridge and it didn't last long; it washed away in a flood 11 months later. In 1875 a proper Congress Avenue Bridge was built, and it lasted until 1910, when the present Congress Avenue Bridge was completed. Today the Congress Avenue Bridge is a tourist attraction, thanks to the millions of Mexican freetailed bats that migrate and roost under the bridge every year. They're a boon to Austin; they come out at night for dinner, consuming hundreds of thousands of insects from the air.

THE 'DILLO BUS

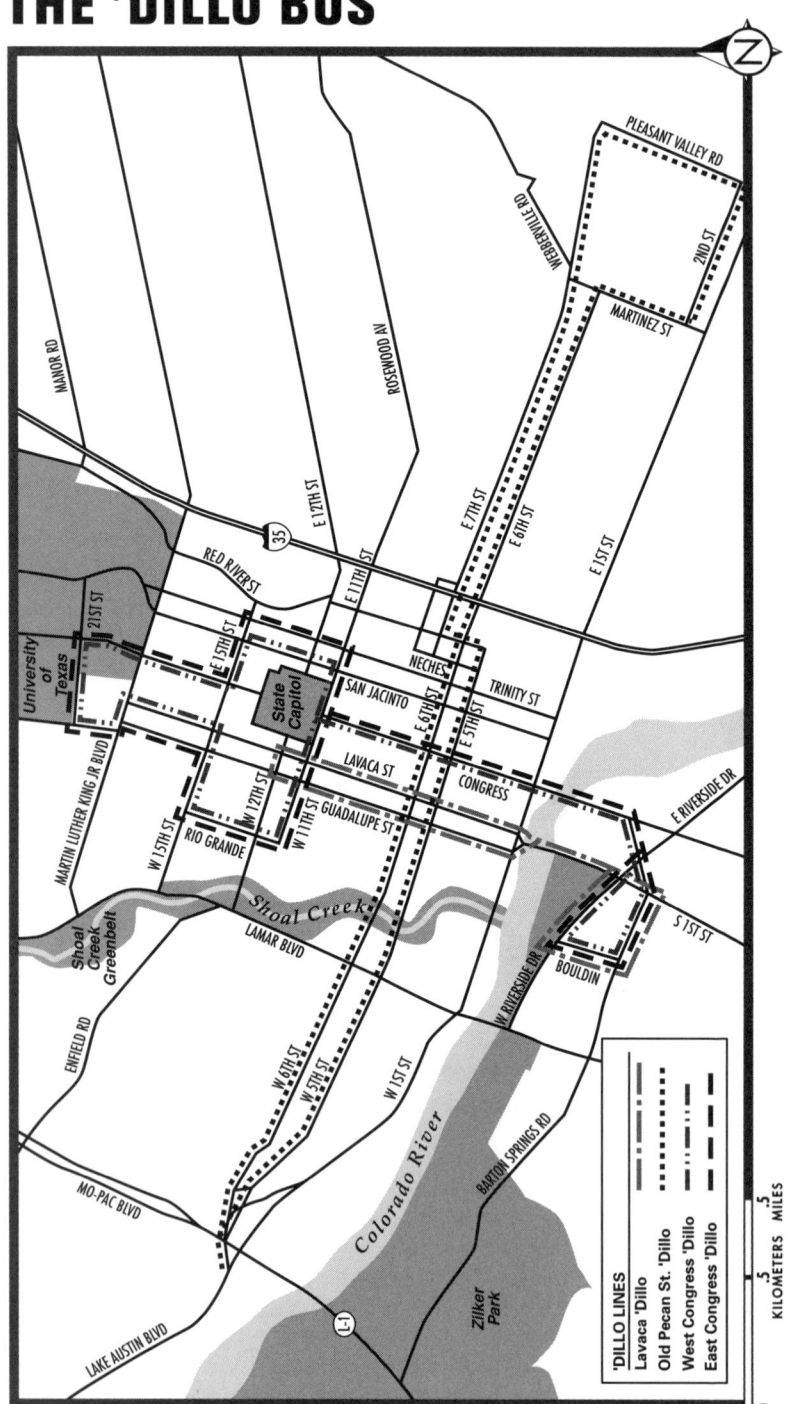

Mon–Thurs 6:30 a.m.–midnight; Fri 6:30 a.m.–1:58 a.m.; Sat 7:25 a.m.–1:53 a.m.; Sun 7:25 a.m.–10:08 p.m. Buses run every 15 to 20 minutes.

The University of Texas Shuttle
512/474-1200
The University shuttle is available to everyone. It runs between the campus and many parts of the city. The cost is 50 cents per trip.

Taxi Service
The city has nine licensed, metered taxicab companies and more than a dozen limousine services. All Austin taxicab companies work 24 hours a day, seven days a week, offering both smoking and nonsmoking cabs. Some take credit cards. Metered service is set by city ordinance and is based on $1.50 the first one-sixth of a mile and $1.50 per mile thereafter. Average fare from the airport to downtown is about $10. Rates to travel to surrounding cities vary among companies.

Ace Taxi, 512/244-1133
American Cab Company, 512/452-9999
Austin Cab Company, 512/478-2222

Transportation for Seniors

Seniors 60 years and older can enjoy special transportation thanks to the Austin Parks and Recreation Department's Senior Support Service. Reserve-a-Ride, provides transportation from your home to meal sites and senior centers between 9:00 a.m. and 1:00 p.m. Contributions of 50 cents each way are encouraged.

For a contribution of $1 each way, Reserve-A-Ride will also arrange transportation to doctors and dentists (non-emergency), lawyers, banks, pharmacies, hair salons, to visit a friend in the hospital, to your volunteer worksite, and to most other social engagements. The rides require a 24-hour notice.

Groups of five or larger (ten or more for out of town journeys) can schedule pleasure trips. Fees range from 50 cents to $10; previous trips have included the San Antonio River Walk, state parks, Hill Country communities, movies, plays, and concerts.

For reservations or more information call 512/480-3012.

If you're driving, in the downtown area you can park free at two Park & Ride lots, one at the City Coliseum (Barton Springs and Bouldin) and the other at Austin High School (MoPac and West 1st Street), then catch the 'Dillo into downtown.

Bastrop Cab Company, 512/321-6666
City Taxi, 512/392-2222
Evergreene, 512/396-0942
Harlem Cab Company, 512/478-2222
Roy's Taxis, 512/482-0000
Yellow Checker, 512/472-1111

Driving in Austin

Not too long ago, Austinites subscribed to the motto "Drive Friendly." Sadly this is no longer true. Perhaps it is because the city is growing so rapidly that traffic is becoming a problem. Rush hour traffic, especially on I-35 and on MoPac, is fast catching up with the kind of five o'clock traffic you find in other large cities. Drivers in Austin are becoming much more aggressive. Motorists rushing through yellow lights, and even running red lights, are becoming all too common, so your best bet is to drive defensively.

Observe left turn lights closely; some are protected with an arrow, some not—usually there is a sign above the light. Speed limits are radar-enforced all over the city, in residential districts as well as major thor-

A Capitol Metro Bus

The Austin Rangers

Downtown, the Austin Downtown Rangers are at your service. Dressed in distinctive uniforms, they are Austin's goodwill ambassadors. On foot and on bicycles, they're on the alert for lost or displaced tourists. They don't carry weapons or make arrests, instead they report criminal activity to the Austin Police Department. Armed only with maps of the city and two-way communication equipment, they provide assistance to visitors, answering questions and reporting problems to city agencies. They range the streets from Riverside Drive to Martin Luther King Boulevard (19th Street) north, and from the I-35 access road on the east and San Antonio Street on the west.

The Rangers are chosen from hundreds of qualified applicants after extensive background checks and personal interviews. They train extensively for downtown duty before they hit the streets. For some, being a Ranger is the first step toward a career with the Austin Police Department. "The Rangers express the friendly nature of Austin. Their presence contributes greatly to the downtown area," says former Mayor Bruce Todd.

oughfares. Right turns on red lights are permitted after a stop; left turns are permitted onto one-way streets after a stop as well.

Parking

State law prohibits parking a vehicle within 20 feet of a crosswalk at an intersection, in front of driveways, and within 30 feet of a traffic signal or stop sign. Sidewalk ramps for persons with disabilities are usually located at crosswalks; state law keeps these areas clear of parked vehicles. The law states that "No person shall park, stop, or stand a vehicle so that it blocks a curb cut or any architectural improvement designed to aid or assist the disabled." The Austin City Code prohibits parking in the sidewalk area or any place designated as "No Parking" by the Traffic Engineer.

Parking meters that take nickels, dimes, and quarters come in several time limits, from 15 minutes to two hours. Be sure to check.

Biking in Austin

The Texas National Resource Conservation Commission (TNRCC) and Bicycle Users Group (BUG) work with the Austin Metropolitan Trails Council,

TIP: AMPCO Parking operates a 24-hour parking hotline, 512/499-7275, with up-to-the-minute updates on airport parking availability and lot closures—a life-saver if you need to catch a flight in a hurry. Radio station 1610 AM also provides additional parking and airport information.

the City of Austin Bicycle Advisory Council, and the Texas Bicycle Coalition to offer advice on the logistics of bicycle commuting and on the safest routes to ride to work. They also offer advice on the best bike shops, safe riding techniques, a cyclist's rights and responsibilities on the road, and the benefits of cycling. They support such major events each year as the Austin Bike-to-Work Day, the MS 150 Ride, the Clean Air Ride, and Pedal for the Planet. For more information call the TNRCC at 512/236-1000. The office is open Mon–Fri, 7:30 a.m.–5 p.m.

A city ordinance requires the wearing of a bicycle helmet along any property that is publicly owned or maintained, including a road or highway, a publicly maintained trail, and any public parks facility. The helmet is required by law to fit properly and not have any structural damage. It also must conform to the standards of the American National Standards Institute, the American Society for Testing and Materials, the Snell Memorial Foundation, or any federal agency having regulatory jurisdiction over bicycle helmets. The ordinance has been enforced since ten days after its final passage on May 9, 1996.

Airports

Robert Mueller Airport

© Permenter & Bigley

**Robert Mueller Municipal Airport
3600 Manor Rd.
(about 5 miles from downtown)
512/472-5439 Aviation Department Administration
512/472-3321 Airport Paging**
Note: For flight information, call the individual airline
With an average of 100 flights a day, the Robert Mueller (MIL-ler) Municipal Airport is ranked the 48th-busiest airport in the continental United States. The 193,388-square-foot building includes 16 gates. The airport provides service to 308 domestic markets and 134 international markets. There is nonstop service to

29 cities. Four lots offer parking with varying fees; 26 rental car companies offer ground transportation.

Austin is a clean-air city, and smoking within the airport terminal is prohibited by law.

Air traffic in the Austin area is growing so heavily—passenger totals for 1994 were up 9.7 percent over 1993 totals, and air cargo activity was up 20 percent—that airport planners have been working for several years to meet this growing demand.

Austin-Bergstrom International Airport
3600 Manor Rd.
512/369-6661 or 512/495-7515

Airport planners have been working for several years to meet the growing demand for more airport facilities. The result is Austin-Bergstrom International Airport at the site of former Bergstrom Air Force Base, which closed in September of 1993. After much controversy between those who wanted the

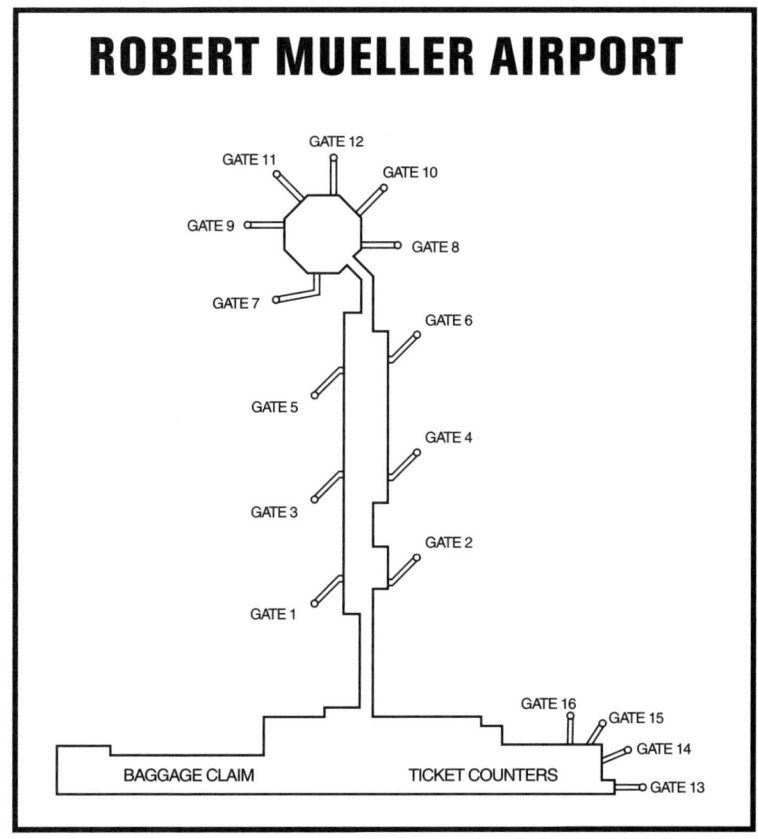

Major Airlines Serving Austin

America West, 800/235-9292
American, 800/433-7300
Continental, 800/525-0280
Delta, 800/221-1212
Northwest, 800/225-2525
Southwest, 800/435-9792
TWA Domestic, 512/454-8900
TWA International, 800/892-4141
United, 800/241-6522
USAir, 800/428-4322

new airport and those who didn't, a 63 percent voter mandate gave the planners the OK to construct a new airport on the Bergstrom site.

The city of Austin acquired 242 buildings when it took over Bergstrom Air Force Base from the Air Force. The city is recycling as much of the Air Force's leftovers as possible, and 69 buildings will probably be reused in the new airport. However, many of these buildings that Austin "inherited" from Bergstrom Air Force Base were poorly maintained and some contained high levels of asbestos. Needless to say, the buildings were removed, in some cases to make room for the future runway, terminal, taxiways, or parking areas.

The airport is scheduled to open in the spring of 1999 and will cost approximately $496 million. In addition, private developers will be responsible for the $100-million cost for other facilities such as air cargo. The Federal Aviation Administration has committed $91 million for the project through 2002. This will be applied to the airport cost. Austin-Bergstrom International Airport will use no federal income taxes, city sales taxes or local property taxes to fund the project. So—if you don't use it, you don't pay for it.

The airport will open with the potential for international passenger air service, which Austin does not have at present. The split-level terminal building is expected to cover 450,000-square-feet.

The Department of Aviation's plan is expected to meet Austin's air traffic needs far into the twenty-first century. In passenger terms, the airport will accommodate non-stop overseas flights, something that Mueller cannot do.

Train Services

The Amtrak Station
250 North Lamar Blvd. and West Cesar Chavez
(a block north of Town Lake)
800/872-7245 (tickets, reservations, and information)
The Amtrak Eagle is a two-level passenger train, the only train service out of Austin. It provides daily direct service to major United States hubs. Trains leave for San Antonio, New Orleans, and Los Angeles on Monday, Wednesday, and Saturday; for Chicago on Sunday, Tuesday, and Thursday. Reservations are required for all trips.

Regional/National Bus Services

Greyhound Bus Lines
916 Koenig Lane (across from Highland Mall Shopping Center)
512/458-3823 or 800/231-2222 (information and schedules)
Greyhound offers daily service to Dallas, San Antonio and Laredo, as well as service to 2,500 other U.S. destinations. Tickets must be purchased at the terminal; reservations are not accepted until the ticket is purchased.

Kerrville Bus Company
916 Koenig Lane (across from Highland Mall Shopping Center)
512/389-0319 or 800/231-2222 (information and schedules)
Kerrville Bus Company offers daily direct service to Kerrville, Houston, Killeen, and Bryan-College Station, with service to numerous Texas cities and towns in between. In Austin, tickets must be purchased at the Greyhound station. Reservations are not accepted.

3
WHERE TO STAY

Although for one reason or another Austin never got around to building a group of historic hotels such as you might find in other large cities, in the early days there were two: the Stephen F. Austin—no longer operating as a hotel—and the Driskill, Austin's pride.

Today, as in any major city, Austin has no dearth of high-rise luxury hotels, but the Driskill still holds a special place. Regardless of the type of accommodation you're seeking—luxury hotel, upscale chain, convenient motel, or homey bed and breakfast—you'll find it in Austin. Luxury hotels are primarily located in the downtown region, near the state capitol and Town Lake. Most chain properties are located north and south along I-35.

Bed and breakfasts are scattered throughout the city, with some of the most charming located in historic neighborhoods. More and more travelers and visitors are finding enjoyment in a change from the anonymity of a hotel, where although the staff may be pleasant, you're handed a key and sent to your room. In a bed and breakfast, your hosts are not only pleasant, they are interested in you; and so, usually, are the other guests. People stay at bed and breakfasts because they enjoy this exchange with other travelers and with gracious hosts. And not to be downplayed is the pleasure of what is usually a filling, and often quite gourmet, breakfast. Wheelchair accessibility is indicated by the ♿ symbol.

Price rating symbols:
$ **Under $50**
$$ **$50 to $75**
$$$ **$75 to $125**
$$$$ **$125 and up**

Note: Prices reflect a general range and may fluctuate depending on season and availability.

The Historic Driskill Hotel

The Driskill Hotel opened in 1886 with a grandeur that was a rarity on the Texas frontier, to say the least. Earlier travelers reported being forced to lodge in establishments with very dirty rooms, and even being forced to share their quarters with other travelers. The names of such establishments have not come down to us, a small loss. But with the Driskill, Austin had something to brag about. The four-story L-shaped building had three grand entrances, arched windows, balconies, columns, corbels, gargoyles, and more. Wide corridors paved with black slate and marble led from the entrances, merging in a magnificent lobby underneath a four-story skylit rotunda. President Lyndon B. Johnson always stayed at the Driskill with Lady Bird; they had their own suite. The hotel has hosted other heads of state, legislators, lobbyists, aspiring and "arrived" socialites, honeymooners, and, of course, visitors to the capital.

DOWNTOWN AUSTIN

Hotels

**AUSTIN MARRIOTT
AT THE CAPITOL**
701 E. 11th St.
Austin, TX 78701
512/478-1111 or 800/228-9290
$$$$　　　　　　　　　　DA
Conveniently located, this hotel includes everything needed to pamper the business or leisure traveler. An American grill serves a casual breakfast, lunch, and dinner; a sports bar and grill provides after-hours fun; and a lobby piano bar provides a soothing end to the day. Work out the travel kinks in the heated indoor/outdoor pool designed for swimming laps, or at the health club, complete with whirlpool and wet/dry sauna. ♿

DOUBLETREE GUEST SUITES
303 W. 15th St.
Austin, TX 78701
512/478-7000 or 800/424-2900
$$$$　　　　　　　　　　DA
This all-suites hotel has 189 accommodations with fully equipped kitchens, including 16 two-bedroom suites (four of which are penthouses). Facilities include an outdoor pool and Jacuzzi, a courtesy shuttle for trips within a 2-mile radius, business and secretarial services, and a restaurant with indoor/outdoor dining. ♿

DRISKILL HOTEL
604 Brazos St.
Austin, TX 78701
512/474-5911 or 800/527-2008
$$$$　　　　　　　　　　DA
Austin's most historic hotel is full of

DOWNTOWN AUSTIN

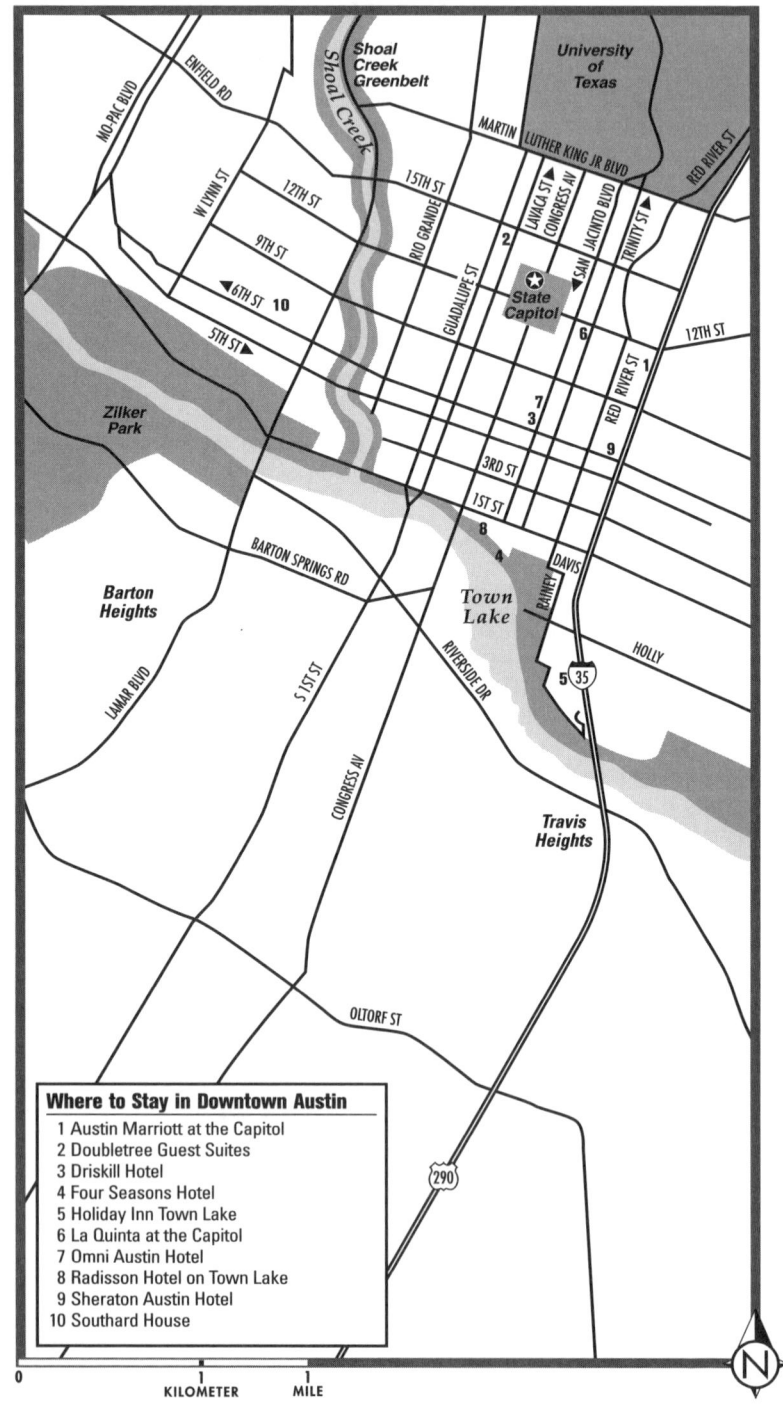

Radisson Hotel on Town Lake, page 30

Texas history, architectural beauties, elegant furnishings, and artwork. Totally renovated and restored with all of the original grandeur intact, it's quite a treat to stay in this hotel, host to dignitaries, heads of state, legislators, and lobbyists—all sort of guests who have shaped Texas' future. The hotel has 177 luxuriously appointed rooms and seven suites, a full service restaurant, lobby piano lounge, 24-hour room service, gift shop, concierge desk, and valet parking—and is right on the corner of Brazos and 6th Street, Austin's famed entertainment district. The Driskill pampers guests with a complimentary coffee and newspaper each morning and a complimentary happy hour each evening. Restaurants, shops, the capitol, and the Governor's Mansion are all within walking distance. ♿

FOUR SEASONS HOTEL
98 San Jacinto Blvd.
Austin, TX 78701
512/478-4500 or 800/332-3442
$$$$ **DA**

The hotel prides itself on pampering guests in the manner of fine European hotels, amidst a Southwest decor that somehow manages to appear elegant even though a rugged crystal and iron chandelier hangs over the lobby. Sofas are upholstered in brown and white steerhide, there are tables of genuine Mission doors with ox yoke legs, and an elk head is mounted over the fireplace. Half of the 292 guest rooms offer views over Town Lake, and there's an outdoor pool overlooking the lake. The hotel is within walking distance of the Convention Center and the 6th Street entertainment district. ♿

HOLIDAY INN TOWN LAKE
20 N. I-35
Austin, TX 78701
512/472-8211 or 800/HOLIDAY
$$$–$$$$ **DA**

Overlooking both Town Lake and I-35, this 319-room hotel is only a mile from central downtown, the 6th Street entertainment district, the Austin Convention Center, the capitol, and the

University of Texas. Amenities include work desks and computer hook-ups in rooms, a restaurant and lounge, a gift shop, valet service, bell service, and complimentary airport shuttle. &

OMNI AUSTIN HOTEL
700 San Jacinto Blvd.
Austin, TX 78701
512/476-3700 or 800/THE OMNI
$$$$ DA

With its high-rise atrium, this sophisticated, 304-room hotel offers all the amenities of a top accommodation for both business and leisure travelers. The Club Floor on the 13th and 14th floors offers restricted access with upgraded amenities including continental breakfast, afternoon hors d'oeuvres, beer and wine, and freshly baked cookies nightly. All guests have use of a fitness center. &

RADISSON HOTEL ON TOWN LAKE
111 E. 1st St.
Austin, TX 78701
512/478-9611 or 800/333-3333
$$–$$$$ DA

Perched at the intersection of Congress Avenue and Town Lake, this hotel includes a health club, an outdoor pool, and a TGI Friday's restaurant. All rooms have hair dryers, coffeemakers, and irons with ironing boards. &

SHERATON AUSTIN HOTEL
500 N. I-35
Austin, TX 78701
512/480-8181 or 800/325-3535
$$$$ DA

The hotel has meeting space, a health club, a pool, and a Jacuzzi that holds 25 people, as well as a restaurant on the 18th floor with a view of Austin. The spacious guest rooms are furnished in Drexel Heritage and are complete with coffeemaker, hair dryer, makeup mirror, and ironing board and iron. &

Top Ten Must-See Things in Austin
By Nancy and Roger Danley
Innkeepers, McCallum House Bed and Breakfast

1. The Texas capitol building and capitol extension.
2. The UT Tower, Campus, and "The Drag."
3. The LBJ Library, especially the model of the Oval Office.
4. Town Lake, especially the hike and bike trail.
5. Zilker Park; don't miss Barton Springs and the gardens.
6. Central Market, the most fascinating market this side of Istanbul.
7. Bats leaving Congress Avenue Bridge at dusk (spring, summer, and early fall).
8. The view from Mount Bonnell.
9. The 6th Street scene.
10. The Wildflower Research Center (spring is best).

Four Seasons Hotel (left), page 29

Motels

LA QUINTA AT THE CAPITOL
300 E. 11th St.
Austin, TX 78701
512/476-1166 or 800/531-5900
$$ DA
The motel has been recently renovated; "Gold Medal Rooms" have all new decor, 25-inch TVs, and speaker phones. Complimentary breakfast and free local calls are offered. ⚐

Bed and Breakfasts

SOUTHARD HOUSE
908 Blanco St.
Austin, TX 78703
512/474-4731
$$–$$$$ DA
Southard House is popular with intellectuals visiting the University of Texas, as well as architects, lawyers, and just plain international folks, too. The b&b's large map of the world is dotted with colored pins showing the home cities of Southard House guests. Airport pickup, special diets, business calls for guests, and other amenities are offered in this restored and convenient Victorian Greek Revival just off busy West 6th Street.

NORTH AUSTIN

Hotels

AUSTIN NORTH HILTON AND TOWERS
6000 Middle Fiskville Rd.
Austin, TX 78752
512/451-5757 or 800/347-0330 or 800/HILTONS
$$$–$$$$ NA
A hotel that says "Welcome to the Hill Country," with a western-motif lobby of stenciled walls, an antler chandelier, and a reception desk of native Texas Limestone. The 332 guest rooms each have an oversized desk, two phones, and an overstuffed chair with ottoman. The pool is surrounded by lush landscaping, and the Cabana Club offers refreshments. The concierge level offers complimentary continental breakfast and afternoon hors d'oeuvres, and 18 meeting rooms. No charge for children in the same room as their parents. ⚐

BEST WESTERN ATRIUM NORTH
7928 Gessner Dr.
Austin, TX 78753
512/339-7311 or 800/468-3708
$$ NA
Located one block west of I-35, this property is built around an enclosed atrium that boasts a heated swimming pool and dry sauna. Some rooms feature Jacuzzi tubs; environmental green rooms are also available. Continental breakfast is included in the daily rate for guests. Local calls, cable TV, and in-room movies round out the amenities. ⚐

DOUBLETREE HOTEL AUSTIN
6505 N. I-35
Austin, TX 78752
512/454-3737 or 800/222-8733
$$–$$$$ NA
Located north of the airport along I-35 at U.S. 290, this hotel, with its Spanish Colonial architecture, is a local landmark. Amenities include 350 guest rooms with generous work areas. The Courtyard Cafe overlooks a multilevel courtyard with greenery and waterscapes. The exercise facility includes a swimming pool and a volleyball court. &

FAIRFIELD INN AUSTIN AIRPORT
959 Reinli St.
Austin, TX 78751
512/302-5550 or 800/228-2800
$$–$$$ NA
Located off I-35 and U.S. 290, 3 miles from Mueller Airport and the University of Texas and 4 miles from downtown, the inn boasts famous Marriott hospitality with down-to-earth prices. In addition to 63 bright and attractive guest rooms, the hotel offers "spa rooms" with personal spas and king-size beds. Complimentary continental breakfast, a heated indoor pool and exercise room, free movie channel, and local phone calls are offered; vending machines and fax and copy services are available. &

HABITAT SUITES HOTEL
500 Highland Mall Blvd.
Austin, TX 78752
512/467-6000 or 800/535-4663
$$$–$$$$ NA
Travelers who want to maintain a "green" environment that utilizes recycled materials, natural products, and no unnecessary chemicals will appreciate this hotel. The eco-friendly property boasts an ionized pool and hot tubs, water and energy conservation measures throughout, with many recycled materials used in the construction. Both one- and two-bedroom suites are available, each with coffeemakers. A full buffet breakfast is served daily.&

HAMPTON INN AUSTIN NORTH
7619 N. I-35
Austin, TX 78752
512/452-3300 or 800-HAMPTON
$$$ NA
Complimentary continental breakfast, free local calls, and cable television with in-room movies are standard features at this property. Also offered: a heated swimming pool and an exercise facility. &

Where to Stay in North Austin

1 Austin Chariot Resort Inn & Conference Center
2 Austin North Hilton and Towers
3 Austin's Wildflower Inn
4 Best Western Atrium North
5 Carrington's Bluff Bed & Breakfast
6 Courtyard by Marriott Austin
7 Days Inn North
8 Days Inn University
9 Doubletree Hotel Austin
10 Drury Inn North
11 Fairfield Inn Austin Airport
12 Four Points Hotel by ITT Sheraton
13 Governor's Inn
14 Habitat Suites Hotel
15 Hampton Inn Austin North
16 Holiday Inn Express
17 The Inn at Pearl Street
18 La Quinta Inn/Suites Highland Mall
19 La Quinta Inn/Suites North
20 La Quinta Inn/Suites-MoPac
21 McCallum House
22 Northpark Executive Suite Hotel
23 Park Inn International
24 Ramada Inn Airport North
25 Ramada Limited Airport North
26 Ramada Limited
27 Rodeway Inn—University
28 Travel Lodge Suites Austin North
29 Traveler's Inn
30 Walnut Forest Motel
31 Woodburn House

NORTH AUSTIN

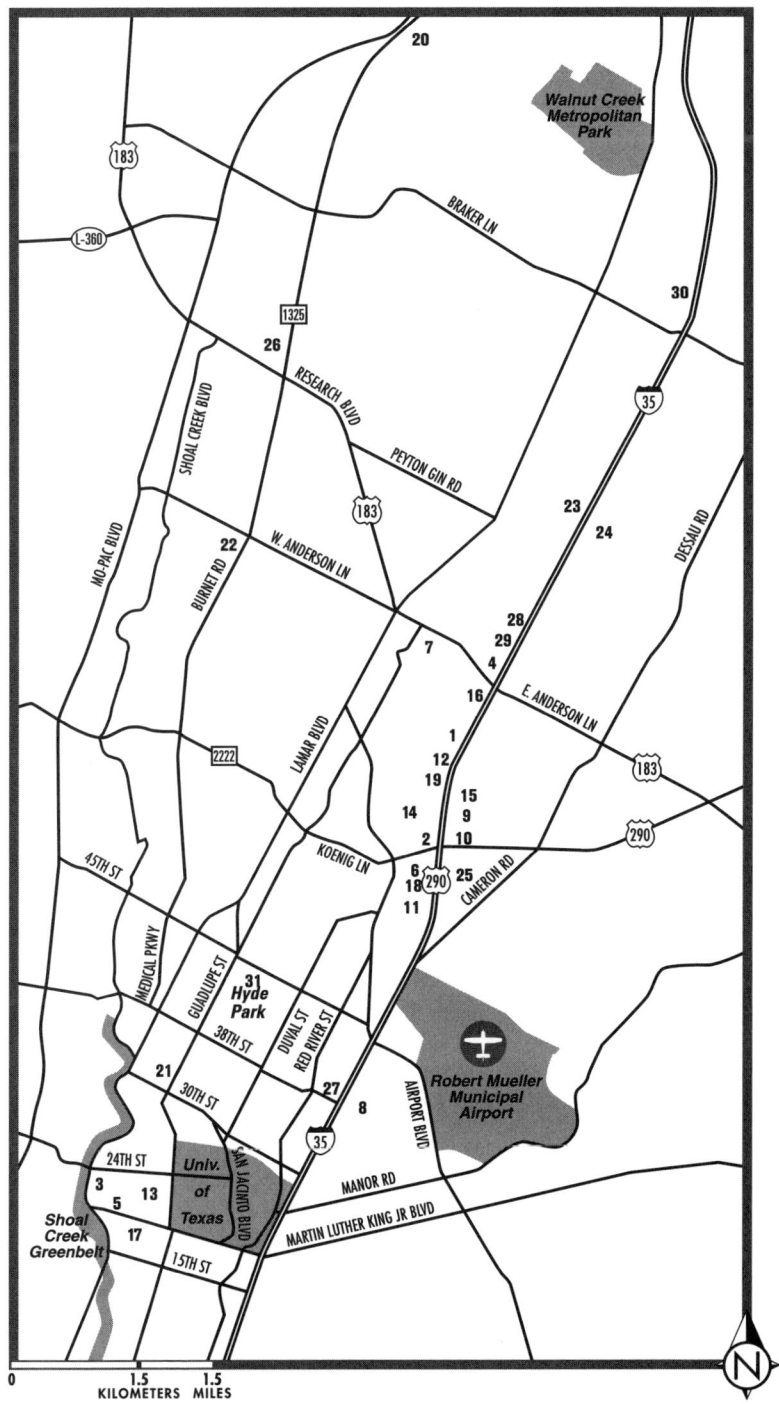

> ## Say it the Austin Way
>
> Want to sound like a local? Here's how to correctly pronounce some of Austin's most common streets and areas.
>
> **Burnet Road**: *BUR-nit Road*
> **Del Valle:** *Del-VAL-ee*
> **Guadalupe:** *GWA-da-loop*
> **Huston** (as in Huston-Tillotson College): *HYOU-stun.*
> **Koenig Lane:** *KAY-nig Lane*
> **Manchaca:** *MAN-shack*
> **Manor:** *MAY-nor*
> **Mueller Airport:** *MILLER Airport*
> **Nueces:** *new-Aces*
> **Texas:** *TEX-sis*

HOLIDAY INN EXPRESS
7622 N. I-35
Austin, TX 78752
512/467-1701 or 800/HOLIDAY
$$ NA
With indoor corridors, the Holiday Inn Express has the feel of a hotel at the price of a motel. Guests are offered a complimentary continental breakfast and use of an outdoor pool. &

NORTHPARK EXECUTIVE SUITE HOTEL
7685 Northcross Dr.
Austin, TX 78757
512/452-9391 or 800/851-9111
$$–$$$$ NA
A property that includes a full buffet breakfast and social hour for guests, as well as in-room VCRs and complimentary movie rental. Visitors can use the facilities at a local health club. &

Motels

AUSTIN CHARIOT RESORT INN & CONFERENCE CENTER
7300 N. I-35
Austin, TX 78752
512/452-9371 or 800/432-9202
$$ NA
Chariot Resort Inn offers a convenient, inexpensive room. The hotel does not include a restaurant, but does have an outdoor pool. Rooms are simple but clean in this conveniently located property. &

COURTYARD BY MARRIOTT AUSTIN
5660 N. I-35
Austin, TX 78751
512/458-2340 or 800/321-2211
$$ NA
Guest can enjoy in-room movies, an outdoor pool and whirlpool, and a small health club.&

DAYS INN NORTH
820 E. Anderson Ln.
Austin, TX 78752
512/835-4311
$$ NA

This basic accommodation offers standard motel rooms as well as an outdoor swimming pool. A restaurant is located nearby. &

DAYS INN UNIVERSITY
3105 N. I-35
Austin, TX 78722
512/478-1631 or 800/725-ROOM
$$ NA
A no-frills property offering inexpensive accommodations in the area of the University of Texas campus. Guests have use of an outdoor swimming pool; a cafe is located next door. &

DRURY INN NORTH
I-35 and St. Johns
Austin, TX 78752
512/467-9500 or 800/325-8300
$$$ NA
Visitors enjoy a buffet breakfast and cocktail hour Monday through Thursday; rooms include coffeemakers. Guests can work out the kinks in the outdoor pool or purchase a daily membership to a local health club for $5. &

FOUR POINTS HOTEL BY ITT SHERATON
7800 N. I-35
Austin, TX 78753
512/836-8520 or 800/325-3535
$$$ NA
Formerly the Howard Johnson, this newly renovated property is located at the intersection of U.S. 183 and I-35, convenient to many stops in far-north Austin. Guests enjoy complimentary breakfast and an outdoor swimming pool. &

RAMADA INN AIRPORT NORTH
9121 N. I-35
Austin, TX 78753
512/836-0079 or 800/843-9077
$ NA
Guests receive a complimentary breakfast and free local calls at this economically priced motel located within easy reach of downtown or north Austin along I-35. &

LA QUINTA INN/SUITES HIGHLAND MALL
5812 N. I-35
Austin, TX 78751
512/459-4381 or 800/531-5900
$$ NA
The motel has been recently renovated; complimentary breakfast and free local calls are offered. &

LA QUINTA INN/SUITES NORTH
7100 N. I-35
Austin, TX 78751
512/452-9401 or 800/531-5900
$$ NA
Rooms boast oversized desks (some also have recliners) and dataport phones with computer hookups; microwaves and refrigerators can be rented in your room. Complimentary breakfast and a swimming pool round out the amenities. Children under 18 are free in parents' room. &

LA QUINTA INN/SUITES-MOPAC
11901 N. MoPac Expwy.
Austin, TX 78759
512/832-2121
$$ NA
All La Quinta inns have been updated with new furnishings in both lobby and guest rooms. Children under 18 are free in parents' room. &

PARK INN INTERNATIONAL
9220 N. I-35
Austin, TX 78753
512/837-7372
$ NA
Located near the intersection of U.S. 183, this hotel includes free HBO,

Renaissance Austin Hotel, page 39

30-channel cable TV, free local calls, king-size beds in the single rooms, and free continental breakfast. Some rooms include refrigerators. &

RAMADA LIMITED AIRPORT NORTH
5526 N. I-35
Austin, TX 78751
512/451-7001 or 800/880-0709
$ NA
With a free shuttle service to the airport and the bus station, this property also includes a complimentary extended continental breakfast daily from 6 a.m. to 10 a.m. with bagels, waffles, and cereal. &

RAMADA LIMITED
9102 Burnet Rd.
Austin, TX 78758
512/835-7070 or 800/880-0709
$$ NA
Free continental breakfast is offered at this property near the intersection of U.S. 183 and Burnet Road. Standard room features include HBO, color TV, whirlpool baths, and a small refrigerator. &

RODEWAY INN-UNIVERSITY
2900 N. I-35
Austin, TX 78705
512/477-6395
$$ NA
Guests have use of an outdoor swimming pool at this motel in the University of Texas campus area. Rooms are simple but comfortable. &

TRAVEL LODGE SUITES AUSTIN NORTH
8300 N. I-35
Austin, TX 78753
512/835-5050 or 800/578-7878
$–$$ NA
A three-story all-suites property offering one- and two-bedroom accommodations. Suites include kitchenettes with microwaves, refrigerators, and coffeemakers. Free breakfast is available daily; a laundry and outdoor pool are also offered. &

TRAVELER'S INN
8128 N. I-35
Austin, TX 78753
512/339-1300 or 800/633-8300
$$ NA
Guests are offered free continental breakfast and free local calls at this conveniently located interstate property. &

WALNUT FOREST MOTEL
11506 N. I-35
Austin, TX 78753
512/835-0864
$ NA
This motel is tucked off busy I-35 under a grove of trees. The simple rooms are clean and comfortable in this property that harks back to the early days of motel travel. &

Bed and Breakfasts

AUSTIN'S WILDFLOWER INN
1200 W. 22nd-1/2 St.
Austin, TX 78705
512/477-9639
$$ NA

This pretty white clapboard house has bright flowers leading up the path, and inside you'll find stenciled flowers brightening up the walls and the stairs—innkeeper Kay is celebrating the Hill Country's famously beautiful spring wildflowers. Lace curtains at the windows bring in lots of sunshine, and the four guest rooms (two with private baths) are light and bright as well. Kay holds the record for variety breakfasts: A guest from Britain stayed almost six weeks, and not one menu was repeated.

CARRINGTON'S BLUFF BED & BREAKFAST
1900 David St.
Austin, TX 78705
512/479-0638
$$–$$$ NA

Bordering Shoal Creek, this estate dates back over 100 years. Located just seven blocks from the University of Texas campus and nine from the State Capitol, the six-room inn offers TV in some rooms and phones in all rooms; two rooms share a bath. No smoking indoors and no children under the age of ten.

GOVERNOR'S INN
611 W. 22nd St.
Austin, TX 78705
512/477-0711
$$–$$$ NA

Built in 1897, this impressive mansion is just two blocks from the University of Texas campus. The neoclassical Victorian home, with high ceilings, lots of white paneling, and several porches, once served time as a fraternity house. Now the wrought-iron gates lead to comfortable rooms named for Texas governors—the Texas Governor's Mansion is practically just around the corner on 11th Street. University students passing by, laughing and happy, add to the warm and youthful atmosphere of the inn.

INN AT PEARL STREET
809 W. MLK at Pearl St.
Austin, TX 78701
512/477-2233 or 800/494-2203
$$$–$$$$ NA

A turn-of-the-century Greek Revival mansion, this is the newest kid on the block of downtown bed and breakfast establishments. Four eclectic guest rooms (and more in the works) are decorated in imaginative styles; the choices are the French Room, the European Room, the Far East Room and the Gothic Suite, all with private

Lake Austin Spa Resort, page 39

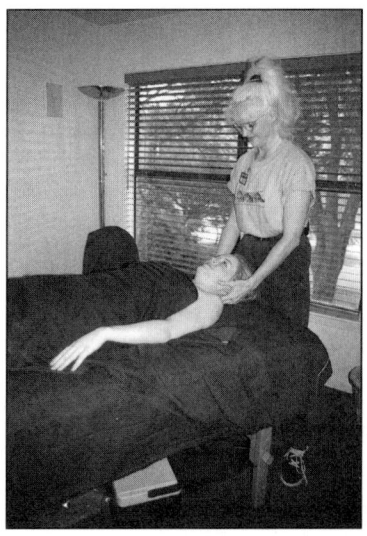

WHERE TO STAY   37

bath. The inn, selected as Austin's 1995 Symphony Designer Showhouse, is surrounded by porches and has a large deck shaded by massive trees. It offers old-world ambiance right in the heart of downtown. Weekdays a continental breakfast is served; weekends it's a full one, with champagne and dessert.

MCCALLUM HOUSE
613 W. 32nd St.
Austin, TX 78705
512/451-6744
$$–$$$ NA
Not only do Innkeepers Nancy and Roger Danley welcome all guests, they make the inn a comfortable home-away-from-home for many visiting professors, which makes for lively breakfast conversation. This bed and breakfast inn is 3/4 mile from the University of Texas. The five guest rooms and suites all have private baths and kitchens; four have private porches. The house has a huge screened-in porch with inviting, white wicker furniture. An early suffragette, Jane Y. McCallum, once lived here with her husband and her five children. As early as 1927, the year the house was built, she felt that 8 million working women needed to vote, and a wonderful banner on the wall of the landing proclaims just that.

WOODBURN HOUSE
4401 Ave. D
Austin, TX 78751
512/458-4335
$$ NA
This bed and breakfast is in Austin's Hyde Park neighborhood, an area filled with lovely old homes. (The Austin Visitors Center recommends this neighborhood for touring.) Woodburn House was named for a former occupant, Bessie Hamilton Woodburn, daughter of a Texas provisional governor after the Civil War. The spacious mansion has porches both upstairs and down, and four guest rooms, all with private baths and lace curtains at their long windows.

NORTHWEST AUSTIN

Hotels

COURTYARD BY MARRIOTT AUSTIN NORTHWEST
9409 Stonelake Blvd.
Austin, TX 78759
512/502-8100 or 800/321-2211
$$–$$$ NWA
Newly completed, this hotel is located convenient to shopping at the Arboretum and Great Hills area. Irons, ironing boards, and coffeemakers are standard in all rooms, as are oversized desk/work areas. Executive rooms include king-size beds, refrigerators, and microwaves; "spa king rooms" also include full-size Jacuzzis. &

HAMPTON INN HOTEL AUSTIN NORTHWEST
3908 W. Braker Ln.
Austin, TX 78759
512/349-9898 or 800/HAMPTON
$$$ NWA
Located at the intersection of MoPac (Loop 1) and Braker Lane, this new 123-room hotel includes 25-inch televisions, coffeemakers, irons, and complimentary HBO. Guests have use of an outdoor pool and an exercise room; dining is located about a mile away in the Arboretum area. &

HOLIDAY INN NORTHWEST PLAZA
8901 Business Park Dr.

Lake Austin Spa Resort

Perched in the rolling hills on a quiet shore of Lake Austin, the Lake Austin Spa Resort combines spa luxury with the rustic atmosphere of a lake retreat. With healthy dining, exercise programs, spa treatments, and many activities, the resort is casual elegance at its best.

Activites range from aerobics classes on a suspended wood floor to tennis, dancing, mountain biking, and even sculling on the lake's calm waters. Guests can try a massage, a facial, a manicure, an aloe vera body masque, an invigorating sea salt scrub, or an aromatherapy scalp conditioning.

Accommodations include 40 cottage rooms with saltillo tile floors, private baths, central air and heat, telephones, cable TV, and king, double, or queen beds. Guests have use of an outdoor pool, an indoor water-aerobics pool, a sauna, a steam and Jacuzzi, training room, a walking trail, and tennis courts.

The resort is located at 1705 South Quinlan Park Road. Call 512/266-2444 or 800/847-5637 for more information.

Austin, TX 78759
512/343-0888 or 800/HOLIDAY
$$$ **NWA**
Tucked just off U.S. 183 and MoPac (Loop 1), this large hotel offers standard rooms with coffeemakers, hair dryers, and Nintendo video games. Guests also have use of an indoor/outdoor heated pool and an exercise room with sauna and whirlpool. Other facilities include a garden atrium restaurant and a sports bar with a 10-foot big-screen TV. ♿

RENAISSANCE AUSTIN HOTEL
9721 Arboretum Blvd.
Austin, TX 78759
512/343-2626 or 800/HOTELS-1
$$$$ **NWA**
Formerly the Stouffer Renaissance Hotel, this elegant accommodation is located in the upscale Arboretum shopping area, with restaurants, boutique shopping, and movie theaters within walking distance. Visitors also have use of a full health club including an indoor/outdoor pool. The hotel offers three restaurants, a lobby bar, and an adjacent nightclub, Tangerines. ♿

Motels

CORPORATE LODGING SUITES
4815 W. Braker Ln., #516
Austin, TX 78759
512/345-8822 or 800/845-6343
$$–$$$ **NWA**
This unique service links travelers with apartments for as little as a

NORTHWEST AUSTIN

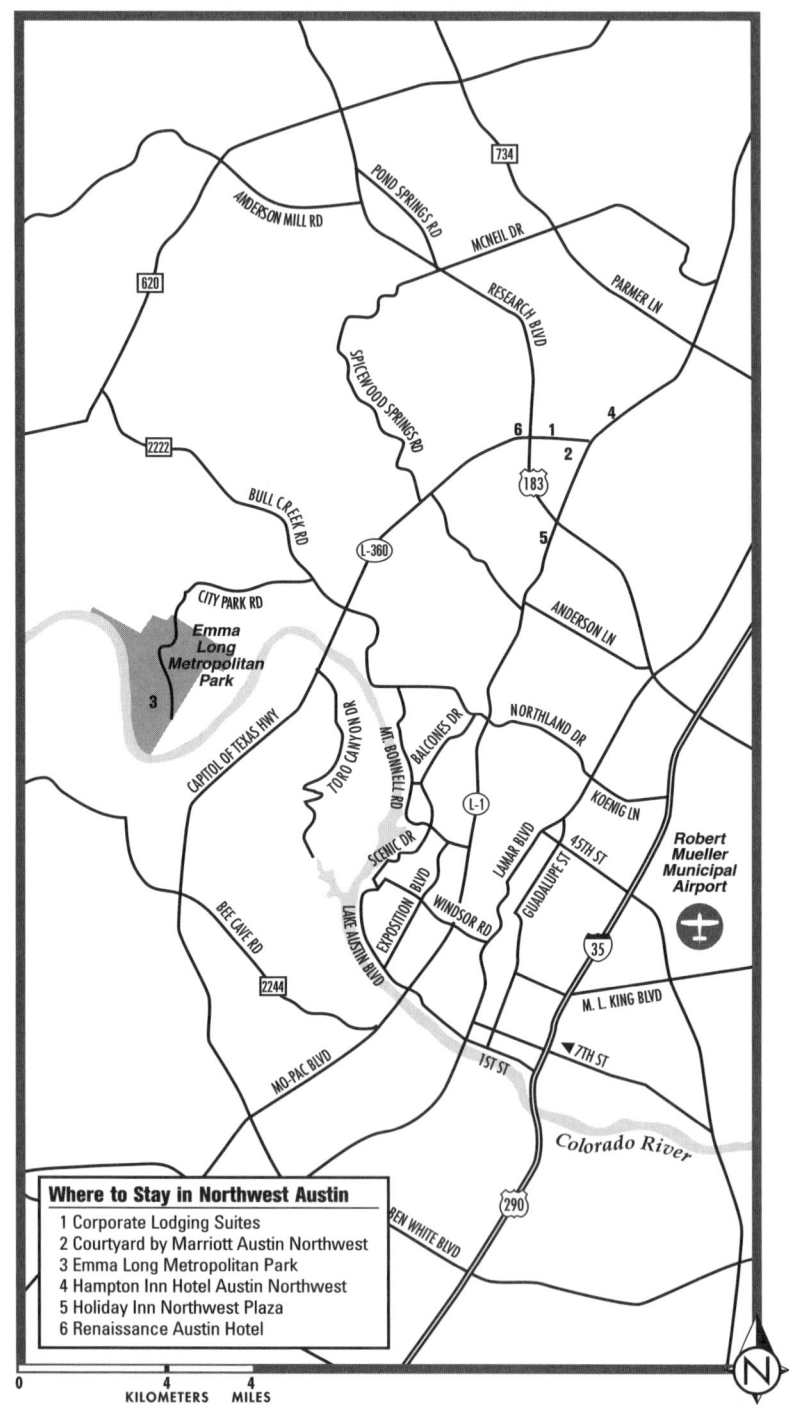

one-night stay. The seven apartment communities are located in far-northwest Austin near the Arboretum and include one- and two-bedroom apartments with varying amenities. Some properties include fireplaces; all are fully furnished and include washer and dryer, TV, VCR, and daily maid service. &

Campgrounds

EMMA LONG METROPOLITAN PARK
6.5 miles off RR 2222
on City Park Rd.
512/346-1831
$ NWA
There are 20 three-way hookups available here, as well as tent sites and all facilities. Camping is $6 per night for a site without utilities (plus a first-day entry fee of $3 per vehicle Mon–Thur or $5 Fri–Sat). Sites with utilities cost $10 per day plus the first-day entry fee.

SOUTHWEST AUSTIN

Hotels

MELBOURNE HOTEL & CONFERENCE CENTER
4611 Bee Caves Rd.
Austin, TX 78746
512/328-4000
$$–$$$ SWA
The Melbourne is a quiet haven in Westlake Hills, a pleasant suburb of Austin. The setting combines the quiet of Hill Country with big-city conveniences. Each of the 55 guest rooms includes a small refrigerator; there is a gazebo in the garden, and conference rooms can accommodate from five to 100 people. &

Motels

HEART OF TEXAS MOTEL
5303 U.S. Hwy 290 West
Austin, Texas 78735
512/892-0644
$–$$ SWA
For a small place, this 30-room motel offers some nice amenities. In addition to king-size beds and recliners, guest rooms have refrigerators and microwaves, cable TV with HBO, remote control, and free local calls. Along with a swimming pool, guests can enjoy a putting green and horseshoe facilities.

SOUTH AUSTIN

Hotels

EMBASSY SUITES
300 South Congress Ave.
Austin, TX 78704
512/469-9000 or 800/EMBASSY
$$$$ SA
Located just south of the river on the corner of Barton Springs Road, the Embassy has 262 suites, both smoking and nonsmoking, opening directly onto a plant-filled, skylit atrium. Each suite contains two TVs, two telephones, wet bar, microwave, refrigerator, coffeemaker, ironing board and iron, and hair dryer. Children under 12 stay free in same suite as parents. &

HOLIDAY INN SOUTH
3401 S. I-35
Austin, TX 78741
512/448-2444 or 800/HOLIDAY
$$$ SA
Every convenience is provided at this recently redecorated luxury hotel. Each of the 190 oversized rooms and 20 elegant suites features a desk

SOUTHWEST AUSTIN

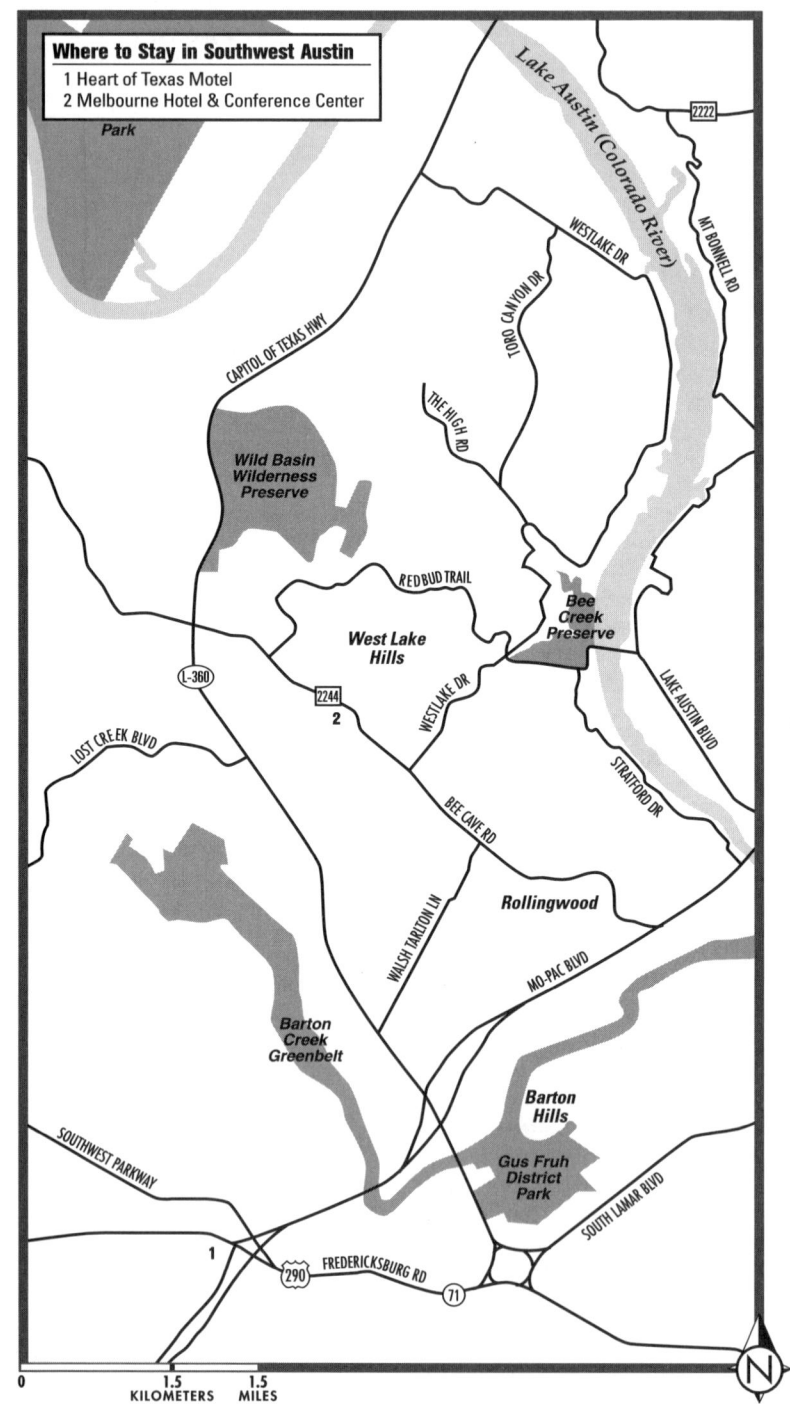

area, telephone, modem hook-up, refrigerator/freezer, coffeemaker, remote control color TV, HBO, and pay-per-view movies. A Country Kitchen Restaurant, a lobby lounge, and a swimming pool, as well as complimentary airport transportation, free parking, room and valet service, and on-site laundry facilities add to guest comforts. &

HYATT REGENCY AUSTIN
208 Barton Springs Rd.
Austin, TX 78704
512/477-1234 or 800/233-1234
$$$$ SA
The 446-room hotel, which includes 18 suites, is located on the south shores of Town Lake, close to Palmer Auditorium and right on Austin's 9-mile hike-and-bike-trail. It's also convenient to the Austin Convention Center, the Capitol, the University of Texas, and 6th Street, Austin's famed entertainment district. The hotel has two restaurants and two lounges, a fully equipped health club, and an outdoor pool and whirlpool, as well as complete conference, meeting, and banquet facilities. Guest rooms have hairdryers, irons and ironing boards, and voice mail. &

OMNI AUSTIN SOUTHPARK
4140 Governor's Row
Austin, TX 78744
512/448-2222
$$$$ SA
This was until very recently a Wyndham Hotel. On the eastside of I-35, it offers meeting space, a restaurant, health club and pool, and free parking. &

Motels
AUSTIN MOTEL
1220 S. Congress Ave.

Austin, TX 78704
512/441-1157
$–$$$ SA
This historic motel with beautiful Spanish styling and a pool has been renovated. It offers free HBO and free coffee and is located just over a mile south of Town Lake.

BEST WESTERN SEVILLE
PLAZA INN
4323 S. I-35
Austin, TX 78744
512/447-5511 or 800/528-1234
$$ SA
Local telephone calls are free from this motel, which also has guest laundry and in-room coffee. Amenities include HBO, a pool, and continental breakfast. The motel is on the Interstate near Ben White Boulevard close to U.S. 90 and U.S. 71. &

DAYS INN SOUTH
4220 S. I-35
Austin, TX 78745

The historic Driskill Hotel, page 27

WHERE TO STAY

SOUTH AUSTIN

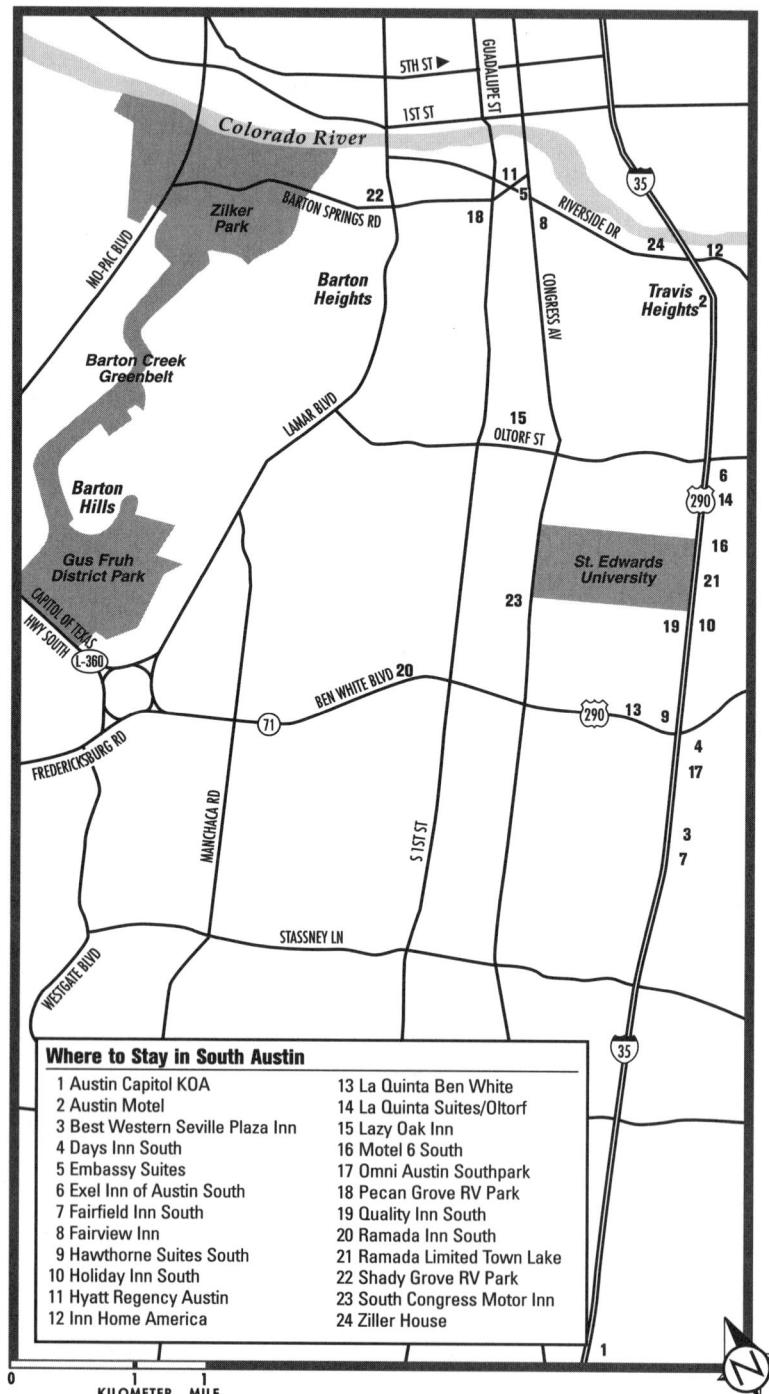

Where to Stay in South Austin

1. Austin Capitol KOA
2. Austin Motel
3. Best Western Seville Plaza Inn
4. Days Inn South
5. Embassy Suites
6. Exel Inn of Austin South
7. Fairfield Inn South
8. Fairview Inn
9. Hawthorne Suites South
10. Holiday Inn South
11. Hyatt Regency Austin
12. Inn Home America
13. La Quinta Ben White
14. La Quinta Suites/Oltorf
15. Lazy Oak Inn
16. Motel 6 South
17. Omni Austin Southpark
18. Pecan Grove RV Park
19. Quality Inn South
20. Ramada Inn South
21. Ramada Limited Town Lake
22. Shady Grove RV Park
23. South Congress Motor Inn
24. Ziller House

512/441-9242 or 800/325-2525
$$–$$$ SA
No swimming pool here, but there are Jacuzzi jets in the bathtubs. Rooms also have mini-refrigerators, 25-inch TVs with HBO, cable, and remote control, and free local telephone calls. A complimentary continental breakfast is served in the lobby. &

EXEL INN OF AUSTIN SOUTH
2711 S. I-35
Austin, TX 78741
512/462-9201 or 800/356-8013
$ SA
Guest rooms have remote control TVs and clock/radios, local calls are free. Laundry facilities, a pool, and a complimentary continental breakfast are also offered.

FAIRFIELD INN SOUTH
4525 S. I-35
Austin, TX 78744
512/707-8899 or 800/228-2800
$$ SA
Located off I-35 South, the inn boasts famous Marriott hospitality with down-to-earth prices. In addition to bright and attractive guest rooms, the hotel offers spa rooms with personal spas and king-size beds, plus complimentary continental breakfast, a heated indoor pool and exercise room, a free movie channel, and free local phone calls. Fax and copy services are available. &

HAWTHORNE SUITES SOUTH
4020 S. I-35
Austin, TX 78704
512/440-7722 or 800/527-1133
$$$–$$$$ SA
These suites come with fully equipped kitchens and irons and ironing boards. Complimentary breakfast and a social hour are offered. Choose an "open-air" suite, with no divisions between the rooms, or a two-story suite. &

INN HOME AMERICA
1001 S. I-35
Austin, TX 78741
512/326-0100
$$$$ SA
All guest rooms and suites have fully equipped kitchens to make you feel at home. Phone numbers are private, local calls are free, and there is voice mail, too. Suites are rented by the day, the week, or the month, with weekly maid service. Ask for a room with a view—of downtown along the lake. &

LA QUINTA BEN WHITE
4200 S. I-35
Austin, TX 78745
512/443-1774 or 800/531-5900
$$ SA
Gold Medal Rooms feature fresh decor with rich wood furniture, expanded bathrooms, and more. A complimentary breakfast includes cereal, fresh fruit, pastries, bagels, juice, milk, and coffee. &

LA QUINTA SUITES/OLTORF
1603 Oltorf
Austin, TX 78741
512/447-6661 and 800/531-5900
$$ SA
La Quinta's fresh new look includes a crisp white exterior with teal trim; offered are a complimentary light breakfast and free local calls. &

MOTEL 6 SOUTH
2707 S. I-35
Austin, TX 78701
512/444-5882 or 800/440-6000
$ SA
Located about 2½ miles south of

downtown, the Motel 6 South has 109 guest rooms, a swimming pool, and TV with cable and HBO. There's coffee in the lobby every morning at 7:00 a.m., and a convenient Kettle Restaurant on the premises. &

QUALITY INN SOUTH
2200 S. I-35
Austin, TX 78704
512/444-0561 or 800/228-5151
$$ SA
Minutes from downtown, the state capitol, 6th Street entertainment district, and Dallas Cowboys training camp at St. Edward's University, this motel is also not far from the Wildflower Research Center. Amenities include a swimming pool and hot tub, a fitness room, complimentary continental breakfast in the lobby, and the Marco Polo restaurant next door. &

RAMADA INN SOUTH
1212 W. Ben White Blvd.
Austin, TX 78704
512/447-0151 or 800/228-2828
$$–$$$ SA
The motel offers both standard rooms and suites, which have full-size Jacuzzi tubs in the center of the rooms. Along with a swimming pool, cable TV, and HBO, guests at the Ramada Inn South get a full all-you-can-eat breakfast of eggs, pancakes, fruit— the works. &

RAMADA LIMITED TOWN LAKE
2915 S. I-35
Austin, TX 78741
512/444-8432
$ SA
This motel, about 2 miles south of downtown, has 58 rooms with TV and HBO, and a pool. A complimentary continental breakfast is offered in the front lobby each morning.

SOUTH CONGRESS MOTOR INN
3012 S. Congress Ave.
Austin, TX 78704
512/443-8383
$ SA
Morning donuts and coffee and a swimming pool are features at this 38-room motor inn. All rooms have cable TV.

Bed and Breakfast

FAIRVIEW INN
1304 Newning Ave.
Austin, TX 78704
512/444-4746 or 800/310-4746
$$$ SA
Built in 1910 and set in large, well-landscaped grounds well off the street and shaded by old oak trees, this Texas Colonial Revival mansion is barely a mile from busy downtown. The lovingly restored home carries an Austin Landmark designation and a 1993 Austin Heritage Award for historic preservation. This neighborhood is known as Travis Heights, and it's safe enough to walk the streets at night. Famous Texans were entertained in the mansion in the past. All the rooms are Texas-size: There are four guest rooms in the big house and two suites in the carriage house in the rear, all of which have private baths.

LAZY OAK INN
211 W. Live Oak
Austin, TX 78704
512/447-8873
$$$ SA
This plantation-style farmhouse, built circa 1911, is barely six minutes from downtown and walking distance to the shops and restaurants on South Congress Avenue. Relax on the front porch or by the backyard fish pond. The Lazy Oak Inn's

rate includes a continental breakfast.

ZILLER HOUSE
800 Edgecliff Terr.
Austin, TX 78704
512/462-0100 or 800/949-5446
$$$ SA

Although it sits on a rock ledge overhanging Town Lake, Ziller House is screened from the street by 2½ acres of greenery. At night the lights of downtown Austin seem close enough to touch. The white Mediterranean-style house has a stucco interior, a perfect setting for its artwork and furniture. There are four guest rooms, each with a private bath and a cabinet containing a microwave, coffeemaker, refrigerator, and utensils, in case you don't want to eat out. Breakfast can be brought to your room if you prefer not to mingle with other guests.

Campgrounds

AUSTIN CAPITOL KOA
7009 S. I-35
Austin, TX 78744
512/444-6322 or 800/284-0206
Daily, weekly, monthly rates.   SA

The campgrounds have 132 three-way hookups, a tent village, eight cabins, and all facilities.

PECAN GROVE RV PARK
1518 Barton Springs Rd.
Austin, TX 78741
512/472-1067
$ SA

Self-contained RVs only at 13 three-way hookups.

SHADY GROVE RV PARK
1600 Barton Springs Rd.
Austin, TX 78741
512/499-8432

$ SA

This RV park offers 50 three-way hookups; electric, water, and cable are included in the price.

EAST AUSTIN

Hotels

EMBASSY SUITES AIRPORT
5901 N. I-35
Austin, TX 78723
512/454-8004 or 800/EMBASSY
$$$ EA

The complimentary amenities of this all-suites property include a full breakfast and a manager's reception in the evenings with both alcoholic and non-alcoholic beverages and snacks. The hotel includes an indoor pool and exercise facility. ♿

Motels

ECONOLODGE
6201 Hwy. 290 East
Austin, TX 78723
512/458-4759 or 800/553-2666
$$ EA

Located at the intersection of I-35 and U.S. 290, this basic but comfortable chain motel includes a complimentary continental breakfast for guests, as well as access to an outdoor swimming pool. ♿

LA QUINTA OLTORF
1603 Oltorf
Austin, TX 78741
512/447-6661 or 800/531-5900
$$ EA

A swimming pool, complimentary breakfast, oversize desks, dataport phones with computer hookups, and microwave/refrigerators are available for guests. ♿

EAST AUSTIN

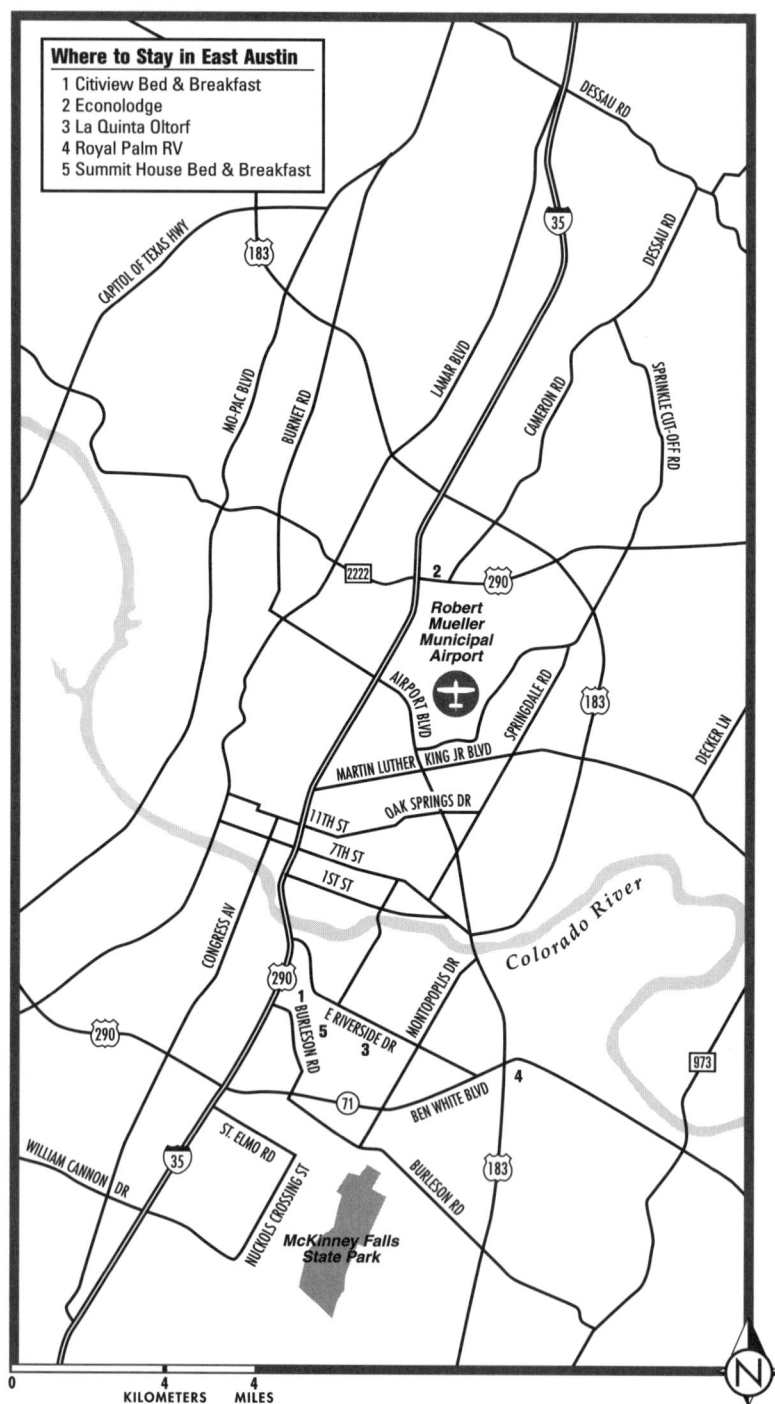

Bed and Breakfast

CITIVIEW BED & BREAKFAST
1405 E. Riverside Dr.
Austin, TX 78741
512/441-2606
$$$–$$$$ EA

This Frank Lloyd Wright–style home from the 1950s is built high on a hill, with picture windows framing a panoramic view of downtown to the north. The decor is art deco, of course, and there's lots of land surrounding the inn.

**SUMMIT HOUSE
BED & BREAKFAST**
1204 Summit St.
Austin, TX 78741
512/445-5304
$$ EA

The Summit House is on top of a hill, hence its name. The guest room has a queen-size bed and a spacious sitting area; a filling, down-home breakfast is served each morning. The house and herb garden are situated on an old Indian campground under 100-year-old oak trees, just minutes from downtown.

Campgrounds

ROYAL PALM RV
7901 East Ben White Blvd.
Austin, TX 78744
512/385-2211
$ EA

There are 32 three-way hookups here along with all facilities—but no tents.

WHERE TO STAY

4
WHERE TO EAT

Austin boasts fine restaurants serving haute cuisine and continental fare, but real Texas dining lies in the small-town diners, the neighborhood cafés, and the smoky barbecue pits across the state.

Cattle rule in Texas, and beef, from T-bone to ground, makes an appearance on every menu and at every backyard cookout. The early cowboy cooks knew that not all meat was like steak; some of it was tough and even stringy. They used Western ingenuity to turn what could have been waste into dishes that award-winning restaurants are now proud to serve. Chicken-fried steak is such a dish, using one of the toughest cuts of meat: the round steak. It's tenderized (the cook just beats the meat into submission), then dipped in an egg and milk batter, floured, and fried to a golden crisp.

Fajitas are a favorite "trash to treasure" Tex-Mex treat. Fajitas were created by chuckwagon cooks who learned that marinating the tough skirt steak in lime juice broke down the meat into chewable consistency. Sliced in narrow strips and grilled, it is now served with cheese, salsa, and guacamole, and rolled into a flour tortilla. Restaurants like to toss the meat onto a hot metal platter with a squirt of lime juice, sending up enough fragrant fajita smoke to make everyone around wish they had ordered this spicy concoction.

The following list of restaurants is just a sampling of what we think are some of the best dining establishments in Austin, a city with hundreds of eateries. The cost rating guide is based upon an appetizer, entrée, and dessert for one person. Wheelchair accessibility is indicated by the ⚿ symbol.

Price rating symbols:
- $ Under $10
- $$ $11 to $20
- $$$$ $21 and up

AMERICAN
East Side Cafe (EA), 76
Good Eats Cafe (NA, SA), 61, 72
Green Pastures (SA), 72
Hut's Hamburgers (DA), 56
Kerbey Lane Cafe (NA, NWA, SA), 62, 66, 73
The Lodge at Lakeview (SWA), 66–67
Ma Ferguson's (NA), 62
Old Pecan Street Cafe (DA), 58
Shady Grove (SA), 74
Threadgill's (NA), 64
Waterloo Ice House (DA), 59

ASIAN
Chinatown (NWA, SWA), 64, 69
Hunan Lion (SA), 73
Korean Garden Restaurant (NA), 62
Mongolian BBQ (DA, NA), 58, 62
Seoul Sushi Bar and Restaurant (SA), 74
Tien Jin Chinese Restaurant (SA), 74

BARBECUE
Artz Rib House (SA), 70
County Line on the Lake (NWA), 66
Five Star Smokehouse (SWA), 69
Green Mesquite (SA), 72
Iron Works Barbecue (DA), 56
Pok-E-Jo's Smokehouse (NWA), 67
Rudy's Country Store & BBQ (NWA), 67
Sam's Bar-B-Cue (EA), 76
Stubb's Bar-B-Q (DA), 58–59

BEST BREAKFAST
Cisco's Bakery, Restaurant and Bar (EA), 74–75
Nau Enfield Drug (DA), 58
Trudy's Texas Star (NA), 64

DELICATESSEN
Katz's (DA), 57

FINE DINING
Bitter End Bistro and Brewery (DA), 52
Jeffrey's (DA), 56
Mezzaluna (DA), 57
Paggi House (SA), 73

GERMAN
Scholz Garten (DA), 63

INTERNATIONAL
Belgian Restaurant L'Estro Armonico (SWA), 69
Brio (DA), 54
Chez Nous (DA), 54
Granite Cafe (DA), 56
Hula Hut (NWA), 66
Jean-Pierre's Upstairs (NA), 62
Louie's 106 (DA), 57

ITALIAN
Aldo's Northwest (NW), 64
Brick Oven (DA), 52–54
Carmelo's Italian Restaurant (DA), 54

MEXICAN
Casita Jorge's (NA), 61
Chuy's (SA), 72
Fonda San Miguel (NA), 61
La Palapa (EA), 76
Las Palomas (SWA), 70
Las Manitas Avenue Cafe (DA), 57
Manuel's Downtown (DA), 57
Mexico Tipico Restaurante (EA), 76
Nuevo Leon (EA), 76

TEX-MEX
El Arroyo (DA), 55
Jalisco Bar (SA), 73
Matt's El Rancho (SA), 73–74
Mesa Hills Cafe (NWA), 67
Ninfa's Mexican Restaurant (NA), 62
Rosie's Tamale House No. 2 (NWA), 67
Texas Chili Parlor (DA), 59
Trudy's Texas Star (NA), 64

SEAFOOD
Boiling Pot (DA), 52
Catfish Parlour (NWA), 64
Cherry Creek Catfish (SA), 70

City Grille (DA), 54
Gilligan's Seafood Restaurant (DA), 55
Joe's Crab Shack (NWA), 66
Pearl's Oyster Bar (NA), 63
Shoreline Grill (DA), 58

SOUTHWEST
Canyon Cafe (SWA), 69
Granite Cafe (DA), 56
Z Tejas Grille (DA), 59

STEAKS
Austin Land and
    Cattle Company (DA), 52
Dan McKlusky's (DA, NWA), 55, 66
The Hoffbrau (DA), 56

VEGETARIAN
Clearwater Cafe (DA), 54
Mr. Natural (EA), 76
West Lynn Cafe (DA), 59

DOWNTOWN AUSTIN

**AUSTIN LAND AND
CATTLE COMPANY**
1205 N. Lamar Blvd., Austin
512/472-1813
$$$ DA
Here, steaks are hand cut, aged properly, and seasoned with a secret family recipe that they won't give out. Start with a salad, escargot, Texas sweet onion pie, or mushrooms battered with Shiner Bock, then move on to favorites like filet mignon, rib eye, or New York strip. Other popular dishes include New Zealand lamb chops with jalap or mint sauce, sauteed mahi-mahi, yellowfin tuna, grilled chicken, and vegetable lasagna. Dinner daily. Reservations recommended. ♿

**THE BITTER END BISTRO AND
BREWERY**

TRIVIA

What a choice! Austin has more restaurants and bars per capita than any other city in the U.S., and Austinites eat out more often than do residents of any other Texas city, including Dallas, Houston, and San Antonio.

311 Colorado St., Austin
512/478-2337
$$$ DA
Its name may include the word "brewery," but don't look for pub grub in this elegant eatery. One of Austin's most lauded restaurants, The Bitter End serves up surprising dishes such as grilled lamb loin with mint harissa, capellini with sun-dried tomatoes, and roasted duck breast with potato pancakes. Lunch Mon–Fri; dinner only Sat–Sun. ♿

THE BOILING POT
700 E. 6th St., Austin
512/472-0985
$$ DA
Don't wear your white shirts to this down-and-dirty seafood joint. Your waitress will robe you up with a plastic bib and hand you a wooden mallet, then set before you your task: a pan filled with spicy boiled shrimp, crab claws, sausage, corn on the cob, and potatoes, all spilled out on the "tablecloth" of white butcher paper. Roll up your sleeves and get to work. Lunch and dinner Fri–Sun; dinner only Mon–Thur. ♿

BRICK OVEN
1209 Red River St., Austin

DOWNTOWN AUSTIN

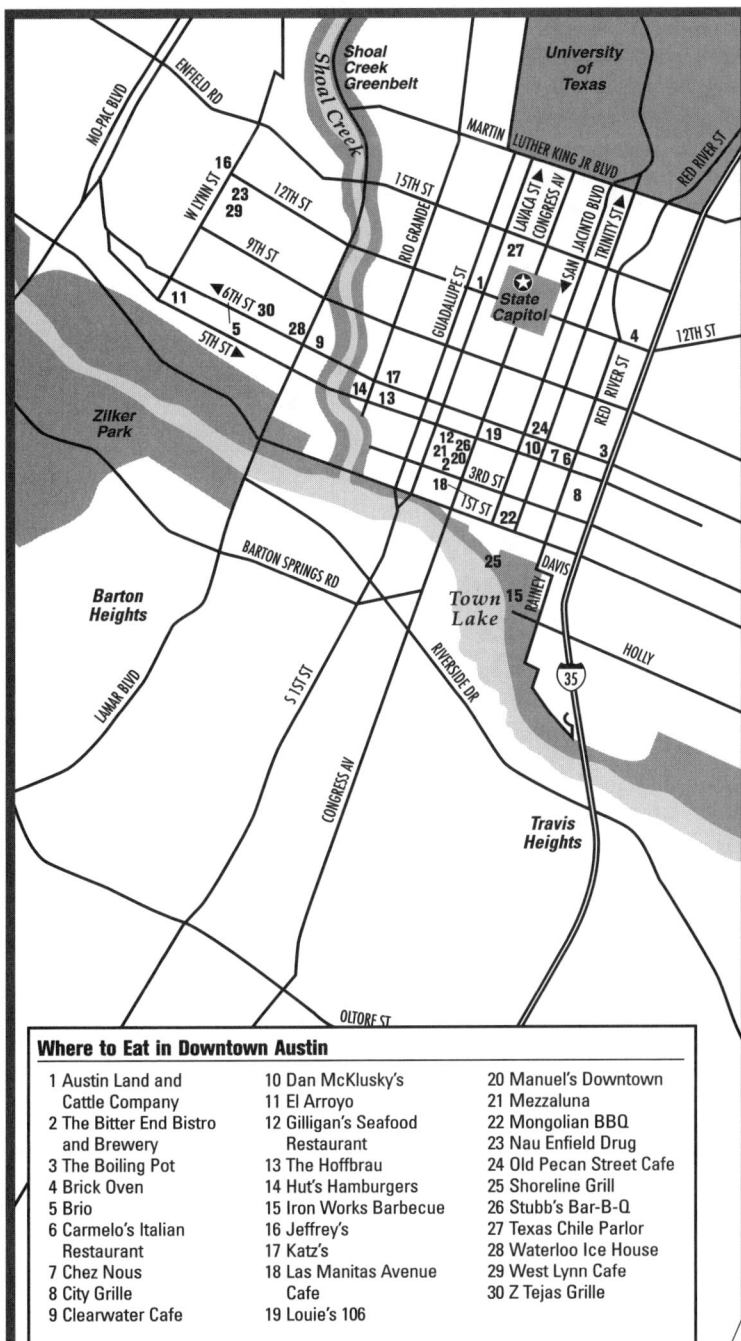

Where to Eat in Downtown Austin

1. Austin Land and Cattle Company
2. The Bitter End Bistro and Brewery
3. The Boiling Pot
4. Brick Oven
5. Brio
6. Carmelo's Italian Restaurant
7. Chez Nous
8. City Grille
9. Clearwater Cafe
10. Dan McKlusky's
11. El Arroyo
12. Gilligan's Seafood Restaurant
13. The Hoffbrau
14. Hut's Hamburgers
15. Iron Works Barbecue
16. Jeffrey's
17. Katz's
18. Las Manitas Avenue Cafe
19. Louie's 106
20. Manuel's Downtown
21. Mezzaluna
22. Mongolian BBQ
23. Nau Enfield Drug
24. Old Pecan Street Cafe
25. Shoreline Grill
26. Stubb's Bar-B-Q
27. Texas Chile Parlor
28. Waterloo Ice House
29. West Lynn Cafe
30. Z Tejas Grille

512/477-7006
$ DA
For over a decade and a half, the Brick Oven has offered some of Austin's finest pizza, elevating itself above the fast food genre to become a city tradition. Today three locations (the others are in northwest Austin on Research Boulevard and in north Austin on West 35th Street) provide diners with real oven-baked pizza as well as other Italian favorites. Lunch and dinner Mon–Sat; dinner only Sun. &

BRIO
1112 W. 6th St., Austin
512/499-0442
$$$–$$$$ DA
Brio's byword is "spirited dining," and both the artistic presentation and the vigorous seasoning live up to it, although it might be a smidgen too spicy for some palates. On up and coming West 6th Street, Brio's might be one of the new kids in town, but it comes with impressive credentials. Chef Raymond Tatum is considered the grand old man of Austin cuisine, and he gives full rein to his attractive and innovative "contemporary Texas cuisine," a flavorful mixture of the Southwest with an Asian and European flair. Dinner only. Reservations accepted. &

CARMELO'S
ITALIAN RESTAURANT
504 E. 5th St., Austin
512/477-7497
$$$ DA
Traditional Southern Italian cuisine is served here, as are delicious veal parmesan or veal marsala, seafood, and chicken. Lunch and dinner Mon–Fri. Reservations recommended. &

CHEZ NOUS
510 Neches St., Austin
512/473-2413
$$ DA
This personable, small French bistro just around the corner from 6th Street serves delicious, authentic French cuisine. The prix fixe menu du jour includes a choice of soup, appetizer or salad, entrée, and dessert. The simple decor is enlivened by a mural of Montmartre on one wall, lace curtains in the windows, flowers (not real) in aperitif bottles, and lots of French posters on other walls. Background music is soft; service is friendly and attentive. Lunch and dinner Tue–Fri, Sat–Sun dinner only.

CITY GRILLE
401 Sabine, Austin
512/479-0817
$$$ DA
You'll find the City Grille, specializing in mesquite grilled steaks and seafood, located in a refurbished warehouse from the 1890s. Old wooden floors and a beamed ceiling contrast with the elegance of candlelight and the linen tablecloths. The beef is certain to be tender and the grilled fish moist and tasty, all in line with the restaurant's popular reputation. Dinner seven days a week. Reservations recommended. &

CLEARWATER CAFE
601 N. Lamar Blvd., Austin
512/476-0902
$ DA
Located at the intersection of 6th Street and Lamar in the massive Whole Foods Market, this cafe features healthy entrées. Eastern dishes prevail but you'll also find a full selection of sandwiches, burgers (meat or veggie), and plenty of fresh fruit and vegetable juices. Lunch and dinner

Top Ten Places to Power Lunch in Austin
by Barbara Redding
Executive Editor of *Ports of Call*,
a publication of Weissmann Travel Reports

1. The Cafe at the Four Seasons Hotel, 98 San Jacinto Blvd., 512/478-4500.
2. Mezzaluna, 310 Colorado, 512/472-6770.
3. Castle Hill Cafe, 1101 West 5th Street, 512/476-0728.
4. Gilligan's Caribbean Grill, 4th and Colorado, 512/474-7474.
5. West Lynn Cafe, 1110 West Lynn, 512/482-0950.
6. Mañuel's, 310 Congress, 512/472-7555
7. Fonda San Miguel, 2330 West Loop Blvd., 512/459-4121.
8. Lupin, 3300 West Anderson Lane, 512/454-6054.
9. Green Pastures, 811 West Live Oak, 512/441-1888.
10. Paggi House, 200 Lee Barton Drive, 512/478-1121.

Mon–Sat; breakfast, lunch, and dinner Sun. ♿

DAN MCKLUSKY'S
301 E. 6th St., Austin
512/473-8924
$$$$ DA
This is a steak-lover's mecca, where wait staff serve up consistently tender steaks. Also "custom combinations" can be ordered: steak and chicken, steak and seafood, steak and lamb, even steak and quail. All served with a generous house salad and your choice of baked or fried potatoes, rice pilaf, or the fresh vegetable of the day. Lunch Mon–Fri; dinner seven days a week. ♿

EL ARROYO
1624 W. 5th St., Austin
512/474-1222
$–$$ DA
Named for the dry arroyo that carves through the lot, El Arroyo serves up popular Tex-Mex dishes, killer margaritas, and Mexican brews. You can dine indoors or outside in this eatery that's a favorite with many longtime Austinites. Lunch and dinner daily. ♿

GILLIGAN'S SEAFOOD RESTAURANT
407 Colorado St., Austin
512/474-7474
$$–$$$ DA
With a name like Gilligan's, you'd expect island cuisine, and that's just what you get at this casually elegant eatery. Don't expect the fun atmosphere of joints like the Hula Hut, however; Gilligan's serves up its island fare atop white tablecloths. Check out the Jamaican jerk or favorites like coconut shrimp. Dinner daily. ♿

WHERE TO EAT

GRANITE CAFE
2905 San Gabriel St., Austin
512/472-6483
$$$ NA
For a decade, the owners of two other popular Austin eateries, Mezzaluna and The Bitter End, have operated the Granite Cafe. This innovative restaurant offers dishes with a Southwest flair such as Southwestern rubbed Texas rib eye, and chicken quesadillas with sour cream and smoked tomato salsa. Open for lunch and dinner daily. &

THE HOFFBRAU
613 W. 6th St., Austin
512/472-0822
$–$$ DA
Since 1934, grilled steaks and chicken have satisfied hungry downtown employees at this casual eatery. Lunch and dinner Mon–Fri.

HUT'S HAMBURGERS
807 W. 6th St., Austin
512/472-0693
$ DA
Since 1939 this hip-hopping joint has been serving up some of Austin's most popular burgers. Over 20 types of burgers—from the Wolfman Jack to the Big Bopper—grace the menu, which also includes chicken-fried steak, salads, and a daily special. Save room for the Texas-size onion rings. Lunch and dinner daily. &

IRON WORKS BARBECUE
100 Red River, Austin
512/478-4855
$ DA
The Ironworks for years was just that, an ironworks. The rustic building that housed the Weigel Ironworks now cooks up delicious brisket, chicken, sausage, and ribs near the Convention Center. The classic barbecue plate comes with a choice of two out of three side dishes: beans, salad, and cole slaw. Top this off with a slice of pecan, apple, or cherry pie, or peach cobbler, while you enjoy deciphering the dozens of brands burned into the wooden siding. Lunch and dinner Mon–Fri; lunch only Sat.

JEFFREY'S
1204 West Lynn, Austin
512/477-5584
$$$ DA
Chef David Garrido, recently acclaimed by the James Beard Foundation, makes magic with an amazing array of flavors. For adventurous cuisine, this fine dining establishment in the historic Clarksville neighborhood takes high honors indeed. For starters, Chef Garrido suggests shredded goose on a small blue corn taco sauced with fresh mango puree. Oysters are a specialty, served crispy on root chips (sea sprouts) with habañero honey aioli. Sturgeon, pecan-wood smoked

Katz's

© Permenter & Bigley

> Incidentally (or not so incidentally), all of Austin's restaurants are non-smoking. This caused quite a flap at the time, but things have settled down considerably, and folks seem to eat out as often as before.

for sweetness and served in an orange champagne sauce, is accompanied by a black Oregon truffle in a wine/butter/shallot sauce. Exotic dishes like elk, served with hazelnut wild rice and huckleberry thyme sauce, are also on the menu. But be sure to leave room for desserts too. Dinner only, Mon–Sat. Reservations recommended. ♿

KATZ'S
618 W. 6th St., Austin
512/472-2037
$–$$ **DA**
"We never klose" is the boast of this restaurant, open 24 hours a day. This is where Austinites have been getting their kosher-style deli fix since 1979 when Katz's introduced bagel and deli to the Texas vocabulary. Bagels range from toasted with butter for $1.95 to the legendary cream cheese–slathered roll, thick with lox and green lettuce for $8.50. Chicken soup comes with both noodles and matzoh balls, and homemade blintzes come in a choice of cheese, apple, or blueberry. To top it all off, there's Top of the Marc (see Nightlife) with music and dancing nightly: jazz, rock, and blues. Breakfast, lunch and dinner seven days a week. ♿

LAS MANITAS AVENUE CAFE
211 Congress Ave., Austin
512/472-9357
$–$$ **DA**
Grab a booth up front, take a stool at the counter, or head to the back (walk right on through the kitchen) to the covered patio for some good downtown Tex-Mex. Check out the chalupas, tacos, or enchiladas, or start your morning with breakfast in either American or Tex-Mex style. Breakfast and lunch daily. ♿

LOUIE'S 106
106 E. 6th St., Austin
512/476-1997
$$$ **DA**
Tapas, those delicious appetizers from Spain, are a specialty here, as are pastas, risottos, bouillabaisse, paella, and special meats from the rotisserie. Lunch Mon–Fri; dinner seven days a week. ♿

MANUEL'S DOWNTOWN
310 Congress Ave., Austin
512/472-7555
$$$ **DA**
Manuel's offers interesting variations of such favorites as grilled (not fried) flautas filled with your choice of shredded beef, pork, chicken, or, for vegetarians, black beans and cheese or mushrooms. The chile rellenos are poblano peppers stuffed with sweet corn, cilantro, and cheese. No lard and no preservatives go into anything cooked and served at this lively spot. Lunch and dinner Mon–Fri; brunch and dinner Sat–Sun. ♿

MEZZALUNA
310 Colorado St., Austin
512/472-6770
$$–$$$ **DA**

The fine Italian restaurant offers a variety of pasta dishes. Lunch and dinner Mon–Fri; dinner only Sat–Sun. Reservations recommended. &

MONGOLIAN BBQ
117 San Jacinto, Austin
512/476-3938
$ **DA**
With more than 15 fresh vegetables and three choices of meat, you can create the stir-fry of your dreams in this large and rustic eatery on the corner of San Jacinto and 2nd. After dousing the heaping plateful of raw comestibles with a variety of sauces, watch it sizzle on a Mongolian grill right before your eyes. Down a few steps from the grill, eat on a picnic-style table in a large room with a mirrored wall. Lunch, dinner daily. &

NAU ENFIELD DRUG
1115 West Lynn, Austin
512/476-1221
$ **DA**
This old-fashioned drug store is a longtime favorite with locals. Belly up to the counter or take a booth and enjoy a taste of a real drugstore malt, burger, or sandwich. Breakfasts are very popular as well, when the grill serves up omelets, huevos rancheros, and so many types of breakfast tacos they have a poster listing possible combinations. Try anything from chorizo and potato to egg and cheese. Breakfast and lunch daily. &

OLD PECAN STREET CAFE
310 E. 6th St., Austin
512/478-2491
$–$$ **DA**
The cafe is in a historic building, the Platt-Simpson, which in 1871 was part of a livery stable. In 1901 it became a hardware store. Inside there are original stone walls and wooden floors; outside on the red brick wall is a plaque telling the building's history. The restaurant is easy to spot; the windows are shaded by bright blue awnings. In addition to offering a nice variety of meals, the menu lists certain favorites each night, so if you find something you really like, you can count on it being there. That the pecan pie is a perennial favorite goes without saying. Lunch and dinner Mon–Sat; Sunday brunch. &

SHORELINE GRILL
98 San Jacinto, Austin
512/477-3300
$$$ **DA**
For a ringside seat to see the bats on the Congress Avenue Bridge, this is the place. Especially when you can enjoy a memorable seafood or prime rib meal while overlooking Town Lake. Lunch Mon–Fri; dinner daily. Reservations recommended. &

STUBB'S BAR-B-Q
801 Red River, Austin

Brio, page 54

512/480-0203
$ **DA**

Stubb's is well-known for both its barbecue and its blues, with a long history of featuring both smokin' musicians and slow-cooked meats. Try Stubb's beef and pork link sausage, beef brisket, and either beef or pork spare ribs. Plates are served heaped with traditional side orders such as potato salad, coleslaw, beans, yellow squash, corn on the cob, green beans, stewed tomatoes and okra, country greens, and more. If barbecue's not your thing, you'll find a catch of the day on the menu as well as chicken-fried steak, marinated chicken breast, and other dishes prepared away from the smoker. Lunch and dinner are served; open until 2 a.m. ♿

TEXAS CHILI PARLOR
1409 Lavaca, Austin
512/472-2828
$ **DA**

When out-of-state visitors come to Austin, they look for a real taste of the Lone Star State. And they find it at the Texas Chili Parlor, a funky restaurant that's within walking distance of the Capitol. Saunter up to a bowl of red... and make that "XXX" chili if you're feeling especially brave. Other dishes include Tex-Mex favorites and burgers. Lunch and dinner daily; late-night hours Thursday through Saturday ♿

WATERLOO ICE HOUSE
600 N. Lamar Blvd., Austin
512/472-5400
$ **DA**

Burgers, fries, tacos, nachos, chicken, chicken-fried steak, and once-in-a-while specials are to be had in this informal eatery where everything is prepared from scratch. Waterloo also boasts an extensive beer selection. Lunch and dinner daily. ♿

WEST LYNN CAFE
1110 West Lynn, Austin
512/482-0950
$ **DA**

The innovative menu of this vegetarian restaurant includes such dishes as spanokopita, a classic Greek dish of flaky phyllo dough layered with spinach, eggs, and sliced almonds and topped with fresh dill and oregano and ricotta and feta cheeses. Some dishes on the menu can be prepared cholesterol-free and non-dairy if you wish. Sandwiches, salads, smoothies, fresh juices, and natural sodas are also on the menu in this attractive cafe, where you can eat outdoors under an arbor. Lunch and dinner; Sunday brunch. ♿

Z TEJAS GRILLE
1110 W. 6th St., Austin
512/478-5355
$–$$ **DA**

This restaurant is perched atop a flight of outdoor stairs, leading up to both outdoor and indoor dining. The grill is affiliated with Brio's Restaurant next door and shares the same enthusiasm for innovative cuisine with unusual food blends. Crunchy catfish beignets are served with jalapeño tartar sauce, and the chicken and sausage gumbo ya-ya is as tasty as its name is enthusiastic. Voodoo tuna is served with black peppercorn vinaigrette and soy mustard sauce, and z'green salad, of mixed greens with Roma tomatoes and colored peppers, comes with a sun-dried tomato basil dressing. Breakfast, lunch, and dinner daily. ♿

NORTH AUSTIN

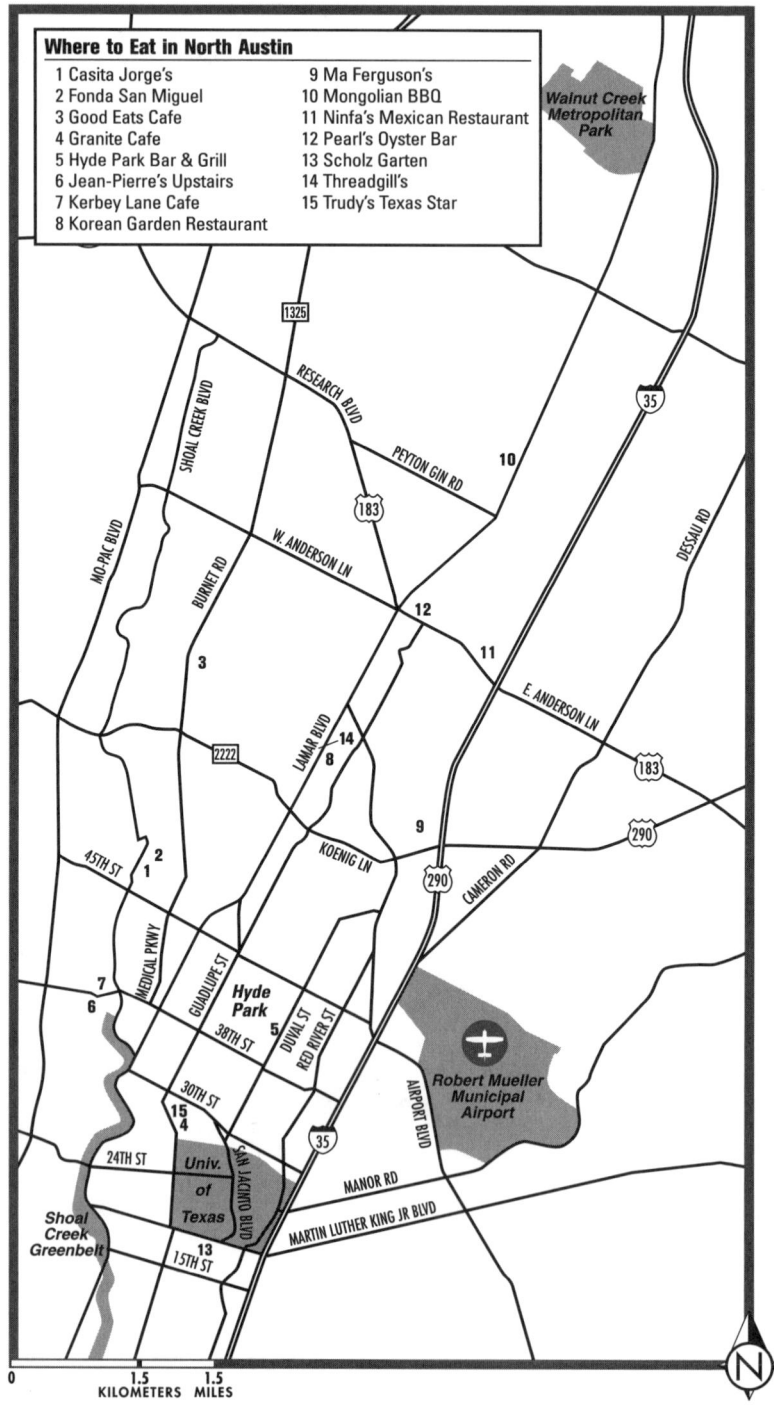

Old Pecan Street Cafe, page 58

NORTH AUSTIN

CASITA JORGE'S
2203 Hancock Dr., Austin
512/454-1980
$$ NA
If you bring along the kids, ask for a table near the aquariums; otherwise opt for patio dining on a nice day. This lively restaurant serves up top-rate Tex-Mex, with popular dishes including enchiladas, fajitas, tacos, and all the usual, dished out with rice and beans. The margaritas are hefty, so take it easy. Lunch and dinner daily. &

FONDA SAN MIGUEL
2330 W. North Loop, Austin
512/459-4121
$$$ NA
Fonda's hacienda Sunday brunch is an Austin treat, as is the classic Mexican cuisine on the regular menu. Here you'll find a beautiful setting of Mexican tiles and artifacts and a plant-filled bar serving unique drinks. Dinner Mon–Sun; brunch Sun 11:30–2. Reservations recommended. &

GOOD EATS CAFE
6801 Burnet Rd., Austin
512/451-2560
$ NA
Like its sister eatery down in South Austin, Good Eats can be counted on for both grilled and lean, fried and steamed—food to suit all-American palates whether you're looking for chicken-fried steak or a heaping plate of steamed vegetables. When Good Eats fries, it's with canola oil only; and on the healthy side of the menu you'll find high-fiber, low-fat, nutrient-dense choices. Daily specials are posted on the chalkboard in this informal cafe with roadside-diner atmosphere and friendly, laid-back help. Breakfast, lunch, and dinner. &

HYDE PARK BAR & GRILL
4206 Duval St., Austin
512/458-3168
$–$$ NA
Hyde Park Grill, a very informal all-American eatery, has super lentil

soup on the menu daily, and there's also a soup of the day if you want a change. We like their stir-fry and the spicy chicken salad, but the spinach salad is delicious, too. Lunch and dinner daily. &

JEAN-PIERRE'S UPSTAIRS
3500 Jefferson, Second Level, Austin
512/454-4811
$$$$ NA

The menu blends continental and Southwest in such dishes as grilled salmon wrapped in apple-smoked bacon and served with a key lime port sauce; or tequila beef tenderloin with a burgundy peppercorn sauce, accompanied with tender julienne vegetables. But be sure to save room for the famous dessert souffles; so far Jean Pierre's is the only restaurant in town to serve them. Open for lunch Mon–Fri; dinner Mon–Sat. Reservations recommended.

KERBEY LANE CAFE
3704 Kerbey Ln., Austin
512/451-1436
$$$ NA

Start your day right with Kerbey Lane's pancakes, sandwiches, crisp salads, and all sorts of imaginative specials. The migas (eggs scrambled with crispy tortilla bits) with spicy red sauce are as good as can be found anywhere. The service is friendly and snappy. Breakfast, lunch, and dinner daily. &

KOREAN GARDEN RESTAURANT
6519 N. Lamar Blvd., Austin
512/302-3149
$$ NA

This restaurant offers Korean and Japanese cuisine, including a new sushi bar. Korean dishes include cho ki gui, smoked yellow fish; kal bi tang, a traditional Korean cow bone broth with noodles; and kimchi soup with pork. Japanese dishes range from udong (a thick noodle) soup, to chicken teriyaki to chicken curry with yakimandoo, a spicy dish. Lunch and dinner daily.

MA FERGUSON'S
6000 Middle Fiskville Rd., Austin
512/206-3030
$$$ NA

Ready for a taste of Texas homecookin'? You'll find it at this restaurant that's named for Miriam Ferguson, the first woman governor of Texas. Go for the chicken-fried steak, fried catfish, German sausage, barbecue brisket, of top sirloin; or get fancy with shrimp mole, seafood pie, or smoked poblano chile relleno. Breakfast, lunch, and dinner daily; closed 2–5 daily. &

MONGOLIAN BBQ
9200 N. Lamar Blvd., Austin
512/837-4898
$ NA

Like its sister restaurant on San Jacinto, grilled veggies are the specialty of the day in this eatery that's a far cry from a typical "BBQ" joint. Lunch and dinner daily. &

NINFA'S MEXICAN RESTAURANT
214 E. Anderson Ln., Austin
512/832-1833
$–$$ NA

Come early for a table on peak Friday and Saturday nights at this popular Tex-Mex hangout. The food is plentiful and mighty tasty, includes all the typical fare from enchiladas to tacos. Don't miss the terrific green salsa served with chips; it's good enough to make a meal itself. Save room for the flour tortillas, made right in the restaurant in view of diners. Lunch and dinner daily. &

Tex-Mex

The designation "Tex-Mex" refers to the particular style of Mexican food found in the Lone Star State. Unlike New Mexico's Mexican food, which might include blue corn tortillas, or California's Mexican food, which relies on avocados and black olives, Tex-Mex depends heavily on ground beef, cheese, and chile sauce. You can find great chicken enchiladas with a flavorful verde tomatillo sauce, vegetarian dishes, or even shrimp enchiladas. But the real Tex-Mex favorite, known affectionately as Regular Plate No. 1, is an order of beef enchiladas, refried beans, and Spanish rice. If you're lucky, leche quemada, a sugary pecan praline, will be brought out with your check.

Tamales, both mild and spicy varieties, are also found on every Tex-Mex menu, but they're most popular during the Christmas season. Stores like Austin's Green and White Grocery sell tamales by the dozen during the holidays when it's popular to bring them to office parties and home get-togethers. Making tamales at home is a time-consuming job, traditionally tackled by large families. Tamales start with the preparation of a hog's head, boiled with garlic, spices, peppers, and cilantro. After cooking, the meat is ground and then simmered with spices. As the filling is prepared, other family members ready the hojas *(corn husks)* used to wrap the tamale. Others prepare the masa, *cornmeal worked with lard and seasonings*, that is spread thinly on the shucks before filling with meat. Finally, the tamales are steamed in huge pots.

PEARL'S OYSTER BAR
9033 Research Blvd., Austin
512/339-7444
$$–$$$ **NA**
You don't even have to come face to face with an oyster in this tiny eatery; you'll find plenty of other dishes to keep you busy. Gumbo, etouffe, shrimp—the list goes on and on. Live music makes this a popular stop with young club hoppers and the place is a lot more fun than its strip center location would lead you to believe. Lunch and dinner daily; late-night hours Thur–Sat. ♿

SCHOLZ GARTEN
1607 San Jacinto, Austin
512/474-1958
$$ **NA**
Since 1866 this restaurant and pub,

just up the street from the capitol, has been privy to many "real deals" put together by the state's movers and shakers. University of Texas students, and their visiting parents, too, have enjoyed the menu mix of bratwurst, sauerkraut, and down-home staples like chicken-fried steak. Lunch and dinner Mon–Sat; closed Sun. &

THREADGILL'S
6416 N. Lamar Blvd., Austin
512/451-5440
$ NA
Threadgill's is an Austin institution, the place for tried-and-true chicken-fried steak and cream gravy on homemade biscuits. It's hard to believe that Threadgills began life as a gas station back in the thirties. Some local pickers started playing outside, crowds came, and the owners began serving beer. Soon food followed, and good-bye gas pumps. Janis Joplin used to sing here, perhaps lured by the huge portions, great vegetables, and fresh home-cooking. You'll find plenty of neon signs and old beer clocks hangin' on the walls to transport you back in time while you chow down on pork roast, liver, and chicken and dumplings with black-eyed peas and okra. For downtown diners, a new Threadgill's is now open at 301 W. Riverside Dr. Lunch and dinner daily. &

TRUDY'S TEXAS STAR
409 W. 30th St., Austin
512/477-2935
$$ NA
This UT-area eatery has more atmosphere than its younger siblings in north and south Austin. The green chicken enchiladas, served in all their gooey goodness with rice and beans and flour tortillas, are always popular

fare. Breakfast here includes both American and Tex-Mex dishes; especially good are the migas, scrambled eggs cooked up with strips of corn tortillas and bits of tomato. Breakfast, lunch, and dinner daily; late-night hours until 2 a.m. Fri–Sat. &

NORTHWEST AUSTIN

ALDO'S NORTHWEST
12233 N. FM 620, Austin
512/331-6400
$$ NWA
Although it's located in a strip center, this restaurant is an excellent choice for a quiet, intimate dinner for two. Start with a wine selected from an extensive wine list; follow up with Italian favorites served by an attentive waitstaff. Lunch and dinner Tue–Sun; closed Mon.

CATFISH PARLOUR
11910 Research Blvd., Austin
512/258-1853
$$ NWA
Wear an adjustable belt to this all-you-can-eat restaurant; boneless catfish, mouthwatering hush puppies, pinto beans, and coleslaw will have you going back for more several times. Lunch and dinner Mon–Sat; closed Sun. &

CHINATOWN
3407 Greystone Dr., Austin
512/343-9307
$$ NWA
Located right on the corner of Greystone and MoPac, Chinatown has an elegant air, with white linen tablecloths, attentive waitpersons, and the feel of a restaurant designed to celebrate special events with special dishes. Lunch and dinner daily. &

NORTHWEST AUSTIN

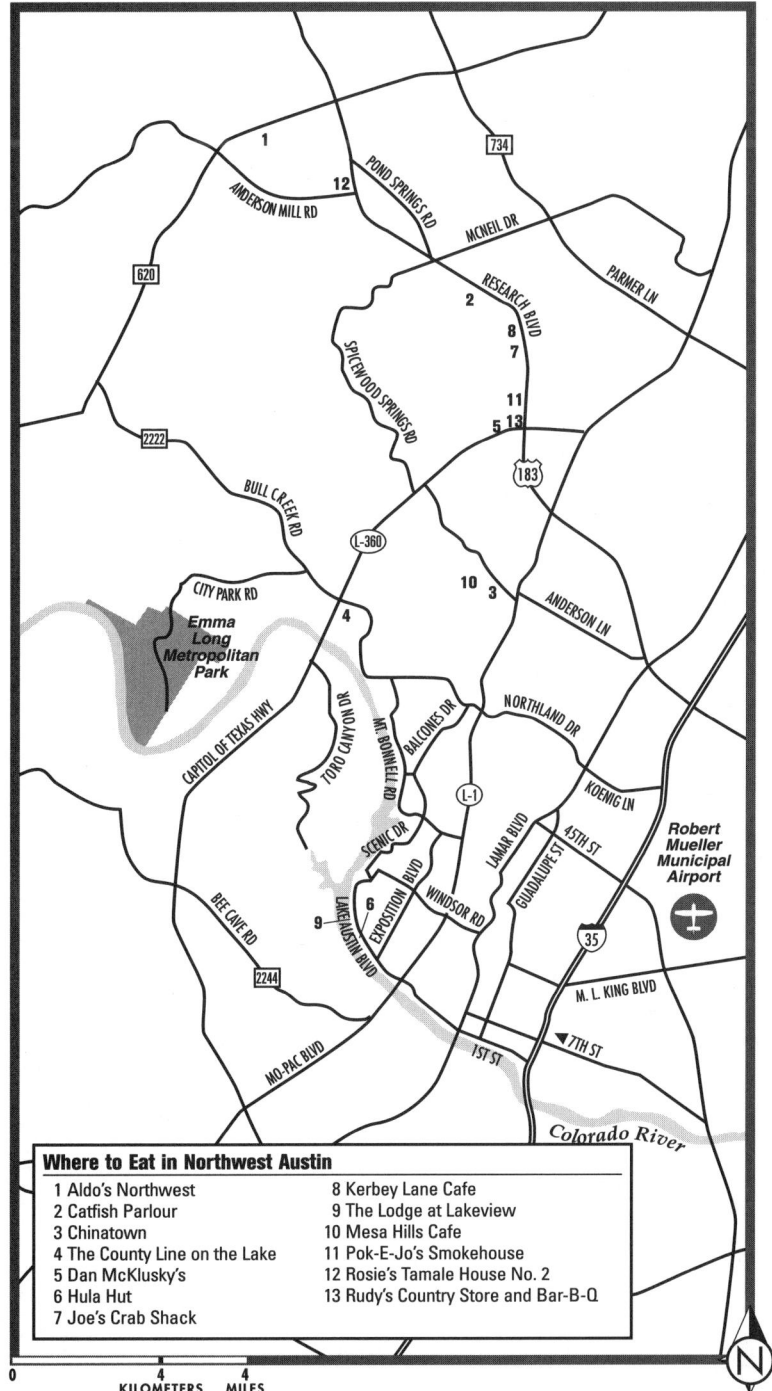

THE COUNTY LINE ON THE LAKE
5204 FM 2222, Austin
512/346-3664
$$ NWA
Always popular, you may have to wait, but it'll be made easier by the beautiful Hill Country view. Continue to enjoy it by eating outdoors if the weather's nice (which is most of the time in the Hill Country!). Enjoy the view from the hill while digging into the big meaty ribs, lean brisket, and special sausage the County Line is famous for throughout the Southwest. The atmosphere is upscale roadhouse, and we watched Bull Creek as it runs into Lake Austin, drinking iced-down beer and frozen margaritas in the Longneck Bar. For dessert, the Kahlua pecan brownie is a must. Lunch and dinner daily. ♿

DAN MCKLUSKY'S
10000 Research Blvd., Austin
512/346-0780
$$$ NWA
Like its downtown cousin, this Arboretum steakhouse serves up corn-fed Omaha steaks in a casually elegant atmosphere. Chicken, seafood, lamb, shrimp, and lobster round out the selections. Lunch weekdays and dinner daily; brunch on Sunday only. ♿

HULA HUT
3826 Lake Austin Blvd., Austin
512/476-4852
$$ NWA
The blend of Tex-Mex and Hawaiian is intriguing, made especially tasty when you choose to dine out over the lake, where boaters tie up their boats by the giant fish figure guarding the pier bar. (There's indoor dining, too, if you prefer.) The menu lists barbecue ribs and chicken tacos, grilled chicken nachos, chicken flautas, and chile con queso along with Hawaiian grilled chicken and grilled fresh-fish tacos stuffed with char-grilled Mahi-Mahi, red cabbage, cilantro, and jalapeño lime sauce. Lunch and dinner daily. ♿

TRIVIA

Austin is often known as "River City," which aptly describes its longtime connection with the Colorado River. Thanks to dams along the river, Austin enjoys two back-to-back lakes located within city limits.

JOE'S CRAB SHACK
11680-A Research Blvd., Austin
512/343-2004
$$–$$$ NWA
This boisterous restaurant serves up Cajun delights in a no-frills, fun atmosphere. Favorites include coconut shrimp, seafood enchiladas, catfish, po'boys, and red beans and rice. Crabs—stone, soft shell, Dungeness, blue, Alaskan king—are sold by market price. Lunch and dinner daily. ♿

KERBEY LANE CAFE
12602 Research Blvd., Austin
512/258-7757
$–$$ NWA
Just off bustling U.S. 183 you'll find a quiet oasis in this cafe that offers the same seriously good meals found at the other two Kerbey Lane locations. Breakfast, lunch, and dinner daily; open 24 hours. ♿

THE LODGE AT LAKEVIEW
3825-B Lake Austin Blvd., Austin

512/476-7372
$$$ **NWA**
Perched right on the edge of Lake Austin, this casually elegant eatery offers a much calmer atmosphere than its neighbor, the Hula Hut. The Lodge, much as its name suggests, exudes a mountain lodge atmosphere, a theme carried out in the menu that includes steaks, seafood, pasta, and burgers. Lunch and dinner are served daily; Sunday brunch also offered. &

MESA HILLS CAFE
3435 Greystone Dr., Austin
512/345-7423
$–$$
Dine inside, or out, taking in an exalted view of downtown Austin while perched high above MoPac on the cafe's pleasant covered patio. Luncheon is served 11–5 with a choice of a dozen platefuls accompanied by rice, beans, and a taco. Lunch and dinner daily. &

POK-E-JO'S SMOKEHOUSE
9828 Great Hills Tr., Austin
512/338-1990
$ **NWA**
Deciding to eat at Pok-E-Jo's is simple; the hard part lies in whether to order the smoky beef ribs the size of nightsticks, the tender pork ribs, the juicy brisket, or the mild or spicy sausage. There's even pork loin, chicken, ham, and sometimes turkey to make your decision that much tougher. Smoked 16 to 20 hours over green mesquite, every choice is a winner. Lunch and dinner are served daily. &

ROSIE'S TAMALE HOUSE NO. 2
13776 Research Blvd., Austin
512/219-7793
$ **NWA**
The plates here are simple Tex-Mex choices: enchiladas, tacos, quesadillas, flautas, and, you guessed it, tamales. This popular eatery is located in a strip center, but its cuisine is straight out of a typical South Texas home kitchen. Open for lunch and dinner daily. &

RUDY'S COUNTRY STORE AND BAR-B-Q
11570 Research Blvd., Austin
512/418-9898
$ **NWA**
Rudy's calls itself "the worst barbecue in Texas" but you sure wouldn't know that from the taste of its barbecue or the size of the crowds that flock to this popular eatery. Rudy's has an extensive menu: pork, baby back, St. Louis, and beef short ribs, plus chicken, prime rib, pork loin, chopped beef, sausage, turkey, and brisket. Start the day with breakfast tacos until 11. Breakfast, lunch, and dinner daily. &

TIP Just beyond the city limits on the shores of Lake Travis stands what's termed the "sunset capital of Texas," the Oasis Cantina del Lago (6550 Comanche Tr., 512/266-2441). Austinites flock to the multiple decks of this restaurant and bar to watch an unparalleled sunset and to enjoy a Tex-Mex dinner, a tangy margarita, and an end to another central Texas day.

SOUTHWEST AUSTIN

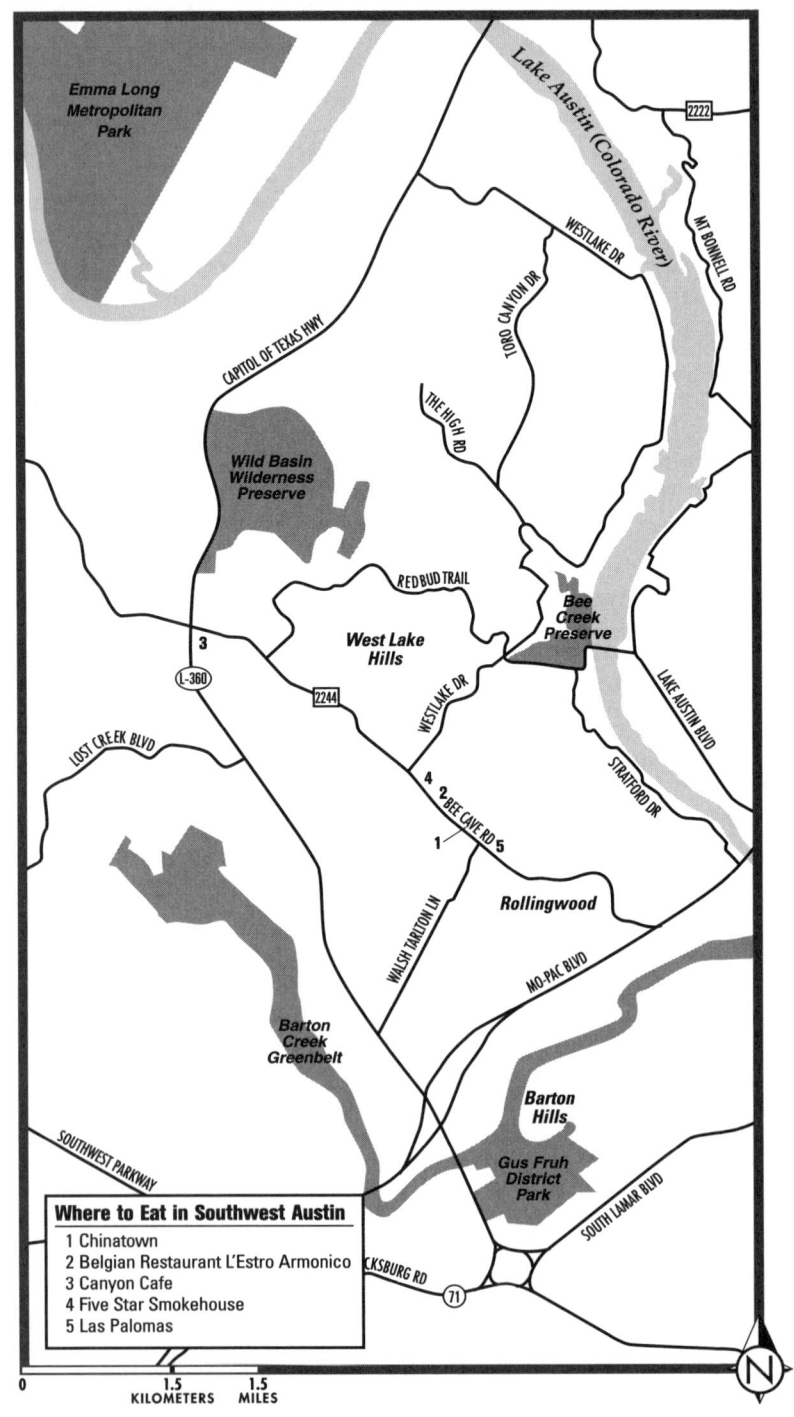

Texas Barbecue

Barbecue ranks with state politics when it comes to provoking heated discussion between Texans. One barbecue joint has a sign over its counter that says it best: "Bar-b-que, sex and death are subjects that provoke intense speculation in most Texans. Out of the three, probably bar-b-que is taken most seriously." You'll find that's true when you ask any Texan for a favorite smokehouse or, heaven forbid, you ask a pit owner for a barbecue recipe. The smoky meats are cooked according to secret methods that many pit masters plan to take to their graves with them, but most recipes call for slow cooking (sometimes 20 hours for brisket) over oak, hickory, or mesquite. The meat is rubbed with dry spices and finished off with a tomato-based sauce. Beef rules most of the Texas barbecue pits in the form of brisket, ribs, sausage, and chopped beef.

SOUTHWEST AUSTIN

BELGIAN RESTAURANT L'ESTRO ARMONICO
3520 Bee Caves Rd., Austin
512/328-0580
$$$ SWA
While deciding between duck in cherry sauce, beef tenderloin with cream and green onion sauce, dover sole in lemon sauce, or chicken tenders stuffed with scallops and sage in a white wine sauce, be sure to save room for dessert. The dessert menu includes Belgian chocolate mousse and a Belgian ice cream sundae with chocolate sauce. Lunch and dinner Mon–Fri; dinner Sat–Sun. Reservations recommended. ♿

CHINATOWN
3300 Bee Caves Rd., Austin
512/327-6588
$–$$ SWA
Chinatown has moved a few blocks west, into the shopping center at Walsh Tarleton, but all 77 items on the menu are the same as before. Shrimp, beef, chicken, and pork, all in rich sauces and in a myriad of combinations, are prepared by the same chef. Lunch and dinner daily. ♿

CANYON CAFE
Loop 360 and Bee Caves Rd., Austin
512/329-0400
$$$ SWA
With the atmosphere of a north woods lodge, this restaurant is housed in a circular building warm with the glow of log pillars, railings, and ceiling. The menu boasts many Southwestern dishes, from

quesadillas to tacos with shrimp. Don't expect fast food service or prices, however; this is nouvelle Southwestern cuisine, with menu surprises like chile-rubbed tuna and tequila chicken pasta. Open for lunch and dinner daily; brunch served on Sunday. &

FIVE STAR SMOKEHOUSE
3638 Bee Caves Rd., Austin
512/328-1800
$ **SWA**
This restaurant boasts an extensive menu. Take your pick from brisket, baby back ribs, pork loin, smoked ham, smoked chicken, smoked turkey, and sausage. Many meats are smoked 12 to 15 hours to reach barbecued bliss. Plates are served with an excellent potato salad, beans, and bread. Save room for the home-baked pies—apple, chocolate, chocolate pecan, buttermilk, Toll House, and key lime—or a piece of old-fashioned peach cobbler. Lunch and dinner daily. &

LAS PALOMAS
3201 Bee Caves Rd., Austin
512/327-9889
$$–$$$ **SWA**
Check out the traditional Mexican fare at this eatery: chicken mole, pork pibil, Veracruz-style dishes, and more. For Tex-Mex lovers, some popular favorites are available as well. Don't miss the live mariachi music on Friday nights. Lunch and dinner. &

SOUTH AUSTIN

ARTZ RIB HOUSE
2330 S. Lamar Blvd., Austin
512/442-8283
$–$$ **SA**

Wrap your hands around either pork or beef ribs at this eatery. Can't decide? Select a combination plate and sample the baby backs, country-style pork ribs, or meaty beef ribs. Other barbecued items include brisket, smoked chicken, sausage (Austin's own Smoky Denmarks), and skewered char-grilled shrimp. The plates are piled high with spicy potato salad, crispy coleslaw, and pinto beans. Lunch and dinner daily. &

CHERRY CREEK CATFISH CO.
5712 Manchaca at Stassney,
Austin
512/440-8810
$$ **SA**
Although it specializes in seafood, you'll find just a little of everything on this eclectic menu. Start with anything from shrimp gumbo to fried green tomatoes to jalapeño peppers, then work your way to blackened catfish, chicken-fried steak, frog legs, barbecue ribs, or a

Oasis Cantina & Restaurant at Lake Travis, page 67

SOUTH AUSTIN

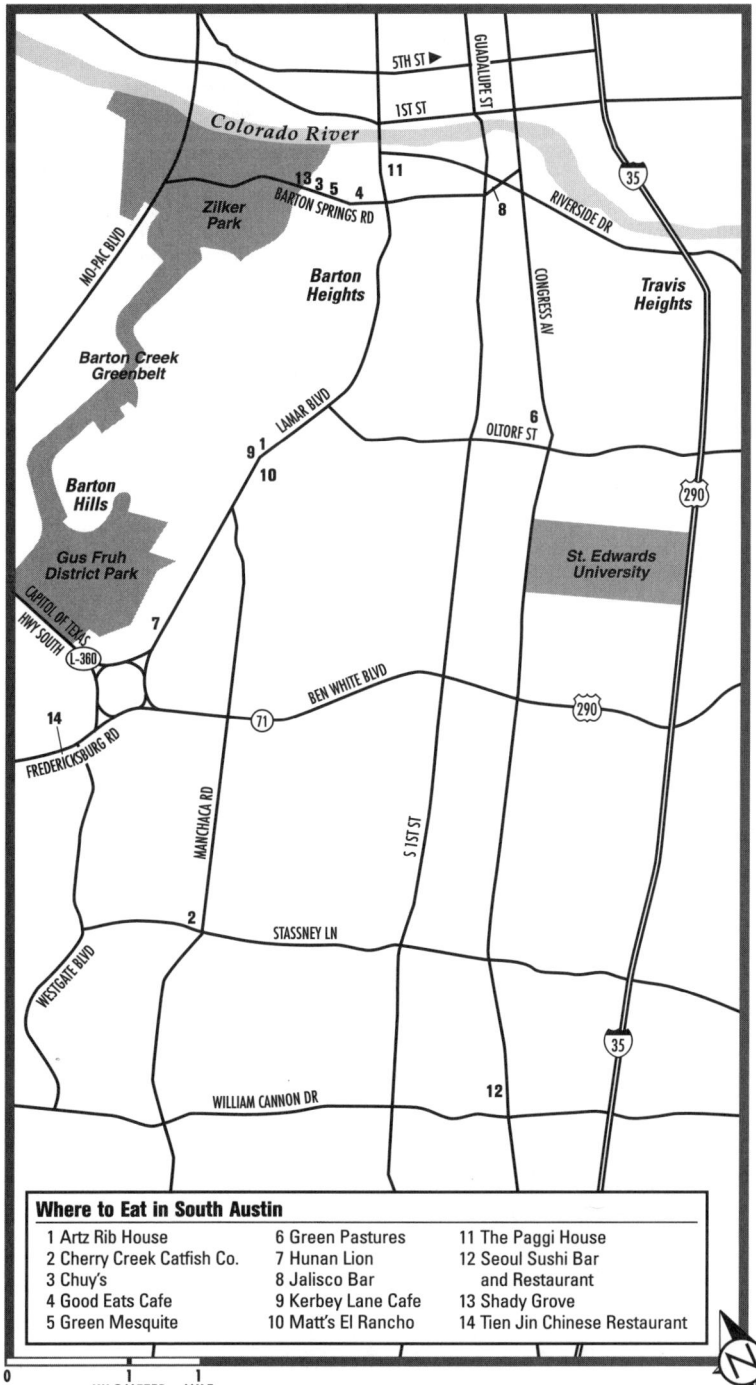

po'boy sandwich. If you're on your way home, Cherry Creek also offers carry-out family packs featuring catfish, shrimp, or ribs. Lunch and dinner daily. &

CHUY'S
1728 Barton Springs Rd., Austin
512/474-4452
$ SA

Chuy's is Austin at its most funky! With 1,000 wooden fish dangling from the ceiling of the bar and hubcaps covering the ceiling of the dining room, the result is hilarious. Walls are painted Mexican pink and green, and piñatas dangle invitingly, just waiting for someone to smack them open. There's a memorial altar to Elvis at the front door, and the crowd most nights testifies to the great taste of the Tex-Mex fare. The menu may be limited but regulars favor the taco salad, the blue corn tortillas, the barbecued chicken tacos, the chips, and the salsa. Lunch and dinner daily. &

GOOD EATS CAFE
1530 Barton Springs Rd., Austin
512/476-8141
$ SA

Tried and true, both grilled and lean, fried and steamed, this café suits all-American palates whether you're looking for chicken-fried steak or a heaping plate of steamed vegetables. When Good Eats fries, it's canola oil only, and on the healthy side of the menu you'll find high-fiber, low-fat, nutrient-dense choices, with daily specials posted on the chalkboard in this informal, café-roadside diner atmosphere with friendly laid-back help. Breakfast, lunch, and dinner daily; breakfast/brunch Sat–Sun. &

GREEN MESQUITE
1400 Barton Springs Rd., Austin
512/479-0485
$ SA

This rustic and homey Austin tradition serves up music on weekends, with local bands playing along with the food. Gosh, there's chicken-fried steak, catfish, jambalaya, and bubba tacos—soft, flour tortillas stuffed with your choice of barbecued beef, turkey, or chicken, topped to the gills with lettuce, tomato, and shredded cheddar cheese; and served with a homemade salsa and a choice of two sides: beans, Cajun rice, big chunky coleslaw, or potato salad. The po-boy sandwiches are as authentic as any you'll get in New Orleans, and of course all the pies are homemade. Lunch and dinner daily. &

GREEN PASTURES
811 W. Live Oak, Austin
512/444-4747
$$$ SA

Shades of the Old South! This white mansion, surrounded by manicured grounds and strutting peacocks, is instant Scarlet O'Hara-Rhett Butler ambiance. Retro Southern gentility and the best Sunday brunch in Texas make this an Austin classic. What everybody likes is not only the good taste of the food, but the sheer abundance of the spread. There's always a large assortment of cheeses and fruits, shrimp, salads, maybe a choice between prime rib and grilled blue marlin tampico (tomato, green pepper, and onion sauce), three or four vegetables, and at least four desserts. The peach and plum strudel is special, and the Green Pastures bread pudding is a must. Lunch and dinner; Sunday buffet. Reservations recommended. &

Jalisco Bar

HUNAN LION
4006 S. Lamar Blvd., Austin
512/447-3388
$$–$$$ **SA**
A statue of a happy Buddha greets you at the entrance to this pretty restaurant with flowered booths, etched glass dividers, and four fish tanks to set a relaxing mood. The Seven Star Platter will do that, too, with Alaskan king crab legs, shrimp, scallops, roast pork, and boneless fried chicken, all stir-fried with mixed vegetables. Other specials of the four-star Mandarin-style cuisine are sesame chicken and Beijing duck. Lunch, dinner ♿

JALISCO BAR
414 BARTON SPRINGS RD., AUSTIN
512/476-4838
$ **SA**
Warm up a chilly day with a bowl of tortilla soup or add some heat to any day with spicy enchiladas, tacos, or fajitas. If you order a slammer, it will be brought to you by a howling waiter, slammed on the table with a flourish, and draw the attention of the entire restaurant. Brace yourself. Lunch, dinner daily.

KERBEY LANE CAFE
2700 S. Lamar Blvd., Austin
512/445-4451
$$ **SA**
Austin couldn't get along without its supply of wholesome food available any hour of the day or night. Healthy meals featuring fresh, locally grown produce are served round-the-clock daily in this light, bright restaurant. A bucolic mural of hills and a plowed green field on one wall is attractive, and the waitstaff wear whatever they're comfortable in. Breakfast, lunch, and dinner daily. ♿

MATT'S EL RANCHO
2613 South Lamar Blvd., Austin
512/462-9333
$–$$ **SA**
This is Tex-Mex Austin style, evolved from grandfather Delphino Martinez's first restaurant in 1925. It's a family restaurant, including the help, since they stay for years. In addition to

WHERE TO EAT

dishes like the enchilada plate (with a sauce of chile con carne), you can try seafood and steak. But chile rellenos are also pretty special, with raisins and pecans part of the filling. Everything is handmade—tortillas, tostadas, even the praline candy—and all the meat is premium. Lunch and dinner daily except Tuesday. &

THE PAGGI HOUSE
200 Lee Barton Dr., Austin
512/478-1121
$$$ SA
Fine continental food is the fare here. Lunch Mon–Fri; dinner Mon–Sat. Reservations recommended. &

SEOUL SUSHI BAR
AND RESTAURANT
6400 S. 1st St., Austin
512/326-5807
$$ SA
The decor is spare and Japanese, with shoji screens offering tables privacy. The food is a nice mix of both Japanese and Korean. The two cuisines go together very well, neither being greasy like some other Asian styles. A soup dinner comes with Korean kimchi, a pickled spicy cabbage, and seasoned bean sprouts. A popular dish is bul gal, tender barbecued ribs marinated in a special sauce. And of course there's sushi: crab, octopus, flounder, tuna, red snapper, squid, shrimp, smoked salmon, salmon roe—the list goes on and on. Lunch and dinner daily. &

SHADY GROVE
1624 Barton Springs Rd., Austin
512/474-9991
$–$$ SA
Relaxed dining is the rule here in yet another laid-back Austin-style eatery where you can dine indoors or out under the pecan trees. Shady Grove is set in a real grove in what was once a trailer park; in fact, the trailer at the end of the patio is put to use as restrooms. Try the special Hippie Sandwich for a real taste treat of grilled zucchini, eggplant, mushrooms, roasted bell peppers, tomato, and arugala on a seven-grain wheat bun dressed with melted mozzarella and pesto mayonnaise. Indoors there's a full bar, rock walls, stone pillars, and a cozy fireplace if needed. Thursday nights there's music under the pecan trees, with local talent like Asleep at the Wheel, The Bad Livers, and such. Lunch and dinner daily. &

TIEN JIN CHINESE RESTAURANT
4601 S. Lamar Blvd. #105, Austin
512/892-6699
$–$$ SA
Cantonese and Szechwan are the styles at this popular Chinese restaurant, with specialties like orange beef, General Tso's chicken, and sesame chicken with the subtitle "Return of the Phoenix." Other menu options include Three Delicacies—fresh shrimp, chicken, and scallops with broccoli, baby corn and snow peas; or the Happy Family—shrimp, chicken, and pork with vegetables. Lunch and dinner daily. &

EAST AUSTIN

CISCO'S RESTAURANT,
BAKERY & BAR
1511 E. 6th St., Austin
512/478-2420
$ EA
Rudy "Cisco" Cisneros was the man who made migas and huevos rancheros famous. This Austin favorite has been serving migas (tortilla chips fried with onion, tomatos, scrambled eggs, melted cheese, sausage, and beans) for years. The bakery, bar, and

EAST AUSTIN

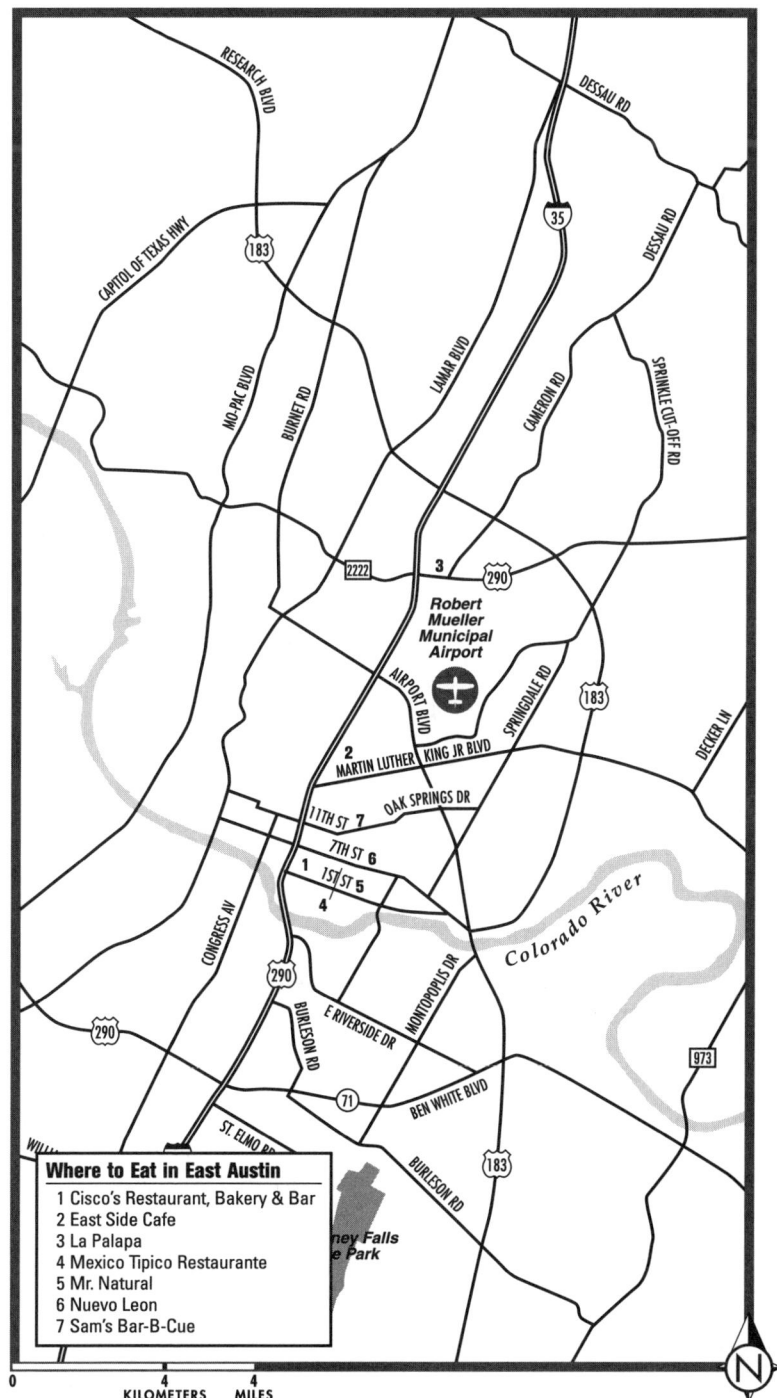

restaurant, a family business, has operated under various guises since 1929. Breakfast and lunch daily. &

EAST SIDE CAFE
2113 Manor Rd., Austin
512/476-5858
$$ **EA**
Dine in any of the several rooms in this 1920s home which sits on 1/3 acre and grows East Side's herbs and vegetables. "Some restaurants talk about fresh food," they say. "We grow it." Chipotle pecan soup, artichoke manicotti, wild mushroom crepes—the menu is eclectic and delicious. Lunch and dinner daily, brunch Sat–Sun. Reservations accepted. &

LA PALAPA
Hwy. 290 E. at Cameron Rd., Austin
512/459-8729
$–$$ **EA**
With its distinctive thatched palm palapa roof, it's tough to miss this restaurant. Tex-Mex favorites such as fajitas and enchiladas top the menu. Lunch and dinner daily. &

MEXICO TIPICO RESTAURANTE
1707 E. 6th St., Austin
512/472-3222
$–$$ **EA**
Known for cabrito, fajitas, and *caldos* (thick soups), Mexico Tipico has mariachi music on Friday and Saturday. Tamales and corn tortillas are hand made; the vegetarian enchiladas are delicious. Breakfast and lunch Tue–Thur; breakfast, lunch, dinner Fri–Sun; closed Monday. &

MR. NATURAL
1901 E. Cesar Chavez St., Austin
512/477-5228
$–$$ **EA**
Tex-Mex and health food don't generally go hand in hand, but at Mr. Natural you'll find favorite foods with a vegetarian twist. Veggie fajitas, enchiladas, chile rellenos, tamales, and salads are offered; vegan dishes are available. Breakfast, lunch, dinner; closed Sun. &

NUEVO LEON
1209 E. 7th St., Austin
512/479-0097
$–$$ **EA**
Although the name that you're about to sample the cuisine of the northern Mexican state of Nuevo Leon, it applies to the cartoon character on the cover of the bright pink menu, a lion juggling a tray of glasses. The cuisine is Tex-Mex, and the Wednesday special (there's a special daily), the Nuevo Leon Burrito, is a winner—a giant flour tortilla stuffed with beef and smothered in Nuevo Leon's chile con carne. It's more than a meal. Lunch and dinner Mon–Fri; breakfast, lunch, and dinner Sat–Sun. &

SAM'S BAR-B-CUE
2000 E. 12th St., Austin
512/478-0378
$ **EA**
Go to Sam's with a big appetite. Plates include ribs, brisket, chicken, spicy sausage, and even mutton. Side dishes include fiery beans spiced with plenty of black pepper and potato salad. You can take out or dine in the small dining room decorated with newspaper clippings featuring the late Stevie Ray Vaughan. The Austin blues musician was a devoted Sam's customer, even making some long-distance call-in orders for Sam's specialties when he was on the road. Lunch and dinner daily. No credit cards. &

5

SIGHTS AND ATTRACTIONS, PUBLIC ART, AND CITY TOURS

There's no denying that touring Austin's many diverse attractions is a capital idea. Regardless of your interest, you'll find plenty of sights not only indoors, but also out, given Austin's average of 300 beautiful sunny days a year. From historic sites to nature sites, from ice-skating on a hot summer day to strutting with peacocks at a historic park, from canoeing on Town Lake to shopping in the West End, there are more than 101 things to see and do. Along the way be sure to notice Austin's art in public places (see page 97 for more information). And for an overall view of Austin and its offerings, try a city tour (see page 101). Note: Maps in this chapter show locations of sights and attractions only.

SIGHTS AND ATTRACTIONS

DOWNTOWN AUSTIN

AUSTIN CONVENTION CENTER
500 E. Cesar Chavez St., Austin
512/476-5461   **DA**
Recognized as one of the most technologically advanced convention centers in the nation, this $75.2-million building covers four city blocks. Works of art include 20 oil paintings by Jill Bedgood of *Texas Botanicals* (west corridor, level 3); a neon and copper sculpture titled *Confabulating Orbits* by Ben M. Livingston (palazzo, level 1); *The Waller Creek Shelves* of limestone, glass, and found objects, by Damian Priour (rotunda, level 1); and *Riffs And Rhythms* by John A. Yancy with Steve Jones, a broken tile mosaic (west corridor, level 1).

AUSTIN HISTORY CENTER
810 Guadalupe St., Austin
512/499-7480   **DA**
Formerly the main library and now known also as the Austin-Travis

County Collection, this beautifully restored 1930s Art Deco building houses print and photo materials relating to Austin's history. Displays in the entrance corridor change regularly. Hours: Mon–Thur 9–9 , Fri–Sat 9–6 , Sun 12–6. Admission: Free.

AUSTIN'S BAT COLONY
Congress Avenue Bridge
at Town Lake, Austin
512/327-9721   DA
Austin has received international attention for its colony of up to 1.5 million Mexican free-tailed bats that reside under the Congress Avenue Bridge during the summer months. Every night at sundown, the bats leave their perch to feast upon the insects of the Hill Country. The best viewing is from the hike-and-bike trail, the bridge, or a free bat viewing area in the parking lot of the *Austin American-Statesman* at 305 South Congress Avenue. The best viewing months are July and August. For more on the bats, check out the information kiosks at the Four Seasons Hotel at 98 San Jacinto Bouelvard and the *Austin American-Statesman* parking lot on the south shore.

AUSTIN PUBLIC LIBRARY
800 Guadalupe St., Austin
512/499-7300   DA
The Main Branch of the Austin library system offers not only books, but adult education, business information, children's programs and services, consumer services, legal and medical information, museums, puppet shows, and films. All in all, it is a well-rounded and extensive public facility. Notice the Art in Public Places piece, *Eagle II*, of Cor-Ten steel by David L. Deming (1976) out in front. Hours: Mon–Thur 9–9, Fri–Sat 9–6, Sun 12–6. Admission: Free.

CAPITOL COMPLEX VISITORS CENTER
E. 11th and Brazos, Austin
512/305-8400   DA
Formerly this 1857 building served as the General Land Office and holds the title as the oldest government office building in the state. Once the workplace of short story writer O. Henry, this building now operates as a visitors center and Texas History Museum, with displays and exhibits about the center of Texas government. Hours: Tue–Fri 9–5, Sat 10–5. Admission: Free.

GERMAN FREE SCHOOL
507 E. 10th St., Austin
512/482-0927   DA
Just off the banks of Waller Creek, this school was constructed by German immigrants in 1857. The building, constructed using a rammed- earth technique, includes two large rooms, gym, and playgrounds. Today the school is used by the German-Texan Heritage Society and the German Free School Guild and hosts educa-

Parking in the capitol and downtown area comes at a premium. The best way to explore is aboard a 'Dillo, the trolley service that starts at the Coliseum's free parking lot at the intersection of West Riverside Drive and Bouldin Avenue. These green trolleys travel up and down the streets from the river to the university.

DOWNTOWN AUSTIN

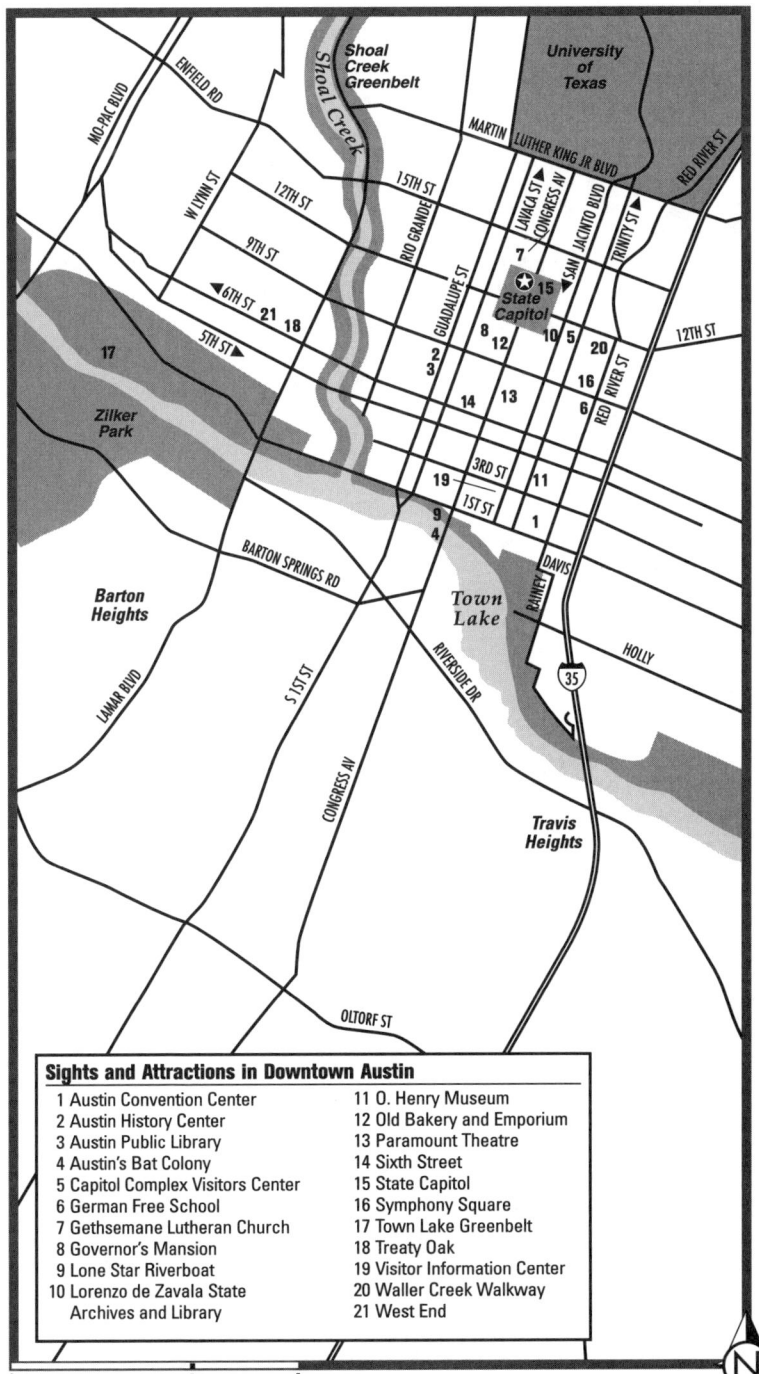

Sights and Attractions in Downtown Austin

1. Austin Convention Center
2. Austin History Center
3. Austin Public Library
4. Austin's Bat Colony
5. Capitol Complex Visitors Center
6. German Free School
7. Gethsemane Lutheran Church
8. Governor's Mansion
9. Lone Star Riverboat
10. Lorenzo de Zavala State Archives and Library
11. O. Henry Museum
12. Old Bakery and Emporium
13. Paramount Theatre
14. Sixth Street
15. State Capitol
16. Symphony Square
17. Town Lake Greenbelt
18. Treaty Oak
19. Visitor Information Center
20. Waller Creek Walkway
21. West End

TRIVIA

The General Land Office was the scene of a comic-opera war back when President Sam Houston and Vice President Mirabeau Lamar were fighting over the site of the state capital. Lamar wanted it to be Austin, and the 1839 Capital Commission so named it. Houston wanted it either in his namesake, Houston, or back in Washington-on-the-Brazos where it began. When the Mexicans invaded Texas in 1842, President Houston sent a small company to seize the republic's archives, housed in the General Land Office. But he was thwarted by the patriotic efforts of one Angelina Eberly, owner of a nearby boarding house. She sounded a warning by setting off a cannon that was usually employed to warn the populace of Indian raids. Houston's men were routed and the archives remained safely stashed away in the Eberly boarding house. This little stand-off has gone down in local history as the "Archives War."

tional programs. Genealogists can use the family history research materials as well. Hours: Thur 1–4. Admission: Free.

GETHSEMANE LUTHERAN CHURCH
1510 Congress Ave., Austin
512/463-6092 DA
This Gothic Revival–style church was built in 1882 and today stands as a reminder of Austin's first Swedish settlers. Today the church serves as the offices of the Texas Historical Commission Main Street Project. Hours: Mon–Fri 8–5. Admission: Free.

GOVERNOR'S MANSION
1010 Colorado St., Austin
512/463-5516 DA
For over 130 years, Texas governors have enjoyed the opulence of this grand home. Visitors are taken past the main staircase, through the formal parlor, and finally into the dining room. Tours (scheduled every 20 minutes) are conducted Monday through Friday from 10 a.m. to noon. Call to check the status of tours; the home is sometimes closed because of incoming dignitaries. Admission: free.

LONE STAR RIVERBOAT
Congress Ave. and S. 1st St., Austin
512/327-1388 DA
Enjoy a 90-minute excursion on Town Lake aboard this paddle wheeler for an unbeatable view of the lake and the city skyline. Hours: 3 p.m. tour Sat–Sun, Sept–Oct and Mar–May; 5:30 p.m. tour Tues–Sun and 10:30 p.m. tour Fri, June–Aug. Admission: $9 adults, $7 seniors, $6 children under 12.

LORENZO DE ZAVALA STATE ARCHIVES AND LIBRARY
1201 Brazos, Austin
512/463-5455 DA
Located just east of the capitol, this building houses the archives of state government, including important genealogical records. Stop by the public areas on the first floor for a look at historic documents or to trace your

family's roots in the Lone Star State. Hours: Library, Mon–Fri 8–5 p.m.; Genealogy, Tue–Sat 8–5. Admission: Free.

O. HENRY HOME AND MUSEUM
409 E. 5th St., Austin
512/472-1903 DA
This modest home, built in 1891, was the address of William Sidney Porter, better known as short story writer O. Henry, from 1893 to 1895. Today the cottage, recently renovated, contains the writer's personal belongings. Hours: Wed–Sun noon–5. Admission: Free; donations appreciated.

OLD BAKERY AND EMPORIUM
1006 Congress Ave., Austin
512/477-5961 DA
You'll find everything from bread to knitted breadwarmers in this historic structure that first opened in 1876. Notice the limestone eagle by John Didelot, on top of the building, installed in 1876. Downstairs, the bakery offers fresh-out-of-the-oven treats; upstairs, senior citizens sell their hand-crafted wares. Hours: Mon–Fri 9–4, Sat 10–3. Admission: Free.

PARAMOUNT THEATRE
713 Congress Ave., Austin
512/472-5411 DA
This old theater, built in 1915, has been expertly restored and is used primarily for the performing arts (with the exception of a classic movie now and then), which was the case when the neoclassical moving picture palace was built—Sarah Bernhardt trod the boards here. The box office is open Mon–Fri 12–5:30; weekends if a performance is scheduled. For films there is a rather tough policy—even infants need a ticket.

SIXTH STREET
6th St. from I-35 to Congress Ave., Austin DA
Known for both its historic architecture and its nationally recognized nightlife, this stretch of 6th Street constitutes Austin's entertainment district. Daytime visitors come to shop its eclectic boutiques, view historic buildings on self-guided tours, and dine its popular restaurants; night owls enjoy late-night revelry that lasts until 2 a.m.

STATE CAPITOL
11th St. and Congress Ave., Austin

MacGregor Park (Hippie Hollow)

This day-use county park covers 109 acres of rugged ledges and hiking trails along Lake Travis and is a popular swimming spot. But you have to 18 years old to enter. Why? Clothing at MacGregor Park—also known as "Hippie Hollow"—is optional! MacGregor Park, located on Comanche Trail, 2.5 miles off the RM 620, is open from 9 a.m. to 9 p.m. There is a $5 admission charge per vehicle, and pets, glass bottles, and ground fires are prohibited.

TRIVIA

The Texas State Capitol is 7 feet higher than the United States Capitol.

512/463-0063   **DA**

You might think that Texas' motto is "The bigger, the better," especially after a visit to the state capitol. Taller than its national counterpart, the pink granite building houses the governor's office, the Texas legislature, and several other executive state agencies. Recently the building underwent a major facelift. Guided tours depart from the first floor rotunda daily but have been suspended for a major renovation. Hours: Mon–Fri 8:30–4:30; Sat 9:30–4:30; Sun 12:30–4:30. Admission: Free

SYMPHONY SQUARE
Red River St. at 11th St.,
Austin   **DA**

The state gave the area to the city in 1982. Waller Creek turns subterranean under the square where there are four restored more-than-a-century-old buildings. The Jeremiah Hamilton home is the only original one—the other three were moved from other locations. Jeremiah Hamilton had been the slave of A.J. Hamilton, a governor during Reconstruction. He was a carpenter and he built this limestone, two-story house, making it triangular in order to wedge it into the triangular lot bordered by Waller Creek, Red River, and 11th Streets. The other three houses date from 1870 (old Wilson Mercantile), 1880 (Doyle House), and 1887 (Hardeman House).

TOWN LAKE GREENBELT
Loop 1 Bridge to South First St.,
Austin   **DA**

The scenic shores that line the north and south sides of Town Lake are home to popular trails where Austinites come to walk, jog, and enjoy the beauty of the city. The best view of the downtown skyline can be seen from the south side of Town Lake.

TREATY OAK
503 Baylor St., Austin   **DA**

This 500- to 600-year-old oak captured the nation's attention in 1989 when it was deliberately poisoned. Today one-third of the original tree, once called the finest example of a tree in North America, is gone, but Austinites are grateful for how much has been saved from the malicious herbicide poisoning, thanks to help from well-wishers throughout the nation.

VISITOR INFORMATION CENTER
201 E. 2nd St., Austin
512/478-0098 or 800/926-2282   **DA**

Stop here for brochures and informa-

Texas State Capitol Building

© Eleanor S. Morris

tion on attractions, trolley and bus routes, dining, and entertainment. Call for a menu of information choices. Hours: Mon–Fri 8:30–5; Sat 9–5; Sun 12–5.

WALLER CREEK WALKWAY
15th St. to Cesar Chavez St., Austin   **DA**
This is a 1.8-mile trail of gravel and concrete along Waller Creek from 15th Street on the north to Cesar Chavez Street on the south. The trail passes along Symphony Square while the creek passes under it. There are ongoing works of art to be seen along the walkway at 500 East Cesar Chavez Street: untitled relief carvings in limestone by David Santos, Ramon Maldonado, Alejandro Bernal, and Tecolete (1983).

WEST END
6th St. between Lamar Blvd. and West Lynn St., Austin   **DA**
This enclave of eclectic shops, restaurants, and offices is a favorite stop with downtown workers for a quiet lunch or some unique shopping. The district is also home of the headquarters of the Austin Lyric Opera, the Austin Independent School District, the Austin Writer's League, the Austin Children's Museum, and Women and their Work Gallery (see Chapter 7).

NORTH AUSTIN

CENTER FOR AMERICAN HISTORY AT THE UNIVERSITY OF TEXAS
Sid Richardson Hall
23rd St. and Red River, Austin
512/495-4515   **NA**
Located next to the LBJ Library on the University of Texas campus, this extensive library houses over 120,000 volumes dealing with the history of the Lone Star State. The stacks are closed, but the materials are available to any researcher. Includes the Barker Collection. Hours: Mon–Sat 9–5. Admission: Free.

THE DRAG
Guadalupe St. from 21st to 25th Streets, Austin   **NA**
Austin's funkiest neighborhood is a collection of unusual shops, trendy coffeehouses, food carts, occasional panhandlers, and more. Located directly across the street from the University of Texas campus, this strip of Guadalupe is always rowdy and a good place to people watch. Hours: Vary by store; peak days Mon–Fri.

ELISABET NEY MUSEUM
304 E. 44th St., Austin
512/458-2255   **NA**
Sculptor Elisabet Ney was one of Texas' most colorful characters. Her restored home and studio exhibits the work of the first prominent sculptor in Texas as well as many of her personal belongings. The first floor contains two large sculpture rooms, a small entranceway, and a parlor. Ney's bedroom, which was seldom used (she usually slept outside in a hammock), is on the second floor, and a third-floor tower room, reached by a spiral staircase, was the study of Dr. Montgomery, Ney's husband who made his home near Houston. With its tower and stone columns, you may think this studio resembles a tiny European castle, but throughout the building are many Texas touches: bronze stars which decorate the balcony balustrade, cedar rails on the banister, and walls of native limestone. Hours: Wed–Sat 10–5, Sun 12–5. Admission: Free.

NORTH AUSTIN

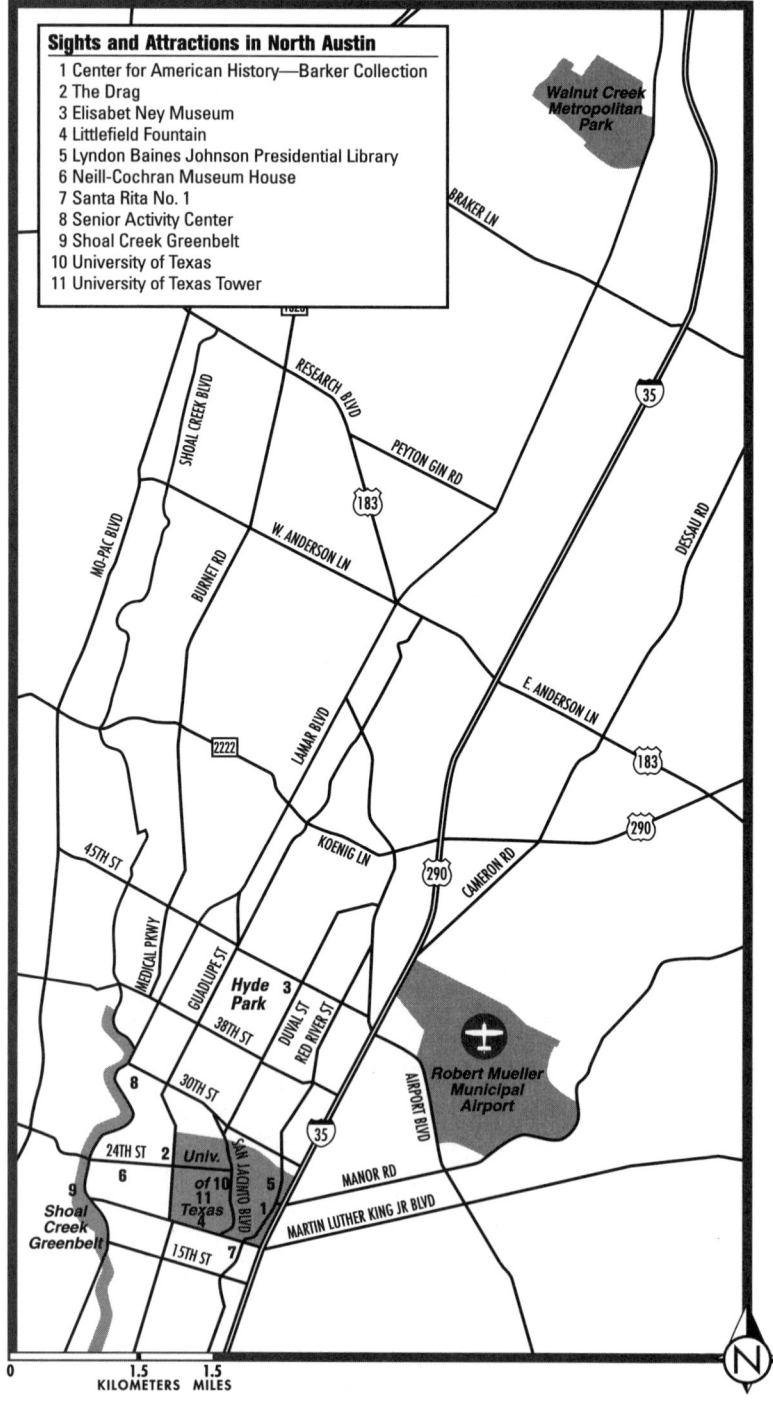

LITTLEFIELD FOUNTAIN
University of Texas Campus, South Mall
21st St. between Guadalupe and Speedway, Austin   **NA**

This bronze by Pompeo Coppini (1933) was commissioned by Major George Washington Littlefield in honor of those of the university who gave their lives in World War I. The three-tiered fountain represents the Navy on one side, the Army on the other; and in the center a ship is led by three seahorses, two ridden by Tritons. "Meet me by Littlefield Fountain" is for Austinites the equal of New Yorkers' "Meet me under the clock at Grand Central."

LYNDON BAINES JOHNSON PRESIDENTIAL LIBRARY AND MUSEUM
2313 Red River St., Austin
512/916-5136   **NA**

No visit to Austin would be complete without a stop at the LBJ Library and Museum. Located on the campus of the University of Texas, this impressive facility serves as a reminder of the Hill Country's most famous resident. The eight-story library, constructed of travertine marble, is the repository for all 35 million documents produced during the LBJ administration. The files, housed in red, acid-free boxes stamped with the gold presidential seal, are open only to scholars and researchers. But a wealth of other exhibits and displays are open to the public on the three museum floors of the library: floors one, two, and eight. They contain over 35,000 historical objects ranging from a ship's passport signed by Thomas Jefferson to a moon rock. Other objects pertain to the Johnson family, foreign affairs, gifts from other countries, and LBJ's special humor.

NEILL-COCHRAN MUSEUM HOUSE
2310 San Gabriel, Austin
512/478-2335   **NA**

Built around 1853, this Greek Revival home was designed by Abner Cook, the builder of the Governor's Mansion. Today the Colonial Dames of America operate the grand home and conduct tours. Hours: Wed–Sun 2–5. Admission: $2.

Loop 360 Bridge, Lake Austin, page 90

Your look at the LBJ Library begins with a 20-minute orientation presentation on the President's early years in the Hill Country, political life in the House and Senate, and finally the White House years.

The first two floors offer films on Johnson's life and career, as well as exhibits featuring jeweled gifts from foreign dignitaries and simpler handmade tokens from appreciative Americans. Visitors also can take in special displays of political, civil rights, and educational memorabilia. The second floor also has a special area for changing exhibits, and the First Lady Theater, where you can take a look at the many contributions made by Lady Bird Johnson.

Don't miss the short elevator ride up to the eighth floor with a reproduction of LBJ's White House Oval Office furnished as it was during his term. Here, too, color transparencies give you a peek into some of the public and private rooms of the White House. Hours: Daily 9–5. Admission: Free.

SANTA RITA NO. 1
Corner of Martin Luther King and Trinity Street   NA
This oil rig, with the name of *Santa Rita*, the saint of the impossible, is in a way the patron saint of the University of Texas, or at least of the university's exchequer. The rig was in the business of pumping oil for 19 years, beginning in 1923 when an oil well in West Texas finally blew in, justifying the faith of a group of investors who gave the claim the name. Oil royalties have been flowing into the Permanent University Fund ever since, and the derrick has been standing on the corner as a memorial, set in motion only for state occasions.

SENIOR ACTIVITY CENTER
2874 Shoal Creek, Austin
512/474-5921   NA
A variety of programs and services are available here for persons 50 or older. Besides workshops, table games, physical fitness classes, tours, and special events, such services as health screening and tax assistance are offered.

SHOAL CREEK GREENBELT
North side of Town Lake between Guadalupe St. and Lamar Blvd., Austin   NA
This 3-mile granite, crushed limestone, and concrete trail winds north to 38th Street, passing Duncan Park, Pease Park, and Bailey Park, winding up at Seider's Spring Park.

UNIVERSITY OF TEXAS
I-35 and Martin Luther King Blvd., Austin
512/471-3434   NA
Start your visit to the sprawling 357-acre UT campus at the visitor information center located in the Arno Nowotny Building, a historic structure built in 1859. The building was formerly an asylum for the blind. Prior to that, the building was once occupied by General George Custer. Tours

NORTHWEST AUSTIN

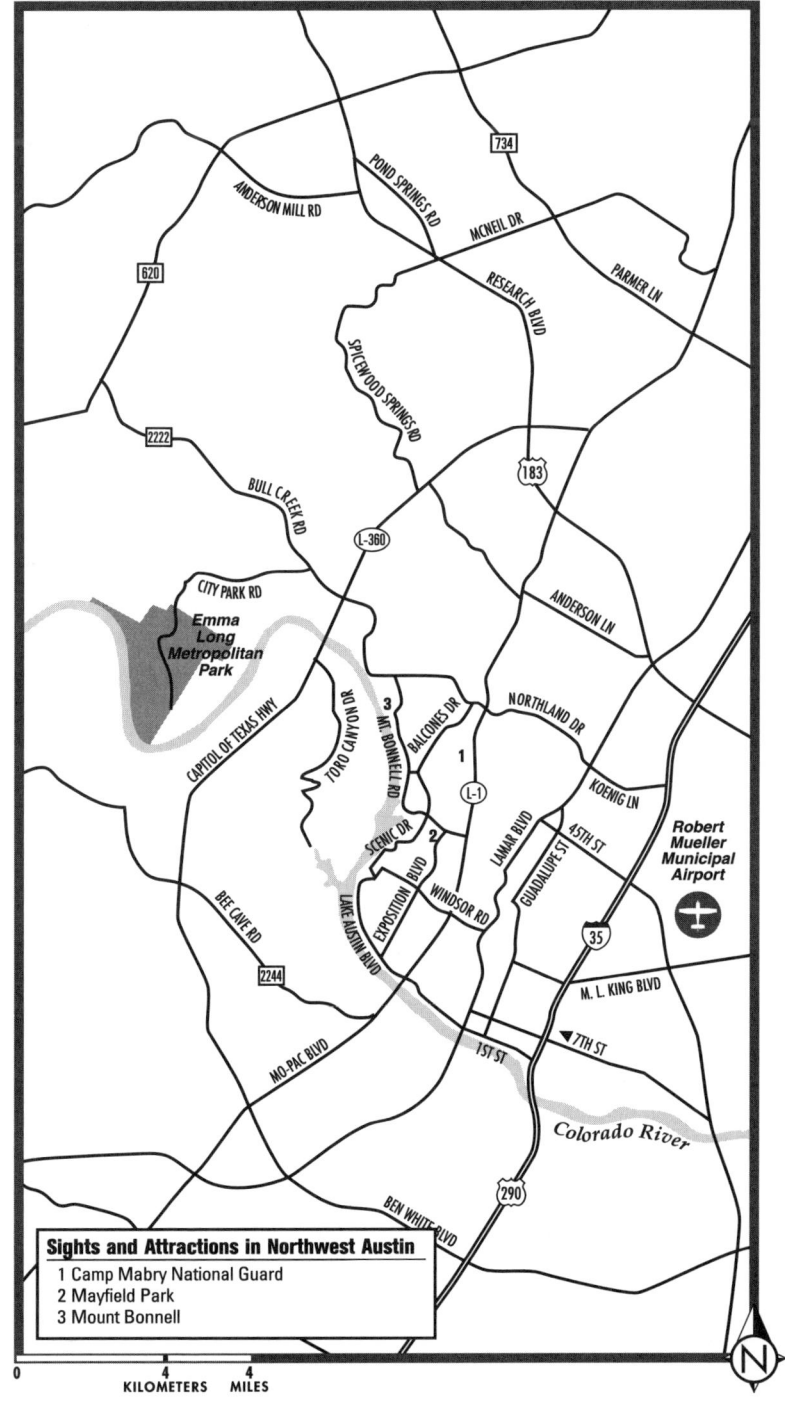

of the campus are offered June–Nov, Mon–Fri 11 and 2; Sat 2 only; Dec–May, Mon–Sat 2 only.

UNIVERSITY OF TEXAS TOWER
Between 21st and 24th Sts.,
Austin
512/475-7348   NA
This tower drew national attention on August 1, 1966 when Charles Whitman opened fire from its balcony, killing over a dozen pedestrians blocks away and wounding 31. Today the tower houses administration offices and the balcony is no longer open to the public.

University of Texas Tower

NORTHWEST AUSTIN

CAMP MABRY NATIONAL GUARD
West 35th St. and Loop 1 (MoPac),
Austin
512/465-5059   NWA
Home of both the Army and Air National Guard, this historic post dates back to 1892 as a summer base for the Texas Volunteer Guard. Today the base includes the Texas Military Forces Museum, an outdoor collection of military artifacts, and a mile-long jogging trail that's popular with locals. Two pieces of sculpture grace the grounds among the artillery: *Audie L. Murphy*, a bronze by Bill Leftwich (1984) in Building No. 82 and the metal *Salute* by Simon G. Michael, Building No. 1. Hours: Open Wed–Sun 2–6, Thur 10–4. Admission: Free; donations accepted.

MAYFIELD PARK
3505 W. 35th St., Austin
512/327-5437   NWA
Take a walk with the peacocks that wander at will in this park on 22 acres of Barrow Creek Cove on Lake Austin.

MOUNT BONNELL
3800 Mount Bonnell Rd.,
Austin   NWA
If you're looking for a scenic overlook of the Hill Country and Lake Austin, here it is. Wear walking shoes for the many steps up to the lookout, where you'll find a view that's well worth the climb. The overlook is located 1 mile past the west end of West 35th Street. Hours: Daily 5–10. Admission: Free.

SOUTHWEST AUSTIN

NATIONAL WILDFLOWER
RESEARCH CENTER
4801 La Crosse Ave., Austin
512/292-4100   SWA
Established by Lady Bird Johnson, this center was founded to research, promote, and preserve native plants. A popular springtime stop for Austinites, the fields bloom with color during peak months and volunteers and docents on hand can tell you how to utilize wildflowers in your own landscaping. Hours: Grounds

SOUTHWEST AUSTIN

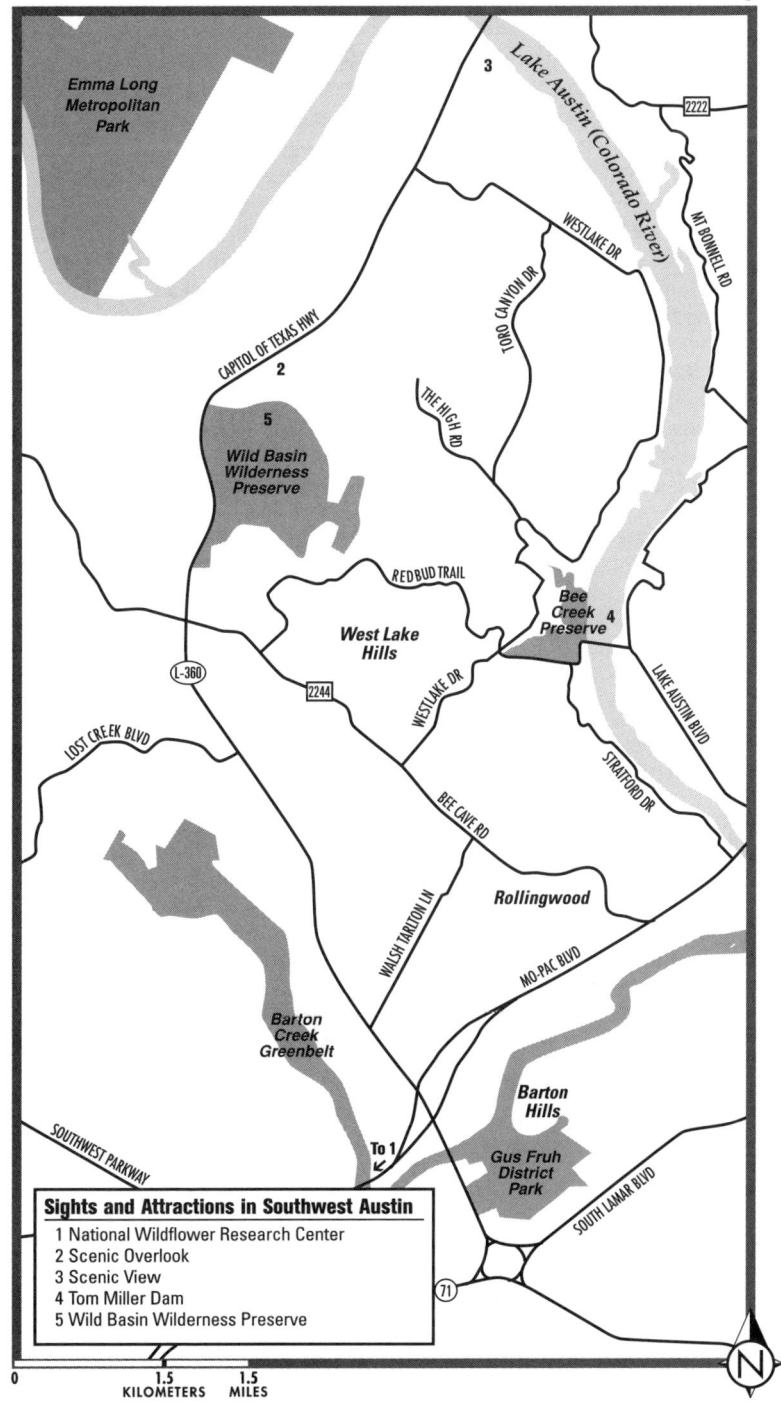

Tue–Sun 9–5:30; Visitors Gallery Tue–Sat 9–4, Sun 1–4; Wild Ideas: The Store Sat 9–5:30, Sun 1–4; Wildflower Cafe Tue–Sat 9–4, Sun 11–4. Admission: $3.50 adults, $2 students and seniors, $1 children 18 months to 5 years.

SCENIC OVERLOOK
Capitol of Texas Highway
Just north of Wild Basin Preserve at 805 N. Loop 360, Austin   SWA
Park your car and look at the Austin skyline far to the east over the hills.

SCENIC VIEW
Pennybacker Bridge, Capitol of Texas Hwy., Austin   SWA
Enjoy the view over Lake Austin from this breathtaking suspension bridge.

TOM MILLER DAM
Red Bud Trail at Lake Austin, Austin
800/776-5272   SWA
Tom Miller Dam is just south of the Walsh Boat Landing, with 4 acres for day-use only, providing picnicking, boat ramps, and access to Lake Austin. It's illegal to climb on the dam, but you can fish in the lake below the dam. Fishermen park along Red Bud Trail and walk down to the lake shore to cast their lines, hoping to catch catfish and bass.

WILD BASIN WILDERNESS PRESERVE
805 N. Loop 360, Austin
512/327-7622   SWA
For a close look at the terrain, flora, and fauna of the Hill Country, step out of the city at this wilderness preserve located just minutes from downtown. The 220-acre sanctuary includes 2.5 miles of trails that wind through the brush; an easy-access trail is also available. Hours: Daily dawn to dusk; tours Sat and Sun. $1 adults; 50 cents kids 5–12.

SOUTH AUSTIN

BARTON CREEK GREENBELT
Scottish Woods Trail, Capitol of Texas Hwy., Austin
512/327-5478   SA
From Scottish Woods Trail, off Loop 360 a mile north of MoPac, walk down to this 7.5 mile hiking trail. The natural surface is rocky in spots. Be sure to bring water as there are no drinking fountains on the trail. Call for trail conditions in bad weather.

BARTON SPRINGS POOL
2201-1/2 Barton Springs Rd., Austin
512/867-3080   SA
Even if you don't want to take a dip, stop by for a look at these pristine springs. Year-round, a flow of 68 degree water from the Edwards Aquifer fills this 1,000-foot-long pool, and no matter what the month you'll find some brave souls swimming laps in its chilly depths. Truly a symbol of Austin, this swimming pool is dear to the hearts of Austinites. The pool is usually open from 5–10 , but call for hours since sometimes it closes for maintenance. Admission: $2.50 adults, 25 cents children.

SOUTH AUSTIN SENIOR ACTIVITY CENTER
3911 Manchaca Rd., Austin
512/448-0787   SA
Take a look at the tile mosaic and broken china artwork by Jill Bedgood and Steve Wiman in the lobby and the multi-purpose room here. Titled *Community Quilt*, the work is part of the city's Art in Public Places program. A variety of programs and services are available here for persons

SOUTH AUSTIN

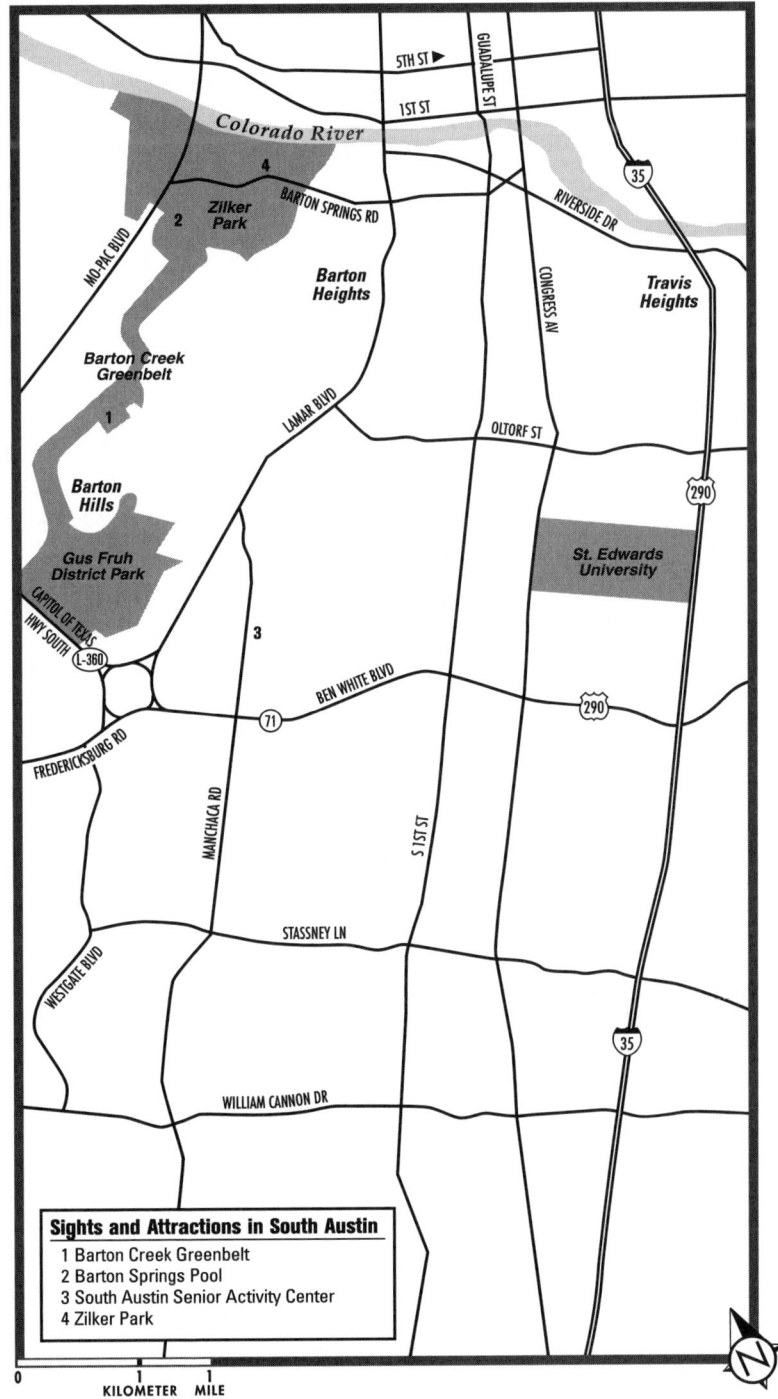

Austin Steam Train

Just outside the northwest boundaries of the city in the community of Cedar Park, the Austin Steam Train offers visitors a look at the Hill Country aboard restored passenger cars that recall the early days of Austin transportation. The Hill Country Flyer transports visitors on a round-trip excursion through the oak- and cedar-dotted hills to the town of Burnet. The 143-ton engine that powers the tourist train once powered both passenger and freight trains, chugging through Texas and Louisiana. In 1956 the mighty engine was retired and donated to the City of Austin as a park display for three decades.

Today five coach cars plus three air-conditioned/heated lounge cars give travelers a chance to travel in style. Once the train is loaded, a loud blow on the steam whistle signals the start of the journey as the train departs Cedar Park. The locomotive heads north along U.S. 183, veering west as it crosses the South San Gabriel. Listen for the clatter of the wheels as the train crosses the river on an old-fashioned wooden trestle.

From the river valley, the train climbs 500 feet as it journeys westward into the hill country. It was along this route that granite was hauled from Marble Falls to Austin for the construction of the capitol. The pink stone was mined from Granite Mountain and loaded on this line. Some of this stone, stacked to capacity on the cars, never made it to the capital city. Chunks of pink granite still lie along the tracks where they fell from the train over a century ago.

Arrival in the town of Burnet is a weekly event enjoyed by the townspeople. Many come out to meet the train and the visitors who enjoy a three-hour stop in their town. Stroll to downtown Burnet where members of the local gunfighters association perform a Wild West gunfight on Town Square for guests.

50 years of age or older. Besides recreational activities like workshops, table games, physical fitness classes, tours, and special events, such services as health screening and tax assistance are also offered.

ZILKER PARK
2100 Barton Springs Rd., Austin
512/478-0098 **SA**
This 400-acre downtown park is where Austinites come to play—whether that means enjoying a game of rugby, flying a kite, playing with the dog, savoring gardens, or having a picnic. Here too you can hike, bike, jog, and fish. It's been a city park since 1917 when the initial acreage was donated by Colonel A. J. Zilker. Throughout the park you'll find picnic tables, playgrounds, ball fields, and group shelters; there is a miniature train, and along Town Lake you can rent rowboats and canoes.

EAST AUSTIN

CELIS BREWERY
2431 Forbes Dr., Austin
512/835-0884 **EA**
Take a tour of a brewery with a huge, shiny, bright copper fermenting tank sitting in the window and visible from the street. Hours: Tours are offered Tue–Sat at 2 and 4; Fri at 5:30. Admission: Free.

THE FRENCH LEGATION MUSEUM
802 San Marcos St., Austin
512/472-8180 **EA**
(see page 120)
This Greek Revival–style residence is the only foreign legation in the country ever built outside of Washington, D.C. The home has a breezeway, with doors at either end to cool the house on hot Texas days. Downstairs, there are four rooms, whose most notable characteristics are their bright and varied colors. Paint experts were consulted when the house was renovated, and paint chips were analyzed to arrive at the colors you see today. Apparently Saligny enjoyed variety—you'll see mustard green walls, pink banisters, and pink baseboards! Behind the house stands a separate kitchen, the only authentic free-standing French Creole kitchen in the United States. The kitchen is filled with French kitchen utensils and furniture dated before 1845, including a handcarved rosewood cabinet built to cool bread when it was removed from the oven, hung from the walls out of the reach of rodents.

A French prayer chair sits meditatively in one corner, near a wedding cake mold, a lacemaker's lamp, and a French butter churn. Tours are conducted Tuesday through Saturday from 1 to 5, and there's a bang-up Bastille Day celebration every July 14th. Hours: Tue–Sun 1–5. Admission: $3 adults; $1 children 11–18; 50 cents children under 10.

Austin's Sixth Street entertainment district, page 81

EAST AUSTIN

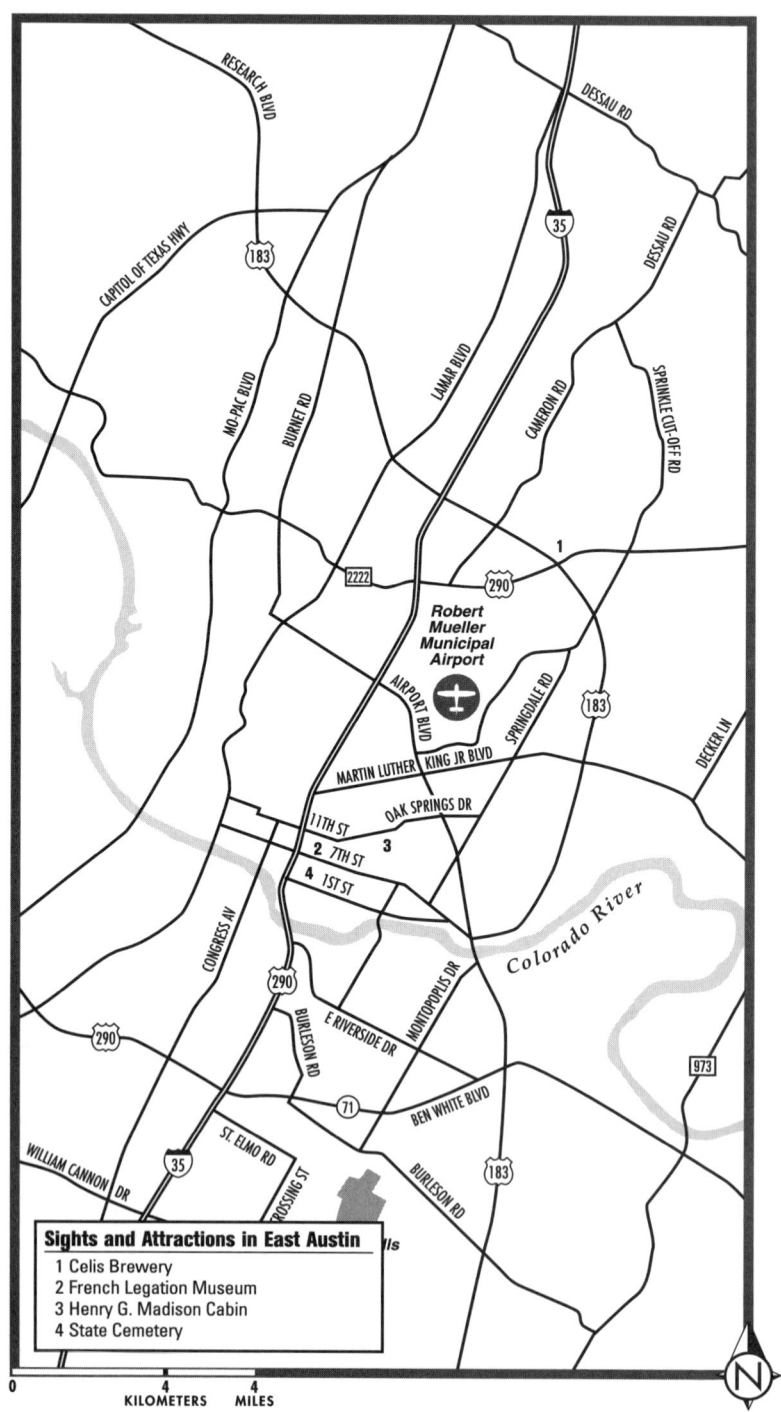

TRIVIA

Wondering why a foreign legation (an official residence and office of a foreign diplomat) was built in Austin? Don't forget: Texas was once a separate country—complete with its own foreign ambassadors!

HENRY G. MADISON CABIN
2300 Rosewood, Austin
512/472-6838   EA

The African-American heritage of Austin is the focus of this 1863 cabin. It's amazing to learn that ten people—two parents and eight children—once lived in this one-room home. Inside, there are historic artifacts. Hours: Daily 8–6; call for free tour. Admission: Free.

STATE CEMETERY
E. 7th St. at Comal St., Austin
512/478-8930   EA

This last resting place of many well-known Texans is known as the "Arlington Cemetery of Texas." Graves include those of Stephen F. Austin, father of Texas, as well as eight former governors.

PUBLIC ART

In 1985 the Art in Public Places (AIPP) ordinance was established in order to preserve and encourage the unique artistic qualities that make Austin special. The ordinance sets aside 1 percent of the total construction cost for all new or remodeled public buildings, parks, parking facilities, and decorative or commemorative structures for the commission, purchase, and installation of art.

A second way in which Austin celebrates and promotes the arts is in the awarding of Cultural Contracts. These contracts allow local nonprofit, tax-exempt cultural arts organizations to apply for funding from the city. The categories that qualify for funding include dance, theater, literature, visual and mixed arts, and music. Thus, for more than a decade, Art in Public Places has made it possible for talented artists known both locally and nationally to enhance public spaces throughout the city. Works of art range from murals and outdoor sculptures to functional works integrated into architecture.

Recommendations are made by an Art in Public Places panel, composed of seven respected local design and visual arts professionals. The panel works closely with project architects and city department and community representatives to secure works of high quality that represent a broad range of media, styles, and cultural sensibilities. Artists have incorporated traditions and objects to create cultural landmarks for all of Austin.

DOWNTOWN AUSTIN

On the north shores of Town Lake, look for the futuristic **Lone Star Gazebo**, made of steel by Rodolfo Ybarra (1995). It's on Cesar Chavez Street just west of Congress at Colorado Street, adjacent to Buford Tower, a memorial to Captain James Buford.

Also on Cesar Chavez Street, west of Lamar Boulevard, is the iron and cast concrete piece, **Opossum Temple and Voodoo Pew**, by Lars Stanley, Robert Phillips, and T. Paul Hernandez (1993). Another work, at 800 Cesar Chavez Street, is the

Seaholm Power Plant metal signage, which was dedicated in 1951.

Heading north and west of Congress Avenue along 4th Street, you'll find **Untitled**, a Cor-Tex steel work by Jerry Hartung (1978) at 208 W. 4th; **Bus Stop**, two long-legged two-dimensional aluminum figures by William King (1986) at 4th and Colorado Streets; and **Prelude** by Itzik Ben Shalom, a bronze in Republic Square Park at 4th and Guadalupe. On the north side of the park is Taylor Fountain, dedicated in 1988. The designer of the limestone work was James A. Turner.

Moving to Austin's famous 6th Street scene, cast your eyes up to the architecture atop the **Driskill Hotel** (604 Brazos on the corner of 6th Street). There you'll see the limestone likenesses of both Colonel Jesse L. Driskill and J.W. Driskill, along with longhorn steer heads and gargoyles. All were completed (with the building) in 1886.

Along 10th Street there are several works of art. **Over the top**, a bronze by Waldine Tauch (dedicated 1971) is at the American Legion Department of Texas, 709 E. 10th Street. **The Source** by John Christiansen, a 1994 bronze, graces Waller Creek Center, 625 E. 10th, while at the State Treasury Building, 200 E. 10th, you'll find Charles Umlauf's bronze, **The American Eagle**. The noted Austin sculptor also sculpted **Abstraction, Form Vii**, to be seen at the Teacher Retirement System of Texas' building at 10000 Red River.

Memorial To World War II Dead on West 11th and Colorado Streets depicts a lone soldier atop a rock, with a tree on his right and flowers on his left, and a panel inscribed with names behind him.

Austin's famous lady sculptor Elisabet Ney did the bronze of **Dr. David Thomas Inglehart** in 1903. It stands at 11th Street and Red River. **Big Rock**, a 1990 limestone by David Santos, can be seen in Waterloo Park at 12th Street and Red River. On 12th Street between Lavaca and Colorado there is the **Memorial to the Builders of the Great State of Texas**, a bronze by Hugo Villa (1938). Charles Umlauf has a work on 12th Street, too. His 1970 bronze **Symbol of Education** graces

Camp Mabry, page 88

the Texas State Teacher's Association Building at 316 W. 12th.

Art on the Capitol Grounds

Nine memorable works of art sit on the capitol grounds, beginning with the **Goddess of Liberty**. Although she is an aluminum replica of the original, she stands just as tall atop the capitol dome. The original statue (now in the Texas Memorial Museum) was dedicated in 1886, the replica in 1986. **The Hiker**, a bronze by Theo Alice Ruggles Kitson (1951) and **The Cowboy**, an action bronze of a cow boy on a bronco leaping over a tall cactus, by Constance Whitney Warren (1921) are testimonies to the Texas lifestyle; the remaining five are testimonies to Texas heroes. **Heroes of the Alamo**, a bronze by Crohl Smith, was erected in 1901. The **Confederate Monument**, a bronze by Pompeo Coppini, was dedicated in 1903. **Terry's Texas Rangers**, another bronze by Pompeo Coppini, was dedicated in 1907, while even earlier, a Volunteer Fireman's Monument was dedicated in 1896. It was replaced by a bronze by J. Segesman, of a fireman holding a small child in his arms, and was rededicated in 1905. **Monument to Memory of Hood's Brigade**, also a bronze work by Pompeo Coppini, was dedicated in 1910.

NORTH AUSTIN

There are 25 pieces of sculpture on the campus of the University Of Texas. Both **Littlefield Fountain** and Alexander Phimister Proctor's **Mustangs** are among the best known, but all are interesting. Charles Umlauf is responsible for several, such as **The Torchbearers**, a bronze in front of the Undergraduate Library on West Mall at Guadalupe and 23rd Street; **Muse**, a bronze on the fourth floor terrace opening off the President's Office in the main building, 2400 Inner Campus Drive; **The Family**, a 1962 bronze at the George Kozmetsky Center For Business Education, 21st Street and Speedway; **Seated Bather II**, a 1965 bronze in the courtyard of the Huntington Art Building at 23rd and San Jacinto Streets; and 1962 bronze **The Three Muses**, in Centennial Park on 15th and Red River Streets.

Pompeo Coppini was a prolific sculptor for Austin, too, with eight historical figures such as Robert Lee, Albert Sidney Johnston, Jefferson Davis, Woodrow Wilson, and James Stephen Hogg, all in 1933; and George Washington, South Mall at 21st Street between Guadalupe and Speedway.

Other interesting works are **Monument Holistic IX** of cold rolled steel by Betty Gold (1981) at Trinity Street north of 23rd Street, and **Stonelith #136**, a limestone and glass piece in the courtyard of the Huntington Art Building at 23rd and San Jacinto Streets. And don't miss the two longhorns, **Texas Longhorn** by Jim Hamilton (1992) at the Alumni Center, San Jacinto Street south of 23rd Street; and **The Texas Longhorn** by Duke Sundt, a 1983 bronze in front of the Frank Erwin Center at Red River just south of Martin Luther King Jr. Boulevard.

Unusual is **Merlin the Magical Sage**, carved from a large oak tree stump by David Kestenbaum. You'll find it at Eastwoods Park—Harris Park Boulevard north of 26th Street. There's a Charles Umlauf sculpture at Austin Community College's Northridge Campus, 11928 Stonehollow Drive. The bronze is titled **Pro-**

Lyndon B. Johnson Library at the University of Texas, page 85

metheus (1990). **Las Mesas Inner Column**, of granite by Jesus Batista Moroles (1986) is in Century Park at 13521 Burnet Road.

NORTHWEST AUSTIN

Up at the Arboretum shopping center you'll find two interesting pieces of sculpture. The **Arboretum Cows**, of marble by Harold Clay, are adjacent to the food court at the mall, 9722 Great Hills Trail. **Untitled**, a metal piece by Tom Torrens, is at Clarksville Pottery, 9722 Great Hills Trail, #380. Along the Capitol of Texas Highway at #8911 you'll find **The Red Check** in steel by Bernar Venet (1986); and at the University of Texas at Austin, Balcones Research Center at Read Granberry and Neils Thompson Drives there is David Slivka'a **Machu Picchu** in wood, nylon webbing, and plaster (1974). **Sanctuary of the Tribal Alligator** is to be found at Hill Elementary School, 8607 Tallwood Drive. Of cast concrete it's by T. Paul Hernandez (1988).

SOUTH AUSTIN

In addition to the Umlauf Sculpture Garden (see museums) there are four public works of art in South Austin. Take a look at the steel architecture details by Lars Stanley (1991) ornamenting Fire Station #17 at 4128 South 1st Street. **Partners**, a bronze by Robert E. Coffee (1994) is at the Sheriff's Association of Texas, 1601 South I-35. An unusual **Wall of Hands** covers the wall of the St. Elmo Service Center at 4411 Meinardus Drive. The cast ceramic tiles are by Tre Arenz (1994). There's a bronze statue of **Jimmy Clay** at the Jimmy Clay Golf Course, 5411 Jimmy Clay, done by Daniel Hawkins (1994).

Also enjoyable is an outdoor sculpture tour of Town Lake and Zilker Park, starting on the south shores of the lake.

In Zilker Park, before you enter the Zilker Botanical Gardens at 2220 Barton Springs Road, notice the main entrance gates. Of steel, by Lars Stanley and Louis Herrera Jr. (1995), they are a garden in themselves, of graceful wrought-steel leaves and vines. Over by Barton Springs Pool, 2201 Barton Springs Road, there are three figures in bronze by Glenna Goodacre (1994) called the **Philosophers' Rock**. The philosophers are J. Frank Dobie, Walter Prescott Webb, and Roy Bedichek. Nearby is the Zilker Park Playscape, also at 2201 Barton Springs Road. The **Phantom Ship**, of cast concrete by Jill Bedgood (1991), seems to be a happy dolphin-type fish among the seaweed.

There are some interesting works along the Town Lake hike-and-bike trail. At Lou Neff Point at the confluence of Town Lake and Barton Creek you'll find the **Lou Neff Point Gazebo** of iron and steel by David Santos and

TRIVIA

In 1885, Austin installed Moonlight Towers, tall street lights that bathed the city in "artificial moonlight." Today one of the 27 original towers still stands at 9th and Guadalupe Streets.

Joe Perez (1993). At Butler Shores on the Town Lake Hike & Bike Trail at Riverside Drive just west of the Lamar Boulevard Bridge, **Untitled** (Chris Kerns Memorial) is of limestone, granite, and found objects by Paul Siebenaler (1992).

At Auditorium Shores, between South 1st Street and Lamar Boulevard, is the **Stevie Ray Vaughan Memorial**, a bronze by Ralph Helmick (1993). At the Auditorium Shores intersection of South 1st Street and Riverside Drive there is the **Bicentennial Fountain**, a granite and Cor-Ten steel by Ken Fowlet, dedicated in 1976.

Moving over to the Dougherty Cultural Arts Center, 1110 Barton Springs Road, you'll find another **Untitled**, a limestone, steel, and wood by David Ellis (1980). **The Gargoyles** at the Zachary Scott Theater Center, 1510 Toomey Road, are of fiberglass and clay by Stephen Ray (1990).

EAST AUSTIN

Along the Holly Street Power Plant (2401 Holly Street west of Congress) is the **Big Arch** of limestone and iron by David Santos and Joe Perez (1992).

Central Access Television Station at 1143 Northwestern Avenue has two works of art: **Outdoor Studio** is of metal, cinder block, and concrete by Laurel Butler and Rita Starpattern (1990); and **Snake Culvert** of cast concrete is by T. Paul Hernandez (1990). A bright artwork is **Color At Play** by Mary Visser, a fantasy piece of concrete and ceramic tile at University Hills Library, 4721 Loyola Lane.

CITY TOURS

(also see page 206)

BREMOND BLOCK
7th, 9th, San Antonio, and
Guadalupe Sts., Austin   DA
This historic block includes nine registered landmarks recognizing the homes constructed at this site from 1850 to 1877. The Austin Convention and Visitors Bureau offers tours of the block departing from the steps of the capitol. Sat–Sun 11 a.m. Free.

CAPITOL GROUNDS TOUR
South steps of capitol, Austin
512/478–0098   DA
Tour the grounds of this stately building for a look at its statues and for tales of its fascinating history. One-hour walking tours depart promptly at the designated hour from the south steps of the capitol. Mar–Nov, Sat 2 p.m.; Sun 9 a.m. Free.

CONGRESS AVENUE/EAST 6TH
STREET WALKING TOURS
South steps of capitol, Austin
512/478–0098   DA
Enjoy a guided walking tour with a look at historic sites such as the 1915 Paramount Theatre, the 1876 Walter Tips Building, and the 1886 Driskill Hotel. Hours: Thur–Sat 9 a.m., 2 p.m. Sun. Admission: Free.

SIGHTS • PUBLIC ART • CITY TOURS

6
KIDS' STUFF

Austin is filled with attractions that kids will enjoy. Austin Family, a free monthly newspaper distributed at local stores, is filled with family-oriented articles, a family activities calendar featuring special children's activities across town, family movie reviews, and more.

Austin's beautiful outdoor attractions are a natural draw for families with young children, who will find educational and entertaining diversions, many at little or no cost. Year-round temperate weather conditions have encouraged the construction of many playscapes and parks throughout the city. Stop by the Austin Convention and Visitors Bureau at 201 E. 2nd Street for a copy of the free "101 Things For Kids to Do in Austin" brochure.

ANIMALS AND THE GREAT OUTDOORS

THE ARBORETUM
10000 Research Blvd., Austin
512/338-4437 **NWA**
This open-air mall may be home to some of Austin's most upscale shopping, but to young visitors it's the location of "the cows." Let the kids climb on top of a life-size cow sculpture on the west side of the mall, then feed the ducks at the lake.

AUSTIN NATURE AND SCIENCE CENTER
301 Nature Center Dr., Austin
512/327-8180 **SWA**
No need to tell the kids "look but don't touch" at this hands-on educational center. Here exhibits teach ecological lessons about natural history, botany, and more amid 80 acres of canyons and meadows just west of Zilker Park. Hours: Mon–Sat 9–5, Sun noon–5. Admission: Free.

DOWNTOWN AUSTIN

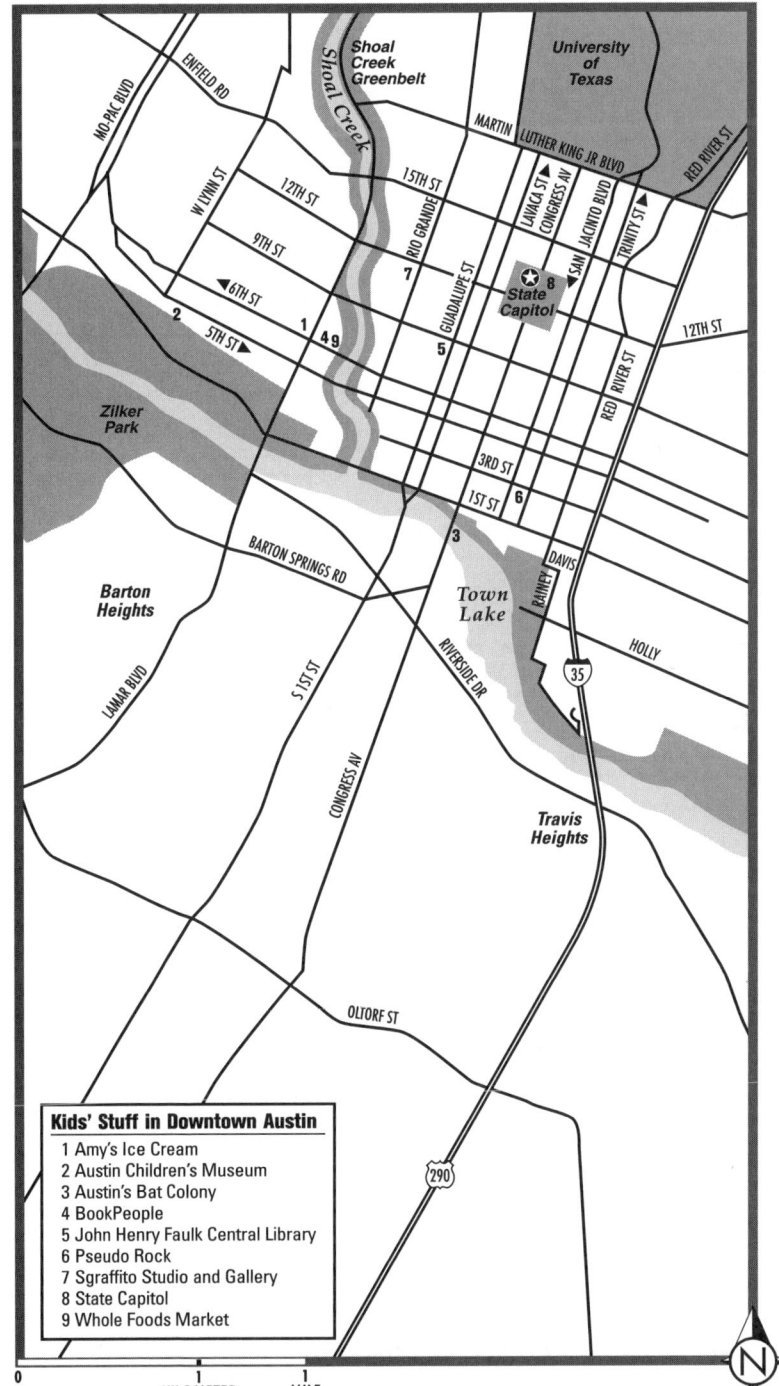

AUSTIN ZOO
10807 Rawhide Terr., Austin
512/288-1490 or 800/291-1490 SWA
This privately owned zoo located near Oak Hill offers pony rides, train rides, a petting zoo, and plenty of exotic creatures to keep the little ones happy. Animal food is offered for sale so young visitors can feed some of the inhabitants by hand. Hours: Daily 10–6. Admission: $4 adults over 12, $3.50 kids 3–12, free children under 3, $3.50 grandparents and seniors.

AUSTIN'S BAT COLONY
Congress Ave. Bridge at Town Lake, Austin
512/327-9721   DA
Watch 1.5 million Mexican free-tailed bats make their departure from the Congress Avenue Bridge on summer nights. The best viewing is from the hike-and-bike trail, the bridge, or a free bat viewing area in the parking lot of the Austin American-Statesman at 305 S. Congress Avenue. The best viewing months are July and August. For more on the bats, check out the information kiosks at the Four Seasons Hotel at 98 San Jacinto Boulevard and across the river in the parking lot of the Austin American-Statesman.

BARTON SPRINGS POOL
2200 Barton Springs Rd., Austin
512/476-9044   SA
Even little non-swimmers will enjoy splashing around the shallow waters on the upstream side of Barton Springs Pool. Restroom and changing facilities are available and food and drink concessions are located just outside the gates, or bring along a picnic lunch to enjoy in the shade of the tall oaks. Hours: Daily 9 a.m.–10 p.m. Admission: $2.50 adults, 25 cents for children.

Inner Space Cavern

Just up I-35 about 20 minutes beyond Austin's northern limits lies the most accessible cavern in Texas. Discovered during the construction of the interstate highway, this cavern is a cool getaway for summer travelers and was once a hideaway for animals as well. A skull of a peccary (a pig-like hoofed mammal) estimated to be a million years old has been found here, along with bones of a giant sloth and a mammoth. After reaching cave level aboard a small trolley, follow your guide for a tour of cave formations, a small lake, and evidence of those prehistoric visitors. The cavern is located off I-35 west of Austin, exit 259, in Georgetown. It's open 10–5 daily during winter months; 9–6 daily from Memorial Day through Labor Day. For more information, call 512/863-5545.

For the budding novelist in your family, check out the Austin Writer's League Creative Writing Camp, held every summer for middle school students. The AWL also sponsors weekend workshops for young writers. For details, call 512/499-8914.

JOURDAN-BACHMAN PIONEER FARM
11418 Sprinkle Cut-Off Rd., Austin
512/837-1215   EA
This attraction is well worth the drive to introduce youngsters to life in rural central Texas in the 1880s. The living history museum is built on a 2,000-acre cotton farm and populated with docents who carry on the chores of the period. Children can watch a blacksmith shoe a horse or a family cooking their meals over a wood-burning stove. Energetic youngsters can even pitch in and help plant or pick cotton or scrub clothes on a washboard. Admission: $3 adults, $2 children 3–12, free children under 3. (Not shown on map in this chapter)

LONE STAR RIVERBOAT
Congress Ave. at S. 1st St., Austin
512/327-1388   SA
You and your child will feel like Tom Sawyer aboard an old-fashioned paddlewheeler. The 90-minute trip offers a great city view. Hours: Sept–Oct and Mar–May, Sat–Sun at 3 p.m.; June–Aug, Tue–Sun 5:30 and Fri 10:30. Admission: $9 adults, $7 seniors, $6 children under 12.

NATIONAL WILDFLOWER RESEARCH CENTER
4801 La Cross Ave., Austin
512-292-4100   SWA
Young botanists can enjoy the children's garden, specially designed to please young visitors. A Children's Little House is especially inviting to young travelers. Hours: Tue–Sun 9–5:30. Admission: $3.50 adults; $2 students and seniors; $1 children 18 mos.–5 years.

OL' CACTUS JACK
13433 W. Hwy. 71, Bee Caves
512/263-2388   SWA
Kids at least 8 years old will enjoy a trail ride over 300 acres of the Hill Country on this ranch. An hour's ride costs $20 for one person, $15 for two or more.

VALLEY CREEK STABLES
8601 Bluff Springs Rd., Austin
512/282-6248   SWA
Kids 6 and up can ride on their own horse at this regular trail ride every Wednesday evening at 5:30; other hourly trail rides are by appointment. For three or more persons the charge is $25 per person; $35 per couple or individual.

ZILKER BOTANICAL GARDEN
Zilker Park, Austin
512/477-8672   SA
In the Pioneer Settlement in Zilker Botanical Garden in Zilker Park you'll see a collection of historic cabins from Austin's early days. The Esperanza School House was built in the Spicewood Springs area and was in use until about 1873. The Swedish Pioneer Cabin is one of the best preserved log houses in the country. The blacksmith shop contains equipment

NORTH AUSTIN

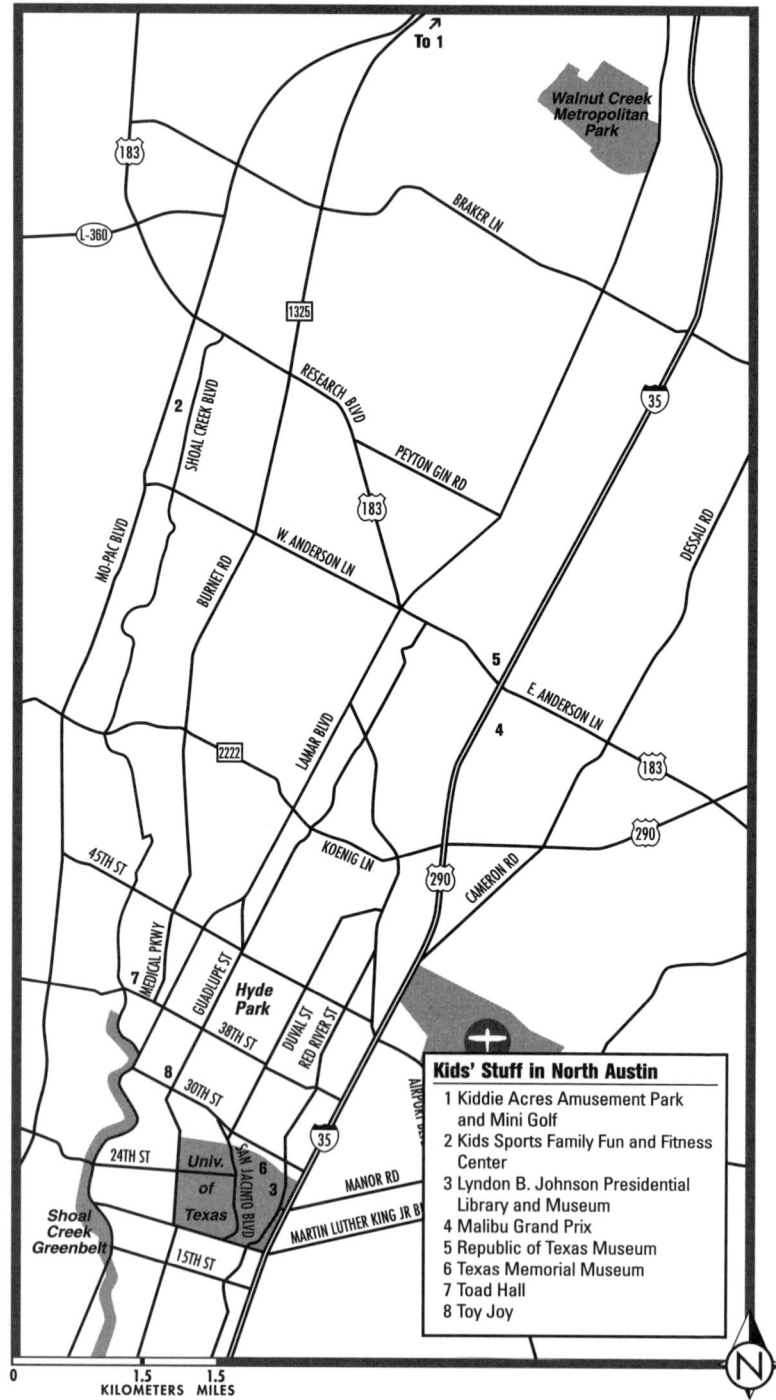

Austin Nature and Science Center, page 100

used by pioneer blacksmiths to make and shape hand-forged metal implements, and the Mamie Wilson Rowe Summer House is made of cypress wood. If you look closely, you may see some of the original square nails. Jan–Feb, Mon–Fri 8:30–4:30, Sat–Sun 1–5; Mar–Dec, Mon–Fri 8:30–4:30, Sat 10–5, Sun 1–5. Admission: Free.

ZILKER DINOSAUR TRACKWAYS
Zilker Park
Barton Springs Rd., Austin   SA
Once restricted to tours only, these invaluable relics of 100 million years ago are now open to the public, but the public is requested to please tread carefully, with soft-soled shoes. The archeologists who discovered the tracks in 1991, of what is believed to be an ornithomimus, an ostrich-like dinosaur, say that 30 to 40 percent of the track definitions have been lost due to carelessness.

ZILKER PARK CANOE RENTALS
2000 Barton Springs Rd., Austin
512/478-3852   SA
Explore Town Lake aboard a canoe for an afternoon of adventure. Hours: 11–dusk. Admission: $6 per hour, $20 per day.

ZILKER RAILROAD
Zilker Park, Austin
512/478-8167   SA
Jump aboard this pint-sized train for a 3-mile, 20-minute ride through picturesque Zilker Park. The railroad winds past the children's playground and along the hike-and-bike trail. Board at the station at Barton Springs Pool, across from the concession stand. Hours: Weather permitting 10–5. Admission: $2 adults, $1.25 children and seniors.

MUSEUMS

AUSTIN CHILDREN'S MUSEUM
1501 W. 5th St., Austin
512/472-2499   DA
The Children's Museum sets out to make learning fun through hands-on exhibits on all facets of science and technology. Some popular permanent exhibits include the Whole

NORTHWEST AUSTIN

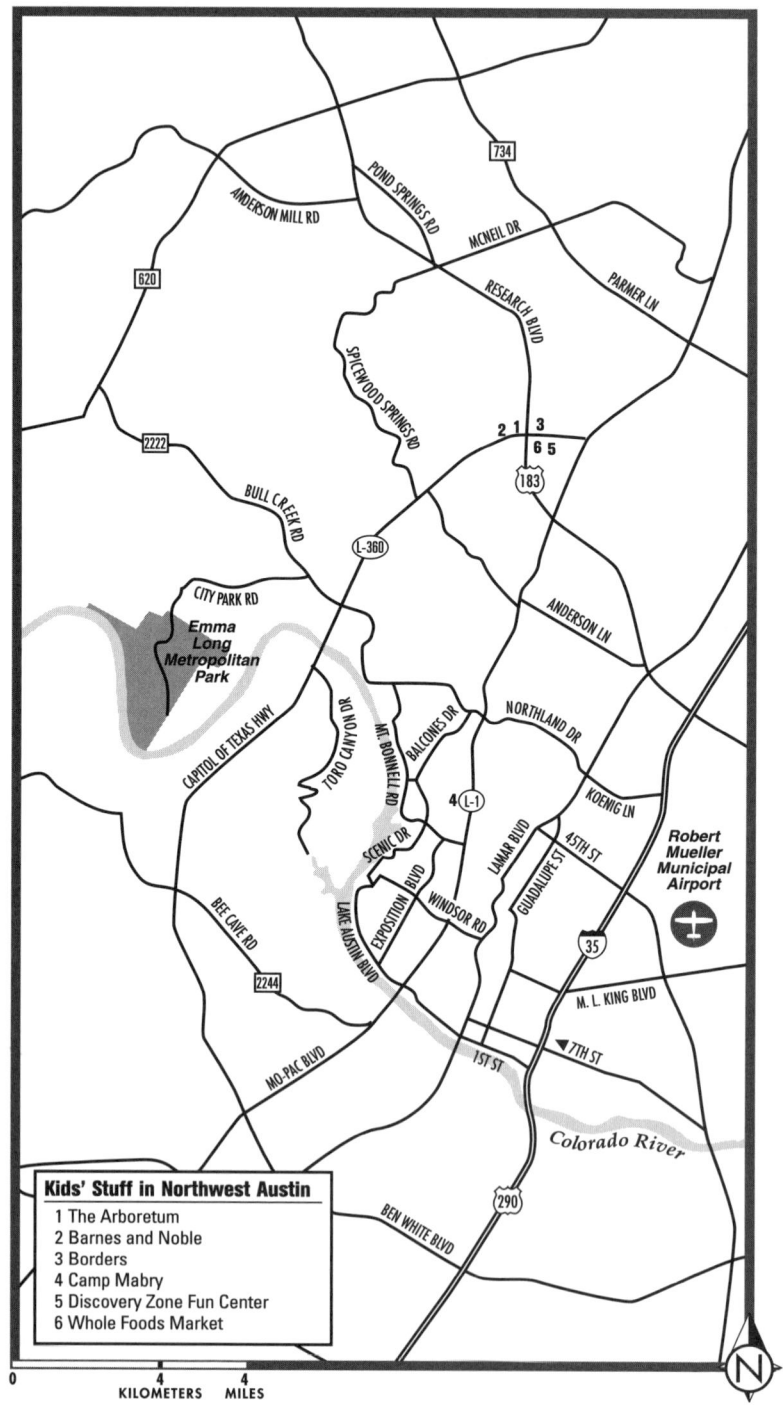

Child-Size Festivals

Austin hosts festivals and special events year-round and several of these celebrations are designed for the younger residents and visitors. Check out these annual events sure to please kids of all ages:

March: *Austin-Travis County Livestock Show and PRCA Rodeo offers youngsters a chance to feel like a cowboy. Watch professionals compete and schoolchildren show their prize-winning livestock. 512/467-9814.*

April: *Celebrate spring at Safari, a family festival that recognizes nature and the environment. Sponsored by the Austin Nature Center. 512/327-8180.*

June–August: *Symphony Square hosts Children's Day Art Park with storytellers and musicians. 512/476-6064.*

October: *Boo! Ghosts and ghouls make their appearance at two events designed to delight, not terrify, young visitors. The Austin Children's Museum (512/472-2494) hosts Gruseum, a costumed celebration for young children. The Jourdan-Bachman Pioneer Farm (512/837-1215) celebrates the season with a Halloween haunt. And finally, bring your costumed youngster to the Austin Symphony's (512/476-6064) annual Halloween concert for kids.*

December: *Austin becomes the land of Dickens at the Victorian Christmas on 6th Street (512/478-8704). Booths sell period costumes and accessories, and carolers share the spirit of the season. Zilker Park lights up with Yulefest and the Trail of Lights (512/397-1463), a magical wonderland of lights.*

Foods Market where children learn about nutrition as they "play store," the Sound Track Studio where they learn about recording technology with keyboards and microphones, and the Music Room where they can make music and dance. Hours: Tue–Sat 10–5, Sun noon–5. Admission: $2.50, free for children under 2.

CAMP MABRY NATIONAL GUARD
W. 35th St. and Loop 1 (MoPac), Austin
512/406-6967   NWA
Any kids wanting to play soldier can head down to Camp Mabry, headquarters of the Texas Army and Air National Guard, for a look at the airplanes, helicopters, cannons, and

> The Austin Symphony Orchestra regularly schedules kids-oriented concerts and activities such as the Children's Halloween Concert, Children's Day Art Park, and more. For information, call 512/476-6064.

even tanks along the walking trail. If that piques your youngster's interest, stop by the Military Forces Museum for a look at military memorabilia. Hours: Museum Wed 1–5, Thur–Sun 10–4, closed Mon–Tue.

**LYNDON B. JOHNSON
PRESIDENTIAL LIBRARY
AND MUSEUM
2313 Red River, Austin
512/482-5136   NA**
Bring the little ones to awe at the six floors of red, gold-sealed boxes containing the public papers of LBJ's career. Children enjoy a look at the moon rock, gifts given to the President from people around the world, and especially the top-floor replica of the oval office. Buy an inexpensive souvenir in the gift shop then go outside for a picnic by the fountain. Hours: Daily except Christmas 9–5. Admission: Free.

**REPUBLIC OF TEXAS MUSEUM
510 E. Anderson Ln., Austin
512/339-1997   NA**
Take the kids to play in "Great Grandma's Backyard" at this historic museum focusing on the years when Texas was an independent republic. Children enjoy the hands-on collection of artifacts that recall Texas' early days in this museum run by the Daughters of the Republic of Texas. Hours: Mon–Fri 10–4. Admission: $2 adults, $1 children.

**STATE CAPITOL
11th St. at Congress Ave., Austin
512/478-0098   DA**
One of the top field trip destinations in Texas, this truly Texas-size building leaves young travelers dwarfed by its massive proportions. Paintings of Texas heroes will also impress youngsters. Starting at the rotunda star, visitors can tour the recently restored structure, and if the legislature's in session, even sit in and watch Texas government at work. Enter the third floor balconies for a view of the House and Senate chambers. The legislature meets from January through May in odd numbered years.

**TEXAS MEMORIAL MUSEUM
2400 Trinity St., Austin
512/471-1604   NA**
Take your little dinosaur lover to this museum on the University of Texas campus. Youngsters also enjoy a look at the gem and mineral collection and the wildlife dioramas. Hours: Mon–Fri 9–5, Sat 10–5, Sun 1–5. Admission: Free.

**WILD BASIN
WILDERNESS PRESERVE
805 N. Loop 360, Austin
512/327-7622   SWA**
This 220-acre park is the perfect place for a hike, no matter the stamina level of your young hikers. Hours: Daily dawn–dusk; tours Sat

SOUTHWEST AUSTIN

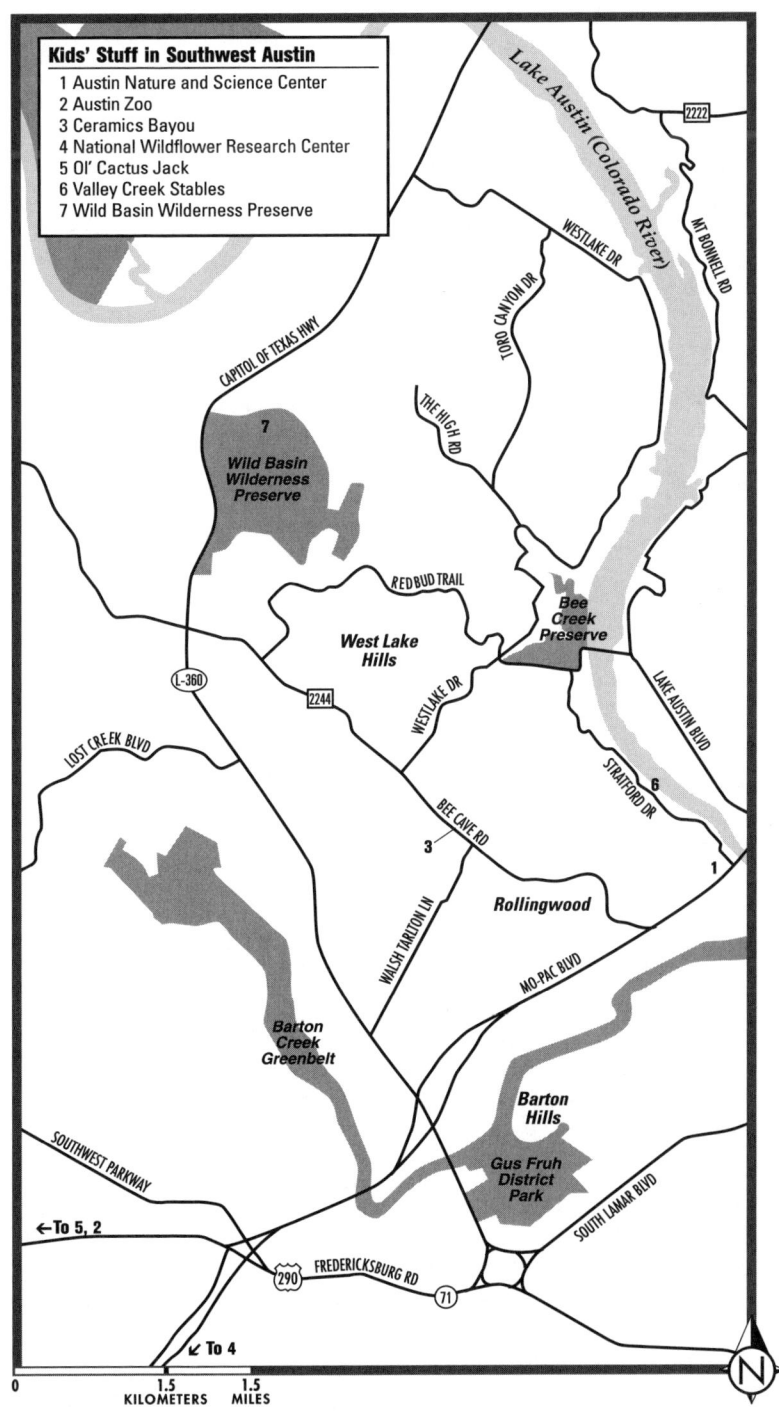

Top Ten Places to Take Preschoolers
By Laurie Kibel
Daycare supervisor for over a decade
and mother of three daughters

1. Austin Zoo, 10807 Rawhide Tr., 512/288-1490.
2. Log Cabin, Wells Branch Park, off Wells Branch Pkwy. on Klattenhoff Dr.
3. Austin Children's Museum, 1501 W. 5th St., 512/472-2499.
4. LBJ Library and Presidential Museum, 2313 Red River, 512/482-5136.
5. Texas Memorial Museum, 2400 Trinity St., 512/471-1604.
6. Ice-skating at Northcross Mall, 512/451-5102.
7. Zachary Scott Theater, 1510 Toomey Rd., 512/476-0594.
8. Kid's Sports, 8015 Shoal Creek Blvd., 512/452-8775.
9. Inner Space Cavern, west off I-35, exit 259, Georgetown 512/863-5545.
10. Roller-skating at Skateworld, 9514 W. Anderson Mill Rd., 512/258-8886.

and Sun (call for times). Admission: $1 adults ; 50¢ children 5–12.

PUPPETS AND THEATER

BARNES AND NOBLE
10000 Research Blvd., Austin
512/418-8985 **NWA**
This two-story bookseller has a separate children's section that encourages young readers to take a place on the floor and curl up with a good book. Regularly scheduled children's events, puppet shows, and readings make this a favorite stop for families. Hours: Daily 9 a.m.–11 p.m.

BOOKPEOPLE
6th St. and Lamar Blvd., Austin
512/472-5050 **DA**
Austin's largest bookstore has weekly events for children at 10:30 a.m. on Tuesday and Wednesday and 2 p.m. on Saturday, including puppet shows and readings.

BORDERS
10225 Research Blvd., Austin
512/795-9553 **NWA**
Pre-schoolers enjoy storytime every Thursday at 10:30. The Children's Department also schedules special events ranging from tea parties to puppet shows to career awareness.

ZACHARY SCOTT THEATRE
1510 Toomey Rd., Austin
512/476-0594 **SA**
Enroll your budding actor or actress in a children's class at the performing arts school for lessons in creative drama, singing, comedy, play writing, and more. Sessions

Branch Libraries

Check with these branch libraries for information about childrens' story times.

Carver, 1161 Angelina, 512/472-8954
Dove Springs, 5405 South Pleasant Valley Rd., 512/462-1452
Govalle, 4704-A East Cesar Chavez St., 512/385-2670
Howson, 2500 Exposition Blvd., 512/499-7599
Little Walnut Creek, 835 West Rundberg Ln., 512/836-8975
Manchaca Road, 5500 Manchaca Rd., 512/447-6651
North Loop Area, 2210 Hancock Dr., 512/454-7208
North Village, 2139 West Anderson Ln., 512/458-2239
Oak Hill, 5125 Convict Hill Rd., 512/499-7599
Oak Springs, 3101 Oak Springs Dr., 512/926-4453
Old Quarry, 7051 Village Center Dr., 512/345-4435
Pleasant Hill, 211 East William Cannon Dr., 512/441-7993
Riverside Drive, 2410 East Riverside Dr., 512/448-0776
Spicewood Springs, 8637 Spicewood Springs Rd., 512/258-9070
Terrazas, 1105 East Cesar Chavez St., 512/472-7312
Twin Oaks, 2301 South Congress Ave. #7, 512/442-4664
University Hills, 4721 Loyola Ln., 512/929-0551
Windsor Village, 5811 Berkman Dr. #140, 512/928-0333

are divided by age and include children 5 to 16 years.

LIBRARIES

The Austin Public Library offers a variety of programs including storytimes, films, arts and crafts, and puppet shows. The programs are scheduled at the main library as well as branch libraries scattered throughout the city.

The main library, housed at 800 Guadalupe Street, is named for John Henry Faulk, a well-known Austin humorist and writer. The library system, with an annual budget exceeding $10 million, has over a million holdings.

Youth programs at the Austin Public Library include toddler Storytimes for ages 18 months to 3 years with an adult, preschool Storytimes for young listeners 4 to 5 years old, and Storytimes for all age groups. A Summer Fun Club is offered every year to children 6 to 10 years old. Other programs include films, arts and crafts, and puppet shows.

One of the most recognized library programs is the Victory Program. Victory Program Homework Centers offer free tutoring to young Austinites using VISTA volunteers. The program was named one of the top 50 outstanding programs for youth in U.S. schools and public libraries by the American Library Association.

JOHN HENRY FAULK CENTRAL LIBRARY
800 Guadalupe St., Austin
512/499-7599   DA
This central library was built at a cost of $6 million in 1979. The library offers excellent youth programs and, for school-age children, thorough resources for any school report. Reference assistance is available on the first floor. Hours: Mon–Thur 9–9, Fri–Sat 9–6, Sun noon–6.

STORES KIDS LOVE

AMY'S ICE CREAM
1012 W. 6th St., Austin
512/480-0673   DA
Boisterous waitpersons serve up frivolity and frozen confection at this Austin institution. Select from dozens of varieties of ice cream—and don't be surprised if the servers toss your order amongst themselves. Other locations: 10000 Research Blvd. (NWA), 512/345-1006; 3300 Bee Caves (SWA), 512/328-9859; 3500 Guadalupe St. (NA), 512/458-6895. Hours vary by store; most open daily at noon and close at midnight.

ANNA'S TOY DEPOT
2401 S. Lamar, Austin
512/447-8697   SA
New and used toys rule at this fun-filled store that has everything from daycare supplies to action figures and games. Mon–Sat 10–6, Sun 1–5.

CERAMICS BAYOU
3736 Bee Caves Rd., Austin
512/328-1168   SWA
Kids can paint their own pottery at this fun store that sells coffee mugs, bowls, platters, and pots. They'll even glaze and fire the work, making it safe for dining use or display. Hours: Thur–Fri 10–9, Sat 10–6, Sun noon–5.

DRAGONSNAPS CHILDREN'S CLOTHING
1700 S. Congress Ave., Austin
512/445-9000   SA
This store promises "100% comfortable clothes for kids." Check out the tiny fashions, footwear, and all the latest trinkets designed to impress the playground crowd. Hours: Mon–Sat 10–6.

SGRAFFITO STUDIO AND GALLERY
809 W. 12th, Austin
512/708-9000   DA
Kids will love painting one-of-a-kind ceramics at this studio. Children can select from an artists' palette a rainbow of colors to decorate plates, cups, and ornaments; the studio also is available for parties. Hours: Mon–Wed 11–8, Thur 11–10, Sat 11–6, Sun noon–6.

TERRA TOYS
1708 S. Congress Ave., Austin
512/445-4489   SA
This Austin institution features dollhouses, railroads, science kits, and dolls. You name it, you'll find it in this

SOUTH AUSTIN

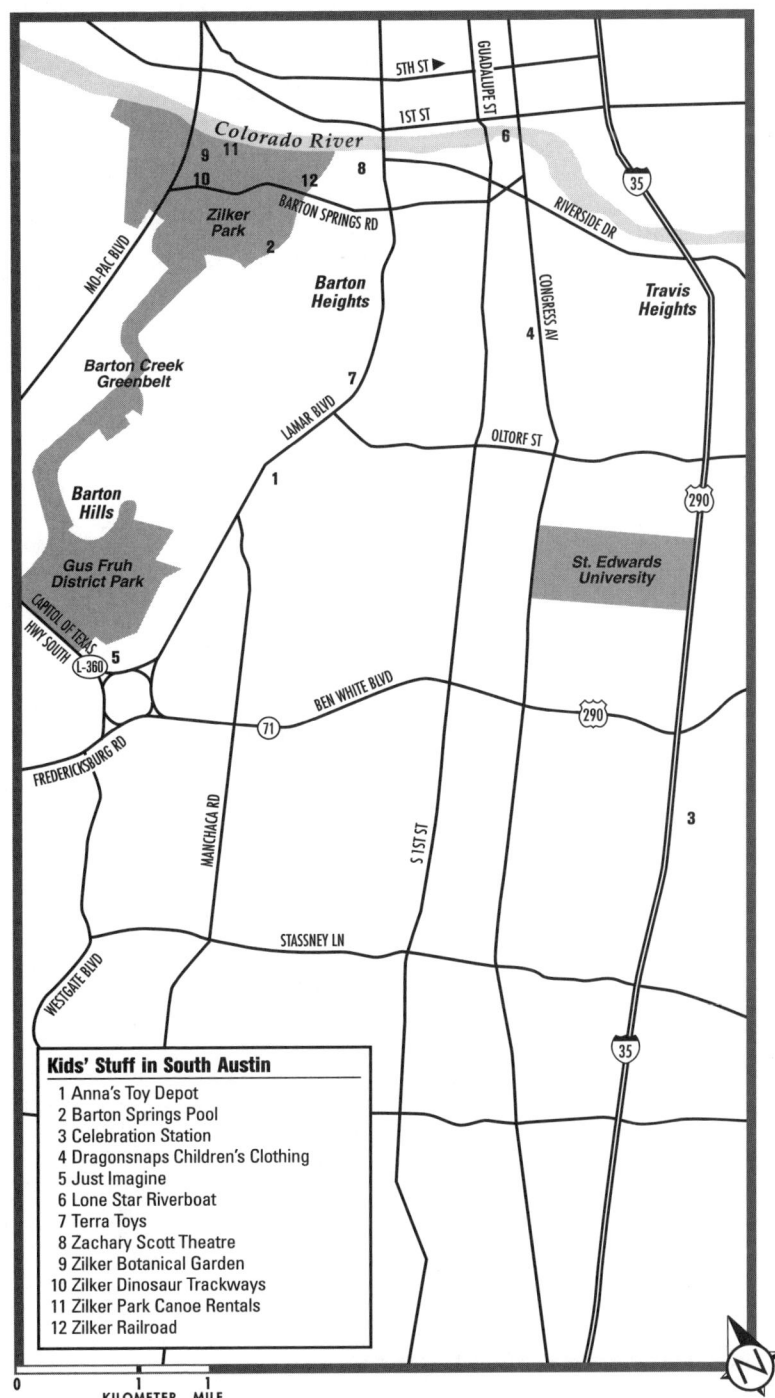

toy palace. Hours: Mon–Sat 10–7, Sun noon–6.

TOAD HALL
1206 W. 38th, Austin
512/323-2665   NA
This children's bookstore is the kind of place the whole family can enjoy, with regularly scheduled puppet shows and readings for little ones, series books and classics for juveniles, and parenting guides for adults. Hours: Mon–Sat 9–7, Sun 1–5.

TOY JOY
2900 Guadalupe St., Austin
512/320-0090   NA
This funky shop is a special favorite with teens who feel they've outgrown toys but still have room for stickers, figurines, and oddities like boxing nuns. Hours: Sun–Thur 10–10, Fri–Sat 10–midnight.

WHOLE FOODS MARKET
6th St. and Lamar Blvd., Austin
512/476-1206   DA
Loop 360 and U.S. 183, Austin
512/345-5003   NWA
Who says food can't be fun? Schedule a children's tour of either of these popular markets. Hours: Daily 8:30 a.m.–10:30 p.m.

FUN AND GAMES

CELEBRATION STATION
4525 S. I-35, Austin
512/448-3533   SA
A popular birthday party venue, Celebration Station entertains children any time with go-karts, batting cages, bumper boats, miniature golf, and more. Rides are priced individually or a play pass gives unlimited access to outdoor attractions. A food court with a pizza restaurant

Blacksmith at Jourdan-Bachman Pioneer Farm, page 103

keeps hungry visitors happy. Hours: Memorial Day–Labor Day 10–10; Sun–Thur 11–10 and Fri–Sat 10–midnight during winter months. Admission: "Pay as You Play" or all-day pass $9.95–$11.95.

DISCOVERY ZONE FUN CENTER
9503 Research Blvd., Austin
512/346-9666   NWA
Another favorite with the birthday party set, this indoor playland has games and playsets for children under 12. Hours: Mon–Thur 10–8, Fri–Sat 10–9, Sun 11–7. Free for adults and children under 1; $3.99 children 1–3, $5.99 children 3–12.

JUST IMAGINE
4220 S. Lamar Blvd., Austin
512/444-8898   SA
Located in Brodie Oaks Shopping Center at Loop 360 and South Lamar, this unique party venue offers kids two hours of fun and also provides all-day fun for $38 per day. Activities include drama, computers, and more. Hours: Mon–Thur 10–8, Fri–Sat 10–9, Sun noon–7.

 If you're looking for an alternative to babysitting, check out the Kids' Night Out at the Hancock Rec Center. The Saturday night fun runs from 6 p.m.–11 p.m. for kids 3–12 and includes movie and popcorn. Kids must be registered by 6 p.m. on Thursday; admission is $10 per child. Call 512/453-7765 for information or to register.

KIDDIE ACRES AMUSEMENT PARK AND MINI GOLF
4800 W. Howard Ln., Austin
512/255-4131   NA
Children under 12 can ride ponies and small amusement park rides at this north Austin playland that's been a longtime favorite with Austinites. Its 18-hole miniature golf course is popular, too. Concessions offer hot dogs, ice cream, and snack foods. Wednesday is discount day when tickets are sold at group rates. Hours: June–August, Tuesday–Sunday 10–7; Sept–Oct, Tuesday–Thursday noon–7, Friday–Sunday noon–9; November–March, Tuesday–Sunday noon–7; April–May, Tuesday–Thursday noon–7, Friday– Sunday noon–9. Admission: $1 per ticket or ten tickets for $8.50; miniature golf rates are $2.50 for adults, $2 for children under 12.

KIDSSPORTS FAMILY FUN AND FITNESS CENTER
8015 Shoal Creek Blvd., Austin
512/452-8775   NA
This high-energy center offers birthday parties, kids' fun, and day camps. Parties include 30 minutes in a private gym doing age-appropriate games, 30 minutes in the party room, and 30 minutes on the adventure challenge course. KidsSports also offers a supervised all-day camp for $22 per day. Hours: summer, Mon–Sat 10–7, Sun noon–6; winter, Mon, Wed, Thur, Sat 10–7; Tue, Fri noon–7 (wee sports gym only), Sun 1–7. Admission: 36 inches tall and under, $4.25; over 36 inches tall, $4.95; adults free.

MALIBU GRAND PRIX
7417 N. I-35, Austin
512/454-3898   NA
Older kiddos can take a turn around the track in three-quarter-size Formula 1 race cars and go-karts or play over 75 kinds of video games, basketball with a moving hoop, and "Big Bertha" where they can throw balls in Bertha's mouth and watch her get bigger at this high-action fun center. Hours: Sun–Thur noon–10, Fri–Sat 11a.m.–midnight. Admission: $2.85–$3.75 for one lap. Need Malibu Grand Prix license, $1.35.

PSEUDO ROCK
200 Trinity St., Austin
512/474-4375   DA
If restless kids have you climbing the walls, let them have their turn at Pseudo Rock, an indoor climbing facility. The 5,000-square-foot place has 35 different climbing adventures for all skill levels and youngsters can learn the basics of rock climbing. Hours: Mon–Fri 10–10, Sat–Sun 10–8. Admission: $8; equipment rental is $5.

7

MUSEUMS AND GALLERIES

There's not a dull museum in lively Austin. Among them are a museum covering the ten-year span of the Republic of Texas, a museum in the house where humorist O. Henry lived, and a museum housing a rare and treasured copy of the Gutenberg Bible. One museum features locally found dinosaur bones; another celebrates the ethnicity of the city. The visual arts by both local and national artists are vibrantly represented in numerous galleries around downtown, north, and south Austin. (Many are located downtown, along 3rd, 4th, and 6th Streets.) At present three vital city museums, the Austin Museum of Art, the Mexican-American Cultural Center, and the George Washington Carver Museum, have come together to plan for a future 86,000-square-foot facility in downtown Austin. While the project builds, visit the three fine museums—and others—at their present locations.

ART MUSEUMS

AUSTIN MUSEUM OF ART AT LAGUNA GLORIA
3809 W. 35th St., Austin
512/458-8191 NWA

Located in a Mediterranean-style villa built in 1916 and now listed on the National Register of Historical Places, the museum is set on 12 green acres of lovely grounds once owned by Stephen F. Austin, who purchased the land in 1832 but died before he could build on it. The museum has become nationally known for its art exhibits, sculpture gardens, and educational programs. The museum building was once the home of Clara Driskill Servier, who is considered a Texas heroine for her work in preserving the Alamo for posterity. The estate was deeded to the Texas Fine Arts Commission in 1943. The grounds, near the middle of the city, are secluded, shady, and spacious, with wandering walks, sunken sculpture gardens, and rock terraces down to the shores of Lake Austin. The museum specializes in American art since 1900, serving as a showcase for modern painters, sculptors, photographers, and architects. There's a museum shop located downtown at 107 W. 6th Street (512/477-0766). Hours: Tue–Sat 10–5, Thur 1–5, Sun noon–5. Admission: $2 adults, $1 children.

AUSTIN MUSEUM OF ART DOWNTOWN
823 Congress Ave., Austin
512/495-9224   **DA**

The Museum of Art Downtown features traveling exhibits of paintings, drawings, poetry, and text. It's mission: to provide dynamic exhibitions focusing on American art of the U.S., Mexico, and the Caribbean are featured each year.

In 1997, construction of a new home for the museum began. Designed by architect Robert Venturi, the four-story, 86,000-square-foot facility will provide generous gallery space, modern classrooms, and a 300-seat, performance-quality auditorium, giving art lovers across Texas a world-class visual arts center. The new building, located at 3rd and Guadalupe, should be open by the year 2002.

ELISABET NEY MUSEUM
304 E. 44th St., Austin
512/458-2255   **NA**

Although she was born in Munster, Germany, in 1833 Elisabet Ney was Texas' first sculptor, and she was famous well before she settled in Austin in 1892. She was the first woman to be accepted into the Munich Art Academy. She sculpted such notables as Bismarck, Garibaldi, and Ludwig II of Bavaria, whose life-size likenesses may be seen in the restored former home and studio today. She and her Scots husband, Dr. Edmund Montgomery, moved to the United States to avoid the Franco-Prussian War. After a 20-year hiatus, she resumed her career in 1892 when she received commissions to model Sam Houston and Stephen F. Austin for the Colombian Exposition in Chicago. Today these marbles are in the capitol, but the plaster models are in the museum. A plaster model of Lady MacBeth, which Ney considered her masterpiece, stands in the full light of the large studio window. Sculpted between 1902 and 1905, the marble statue has been in the Smithsonian in Washington, D.C., since 1916. Hours: Wed–Sat 10–5, Sun noon–5. Admission: Free.

> **TRIVIA**
> Austin has the sixth-highest number of artists per capita in the U.S.

HARRY RANSOM HUMANITIES RESEARCH CENTER
University of Texas Campus
21st and Guadalupe Sts., Austin
512/471-8944   **NA**

Exhibits of twentieth-century American, British, and French literary materials, photography, film, theater arts, and visual arts are displayed on the fourth and seventh floors of the center, and in Leeds Gallery in Flawn Academic Center west of the UT Tower. One of only 48 copies worldwide of the Gutenberg Bible (1449–1450) is on exhibit on the first floor of the Harry Ransom Center. Hours: Mon–Fri 9–4:30, Thur 9–7. Additional hours for the Bible: Sat 9–5, Sun 1–5. Leeds Gallery hours: Mon–Fri 9–4:30. Admission: Free.

DOWNTOWN AUSTIN

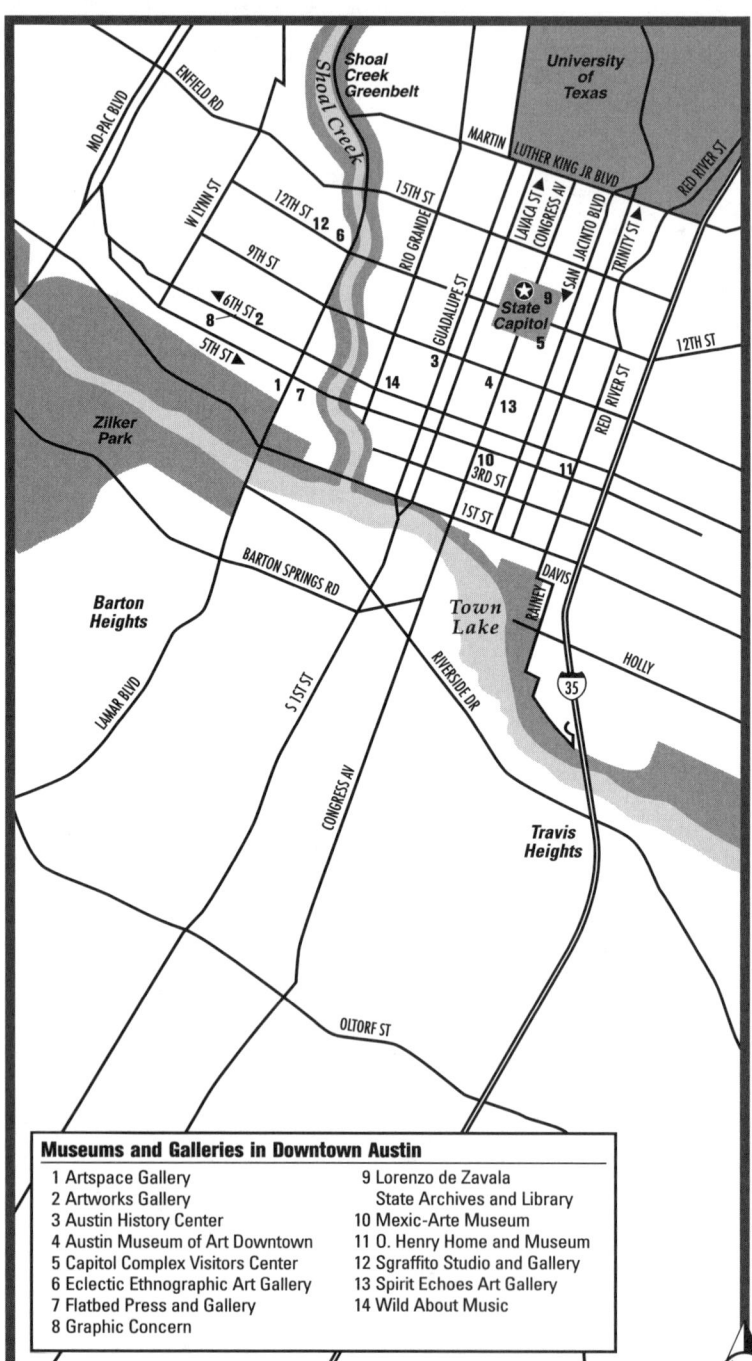

Los Días de los Muertos

Austin's Mexic-Arte Museum celebrates Los Días de los Muertos, the Days of the Dead, with an exhibition, usually the last weekend in October into the first of November. Worship of the Days of the Dead in Mexico has existed since prehistoric times, with the placing of objects for the soul to take along on its journey to the next world. Nowadays in Hispanic culture it's celebrated by communing with departed relatives and friends by sharing food with them, decorating their graves, burning copal, and toasting them. Yellow marigolds, candles, toys, personal mementos, and photographs are placed on an altar, graves are cleaned and weeded, and relatives lay their offerings on the graves. Children make masks of skulls decorated with butterflies and flowers because in Mexican culture, skulls and death are not scary. Los Días de los Muertos is a happy celebration.

HUNTINGTON ART GALLERY
Two locations on the University of Texas campus:
University of Texas Art Building at 23rd and San Jacinto, Austin
Harry Ransom Humanities Research Center at 21st and Guadalupe Sts., Austin
512/471-7324   **NA**
Considered one of the top ten university art galleries in the country, the Huntington is housed in two separate facilities on the university campus. The permanent collections are in the Harry Ransom Humanities Research Center where more than 9,000 works range from ancient to contemporary art from Australia, Europe, Latin America, and the United States. The galleries are home to twentieth-century artwork of both North and Latin America, as well as the Michener Collection of art donated to the university by novelist James Michener and his wife. Temporary exhibits are displayed in the university's Art Building at 23rd and San Jacinto Boulevard. Hours: Mon–Sat 9–5, Sun 1–5. Admission: Free.

MEXIC-ARTE MUSEUM
419 Congress Ave., Austin
512/480-9373   **DA**
"Mexico in Times of Change" is a permanent exhibit with photographs from the Mexican Revolution of 1810 as well as prints showing popular culture from the late nineteenth and early twentieth centuries. Works from Mexican artists are also on display. There is a gift shop. Hours: Mon–Sat 10–6. Admission: Free; suggested donation of $2.

UMLAUF SCULPTURE GARDEN AND MUSEUM
605 Robert E. Lee Rd., Austin
512/445-5582   **SA**
The museum was built with private funds and contains more than 200

TIP

Charles Umlauf's works can also be seen in public institutions across the United States, such as the Smithsonian Institution in Washington, D.C., and the Metropolitan Museum of Art in New York City. In Texas, his works can be seen in public places from Abilene to Waco.

---

sculptures by internationally known sculptor Charles Umlauf. Charles and Angeline Umlauf gave their home, studio, and work to the City of Austin in 1985. The works are displayed by rotation on 6 acres of xeriscaped gardens. The setting is lovely, with a waterfall, streams, and ponds under tall cedar and oak trees. The works are executed in diverse materials, from exotic woods to terra cotta, rich bronzes, and alabasters; they range from detailed realism to lyrical abstractions. There is a ten-minute video in which the late artist tells about his work and philosophy and describes his methodology. Hours: Thur, Sat, and Sun 1–4:30; Fri 10–4:30; Thur in June, July, and Aug 1–8; closed Mon. Admission: $3 adults ; $2 seniors; $1 students; free under 6.

SCIENCE AND HISTORY MUSEUMS

AUSTIN HISTORY CENTER
810 Guadalupe St., Austin
512/499-7480 DA

The center is housed in another of Austin's historical buildings, this one is a beauty, an Art Deco interpretation of Renaissance Revival style. It was built in the 1930s as the main library and is still fondly referred to as "Old Main." (The new building, ultramodern glass and cement, is right next door.) Photographs and exhibits change, but everything ever printed or recorded about Austin and Travis County is zealously collected and protected within its walls, and the library is run by a very helpful and friendly staff. Hours: Mon–Thur 9–9, Fri–Sat 9–6, Sun noon–6. Admission: Free.

CENTER FOR AMERICAN HISTORY AT THE UNIVERSITY OF TEXAS
Sid Richardson Hall
23rd St. and Red River, Austin
512/495-4515 NA

The Texas Collection here has 120,000 volumes of Texana alone. Stephen F. Austin's papers and those of his father Moses Austin are here, as well as the Bexar Archives and other important historical materials dealing with the settling of the state. A closed-stack library, it's open for research to anyone abiding by the rules. Hours: Mon–Sat 9–5. Admission: Free.

CAPITOL COMPLEX VISITORS CENTER
112 E. 11th St., Austin
512/305-8400 DA

The General Land Office, the oldest government building in Texas, has permanent and changing exhibits, information on tours and informative brochures, and a gift shop. Hours: Tue–Fri 9–5, Sat 10–5. Admission: Free.

THE FRENCH LEGATION MUSEUM
802 San Marcos, Austin

512/472-8180 **EA**
Austin's oldest standing building, this Greek Revival bayou-style mansion, built in 1841, is preserved by the Daughters of the Republic of Texas. It was built by Alphonse Dubois de Saligny, named charge d'affaires to the Republic of Texas when Louis Philippe of France recognized the republic in 1839. The parlor contains some furnishings that belonged to Saligny, while others are pieces of the period. The legation's kitchen is the only authentic reproduction of an early Creole kitchen in the United States. Tours are conducted Tuesday through Saturday from 1 to 5 p.m., and there's a bang-up Bastille Day celebration every July 14th. Hours: Tue–Sun 1–5. Admission: $3 adults, $1 children 11–18, 50 cents children under 10.

GEORGE WASHINGTON CARVER MUSEUM
1165 Angelina, Austin
512/472-4809 **EA**
Texas' first African-American neighborhood history museum displays artifacts, videos, oral histories, community-related photographs, and other archival material depicting the local, regional, and national history of African Americans. The museum documents the significant contribution that blacks have made on both city and country levels. The facility includes art exhibits relating to African-American culture and heritage. Hours: Tue–Thur 10–6, Fri–Sat noon–5.

LYNDON B. JOHNSON PRESIDENTIAL LIBRARY AND MUSEUM
2313 Red River, Austin
512/916-5136 **NA**
The library houses 40 million pages from the entire public career of Lyndon Baines Johnson and also those of close associates (used primarily by scholars). Year-round public viewing of the permanent historical and cultural exhibits includes gifts from foreign heads of state, a moon rock, and a replica of the Oval Office. Hours: Daily except Christmas, 9–5. Admission: Free.

LORENZO DE ZAVALA STATE ARCHIVES AND LIBRARY
1201 Brazos, Austin
512/463-5455 **DA**
Some of Texas' most important historic documents and collections are housed here in the Texas State Library, including genealogy records. The library is named for an elected interim vice president of the Texas Republic. The large lobby mural, painted by Peter Rogers in collaboration with Peter Hurd, depicts events and personages of the republic. Also in the lobby are exhibits displaying artifacts of the Texas Republic, and

---

TRIVIA

Alphonse Dubois de Saligny, French charge d'affaires to the Republic of Texas, never occupied the legation; he left in a huff because of the "Pig War." The pigs on a neighboring site ate Saligny's corn, and perhaps even worse, chewed on some table linens that he had purchased in New Orleans on his way to this outpost of civilization. His servant shot the pigs, the animals' owner beat the servant, and the "war" was on.

NORTH AUSTIN

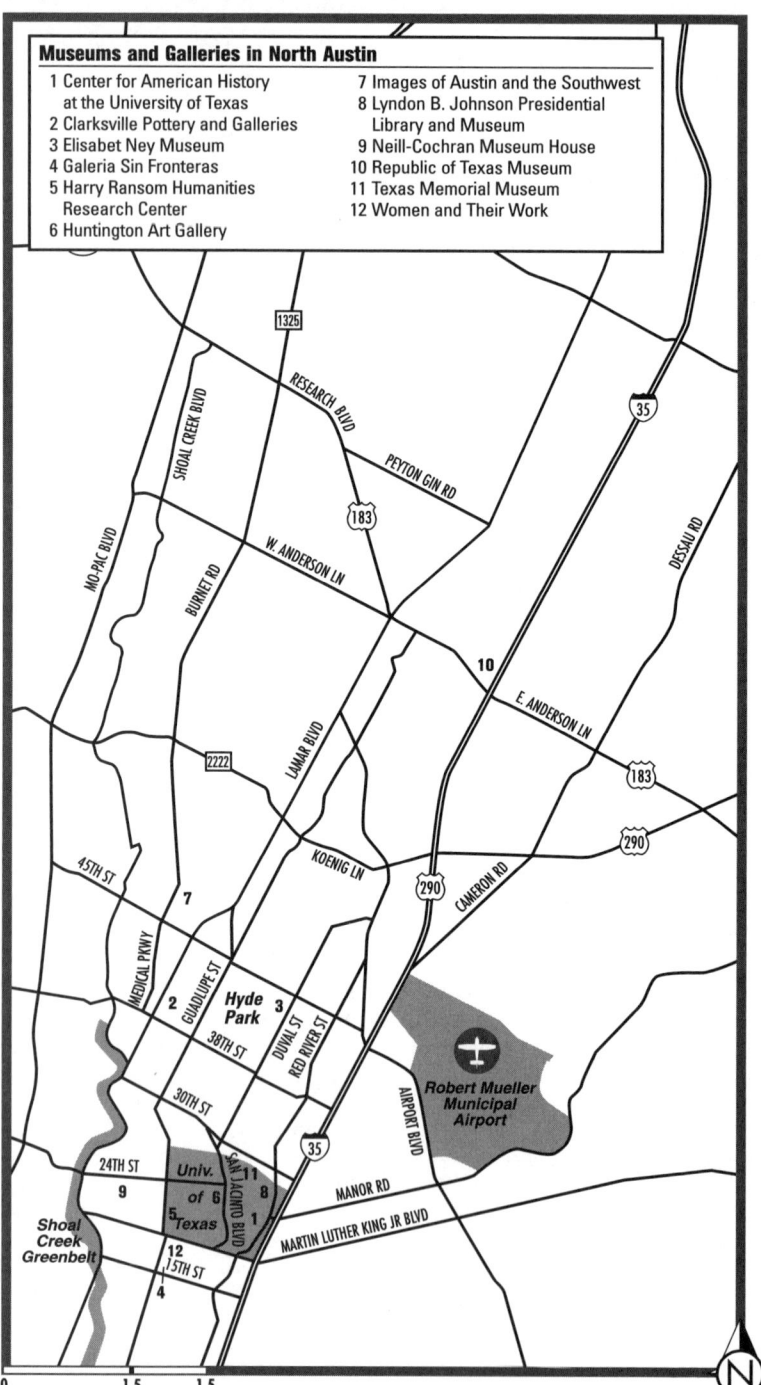

Austin Museum of Art at Laguna Gloria, page 116

on the second floor there is a colorful display of every flag that played a part in Texas history. A large statue of Sam Houston stands at the entrance to the building. Hours: Mon–Fri 8–5. Genealogy Tue–Sat 8–5. Admission: Free.

NEILL-COCHRAN MUSEUM HOUSE
2310 San Gabriel, Austin
512/478-2335 NA
A blend of Greek Revival architecture and native Texas materials makes this mansion a truly unique Austin landmark. Abner Cook, the master builder who also built the Governor's Mansion used native limestone and pine from Bastrop to construct this home in 1855 for Washington L. Hill. It served as a family home to a succession of owners (during the Civil War Federal soldiers were hospitalized here, and some are buried near the house) until purchased in 1958 by the Colonial Dames of America. Hours: Daily except Mon–Tue. Admission: $2.

O. HENRY HOME AND MUSEUM
409 E. 5th St., Austin
512/472-1903 DA
Austin is proud to boast that William Sidney Porter, otherwise known as short story master O. Henry, once lived in Austin, and his Victorian cottage, built circa 1892, contains his desk, writing materials, and other period furnishings. The first weekend in May the museum sponsors the O. Henry Pun Off competition. It's open to the public and adds up to a lot of fun. It's held in the backyard, where both a book fair and a country western band are going on at the same time. All three trophies,—first, second, and third—are of "the rear end of a horse" Hours: Wed–Sun noon–5. Admission: Free.

REPUBLIC OF TEXAS MUSEUM
510 E. Anderson Ln., Austin
512/339-1997 NA
This collection of the Daughters of the Republic of Texas focuses on the ten years of the republic, from 1836 to 1846. Hours: Mon–Fri 10–4. Admission: $2 adults, $1 children.

TIP

In the Pioneer Settlement in Zilker Botanical Garden in Zilker Park you'll see a collection of historic cabins from Austin's early days. The Esperanza School House was built in the Spicewood Springs area and was in use until about 1873. The Swedish Pioneer Cabin is one of the best preserved log houses in the country. The blacksmith shop contains equipment used by pioneer blacksmiths to make and shape hand-forged metal implements, and the Mamie Wilson Rowe Summer House is made of cypress wood. If you look closely, you may see some of the original square nails.

TEXAS MEMORIAL MUSEUM
2400 Trinity St., Austin
512/471-1604   NA
The museum offers an eclectic mixture of both Texas and natural history, including paleontology, antique firearms, wildlife dioramas, Indian artifacts, rare gems and minerals, and the original Goddess of Liberty statue removed from the capitol dome during recent restoration (and replaced with a safer replica). The museum has a gift shop. Hours: Mon–Fri 9–5, Sat 10–5, Sun 1–5. Admission: Free.

GALLERIES

In addition to galleries, often there will be small exhibits in restaurants and such. The Austin American-Statesman lists these in their Thursday XLent entertainment section under "Art in Odd Places." The section also lists art exhibits and galleries, rotating listings weekly as their space permits.

ARTISANS
THE ARBORETUM
10000 Research Blvd., Austin
512/345-3001   NWA
Features various three-dimensional mediums, with contemporary hand-made fine crafted glass, metal, wood, and wire. Hours: Mon–Sat 10–6, Thur 10–8, Sun 1–5.

ARTSPACE GALLERY
403 Baylor St., Austin
512/474-7799   DA
The Artist's Coalition of Austin features work by coalition members. There's a changing exhibit every month, and you might find paintings, sculpture, wood constructions, mixed media, the works. The next-door space is for rent to local artists

The French Legation Museum, page 121

© Permenter & Bigley

GREATER AUSTIN

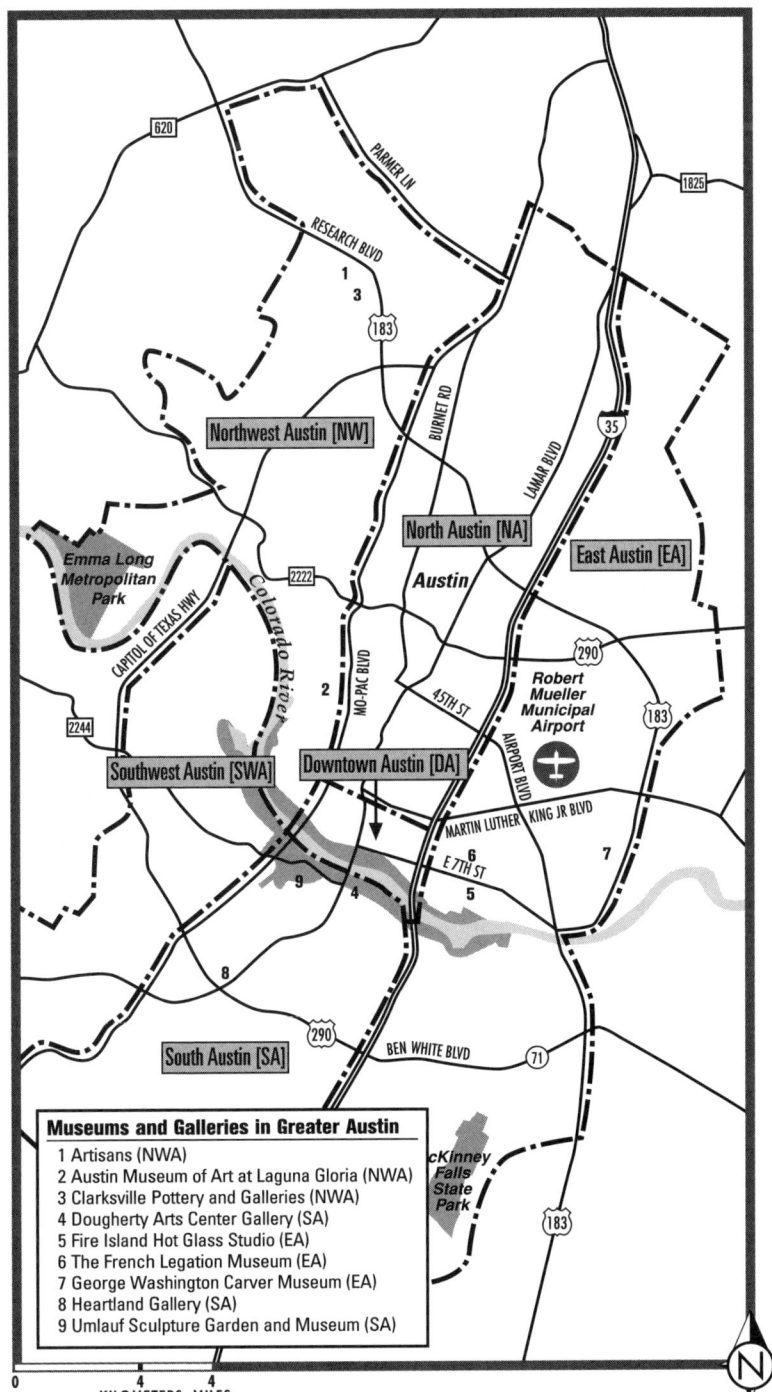

TRIVIA

The Dougherty Arts Center is under the aegis of the Austin Parks and Recreation Department, and as such offers the after-school Isely Artists and Creativity Club programs for youngsters. The staff works hard to plan a fun-filled creative arts curriculum that will expand imagination and encourage interest in both visual and performing arts.

who want to have their own show, so there's always plenty of interest to see in both galleries. Hours: Tue 3–6, Thur 3–8 or by appointment. Open meetings on Mon 6:30.

ARTWORKS GALLERY
1214 6th St., Austin
512/472-1550   DA
Original serigraphs, original watercolors, and classical oils by national and international artists. Also, Bedermier-style furniture. Hours: Mon–Sat 10–6, Sun 1–5.

CLARKSVILLE POTTERY AND GALLERIES
4001 Lamar Blvd., Austin
512/794-8580   NA
9722 Great Hills Tr., Austin
512/454-9079   NWA
This fine crafts gallery represents 300 artists, about a third of them Texans, the rest out of state. The gallery features wooden ware such as boxes and clocks, pottery, blown glass, and gold and silver jewelry. Hours: Mon–Sat 10–6, Thur until 8, Sun noon–6.

DOUGHERTY ARTS CENTER GALLERY
1110 Barton Springs Rd., Austin
512/397-1472   SA
Exhibits here run the gamut of the art world, both locally, nationally, and internationally. Watercolor exhibits, sculpture, student art, faculty art, international children's art, multidisplays of world cultures, even a working metalsmith. Call to see what's on each month. Hours: Mon–Thur 9–9:30, Fri 9–5:30, Sat 10–2. Admission: Free.

ECLECTIC ETHNOGRAPHIC ART GALLERY
916 W. 12th St., Austin
512/477-1816   DA
International folk art, furnishings, and colorful furniture by Texas artists. You'll find hand painted furniture, pre-Colombian artifacts, African art, and etched glass. Hours: Mon–Sat 10–6, Sun noon–6.

FIRE ISLAND HOT GLASS STUDIO
3401 E. 4th St., Austin
512/389-1100   EA
All sorts of hand-blown glass is for sale here, plus, you can watch it being blown. Paperweights, vases, perfume bottles, oil lamps, drinking glasses, Christmas ornaments, glass bead jewelry, fish—even refrigerator magnets. Demonstrations offered every Saturday. Hours: Mon–Fri 8–5, Sat 9–1.

FLATBED PRESS AND GALLERY
912 W. 3rd. St., Austin
512/477-9328   DA
Master printers Katherine Brimberry and Gerald Manson specialize in intaglio, relief, and monotype prints in this print gallery and pub-

Top Ten Artists Studios and Galleries
By Jane Steig Parsons
Chairman of Gallery Galavanteurs,
the University of Texas Ladies Club

1. Umlauf Sculpture Gardens and Museum (130 Charles Umlauf sculptures), 605 Robert E. Lee Rd., 512/445-5582.
2. Gustav Likan Studio (colorist; "Father of acrylics"), 1407 Ridgecrest, 512/327-2591.
3. Dan Pogue Studio (bronze casting and stone sculpture), Cedar Park. By appointment only, 512/441-6717.
4. Michael Frary Studio (watercolor landscapes and oil abstractions), 3409 Spanish Oak. By appointment only, 512/453-0544.
5. Don Herron Clay Works (functional art and utilitarian pottery), 555 Guinevere Ln. By appointment only, 512/328-1043.
6. Terra Rosa Studio (Tim High's fine art prints, drawings, and paintings), 2308 Lawnmont Ave. By appointment only, 512/451-1923.
7. Spicewood Gallery (original paintings, sculpture, glass, porcelain, and jewelry), 1206 W. 38th St., 512/458-6575.
8. Warren Cullar Studio (abstract watercolors and acrylics), 12102 Conrad Rd. By appointment only, 512/250-8868.
9. Spirit Echoes Gallery (exhibiting fine art from 60 artists), 701 Brazos St., 512/320-1492.
10. David Deming Studio (sculptures in bronze and steel), Dripping Springs. By appointment only, 512/441-6717.

lishing workshop. Hours: Mon–Fri 9:30–5, Sat 11–3 or by appointment.

GALERIA SIN FRONTERAS
1701 Guadalupe St., Austin
512/478-9448 NA
You'll find contemporary Latino art—paintings, prints, photographs, mixed media, all mediums; primarily the works of local artists—in this gallery "without boundaries." Hours: Tue–Sat 11–6.

GRAPHIC CONCERN
1202 W. 6th St., Austin
512/472-7428 DA
Featured are original works by many Austin artists, including pastels, photography, glass, and paintings. Hours: Mon–Sat 10–5.

HEARTLAND GALLERY
4006 S. Lamar Blvd., Suite 950
(Brodie Oaks Center), Austin
512/447-1171 SA

Statue of King Ludwig II at the Elisabet Ney Museum, page 117

Specializing in local talent, the gallery sells a wide selection of fine contemporary work by more than 200 artists. Treasures include pottery, raku, jewelry, blown glass, stained glass, metal, wood, and fiber. Hours: Mon–Sat 10–6, Thur 10–9, Sun noon–5.

IMAGES OF AUSTIN AND THE SOUTHWEST
4612 Burnet Rd., Austin
512/451-1229 NA
Paintings, sculpture, furniture, and jewelry with Texas and Southwestern themes are showcased here. Hours: Mon–Sat 10–6.

SGRAFFITO STUDIO AND GALLERY
809 W. 12th St., Austin
512/708-9000 DA
This is a do-it-yourself art place: make your mark on coffee mugs, platters, dog dishes, and more at this ceramics studio. Then the studio applies clear glaze and fires your finished work. In four days it's ready to take home. Hours: Tue–Fri 11–8, Sat 11–6, Sun noon–6.

SPIRIT ECHOES ART GALLERY
701 Brazos, Suite 120, Austin
512/320-1492 DA
The gallery has a wide selection of paintings, monotypes, collage, and prints by more than 60 contemporary artists, with works ranging from realistic gardens of florals to Native American images. Hours: Mon–Fri 9–5:30, Thur until 9, Sat 10–5, Sun 11–2.

WILD ABOUT MUSIC
710 W. 6th St., Austin
512/708-1700 DA
This is a visual, not a vocal, celebration of sound. Everything—paintings, prints, sculptures, serigraphs by both local and national artists—has a music theme or motif. Hours: Mon–Sat 10–7.

WOMEN AND THEIR WORK
1710 Lavaca, Austin
512/477-1064 NA
Although the gallery mainly focuses on the work of Texas women—paintings, prints, photographs, and sculpture—it occasionally showcases works by national as well as local women artists. Hours: Mon–Fri 10–5, Sat–Sun 10–4.

8

PARKS, GARDENS, AND RECREATION AREAS

Austin is known as one of the country's leading innovators when it comes to environmental issues. And with a total of 191 parks keeping it environmentally awake, alive, and aware, it has the distinction of being cited as one of the four best "park" cities in the nation. It's a rare Austin neighborhood that doesn't have its own park, and rarer still to see one empty. No matter how large the city is getting, there are spaces aplenty for fun, fitness, and relaxation for everyone. Both visitors and residents take advantage of the typical 300 beautiful days a year here by enjoying the outdoors.

PARKS AND RECREATION AREAS

Austin's 191 parks are classified according to function, size, and service area. Major park types range from small to large and include 89 neighborhood parks, 12 district parks, nine metropolitan parks, 23 greenbelts, and 29 miles of hike and bike trails. Metropolitan parks, which often include a major water amenity, offer both the largest and most diversified recreational opportunities. Not only do they serve the city population, in some cases they are tourist attractions. Often more than 200 acres in size, they are also usually located on major roadways. Large parking areas accommodate drivers, public transportation serves these areas, and true to Austin's image as an outdoor health-conscious community, access by bicycle or foot by way of hike and bike paths is positively encouraged.

**EMMA LONG
METROPOLITAN PARK
City Park Road 6.2 miles off FM 2222, Austin
512/346-1831**   **NWA**

 The more than 18 miles of well surfaced scenic trails and 14 miles of natural surface trails in Austin are for everyone to enjoy, but there are rules and regulations. Bicycles may be ridden on the trails, but no motorized vehicles are permitted. Keep to the right unless passing, pass on the left, and use verbal warning when it seems necessary. The fastest must give way to the slow: Cyclists must yield to joggers, joggers must yield to walkers, and dogs must be controlled. There is a leash law, and it is enforced.

The 1,150-acre park is on the shores of Lake Austin, but only about 70 acres are developed. The park has a designated swimming area in the lake, with a large sandy beach. Restrooms, dressing rooms, and showers are provided, and lifeguards are on duty noon to 6 on weekends only, Memorial Day through Labor Day. Boats are not allowed in the swimming area nor alongside the swimming docks. A city ordinance prohibits swimming beyond 50 feet from the shoreline. There are two boat ramps, and visitors who have boats but are not staying overnight are restricted to day use of the park. Campers with boats may moor their boats offshore. Park boundaries begin up by Pearce Road, and they include an archery range, a nature trail, and a mountain bike area. The park also has two sand volleyball courts and three sets of volleyball standards.

Contact the Austin Parks and Recreation Department for complete rules and regulations in using the park. Hours: Daily 7–10. Admission: Day use: $3 per vehicle Mon–Thur, $5 per vehicle Fri–Sun and holidays; $1 per pedestrian\bicycle per day. Overnight: $6 camping without utilities per night plus first day entry; $10 Utility (RV) area plus first day entry.

KARST NATURE PRESERVE
3900 Deer Ln., Austin
512/327-5437   SA
The name Karst originally referred to a limestone plateau in Germany, but the word now means any area with limestone rocks, deep fractures, and caves that feed rain water directly into underground lakes and streams. That's exactly what characterizes this 10-acre preserve over the Edwards Aquifer Recharge Zone. The preserve features caves, sinkholes, and honeycomb outcroppings along the 1/8-mile trail, a 20-minute, pleasant, winding walk.

MARY MOORE SEARIGHT PARK
907 Slaughter Ln., Austin
512/440-5150   SWA
This 344-acre park creates a large facility for the South Austin area, comparable to Zilker Park in downtown Austin. (See Zilker Park below.) The park contains a picnic pavilion, volleyball courts, a disc golf course, a nature interpretation center, baseball field, basketball and tennis courts, soccer field, 1.5 miles of hiking and bicycle trails, an equestrian center and a 2-mile equestrian trail, a model

SOUTHWEST AUSTIN

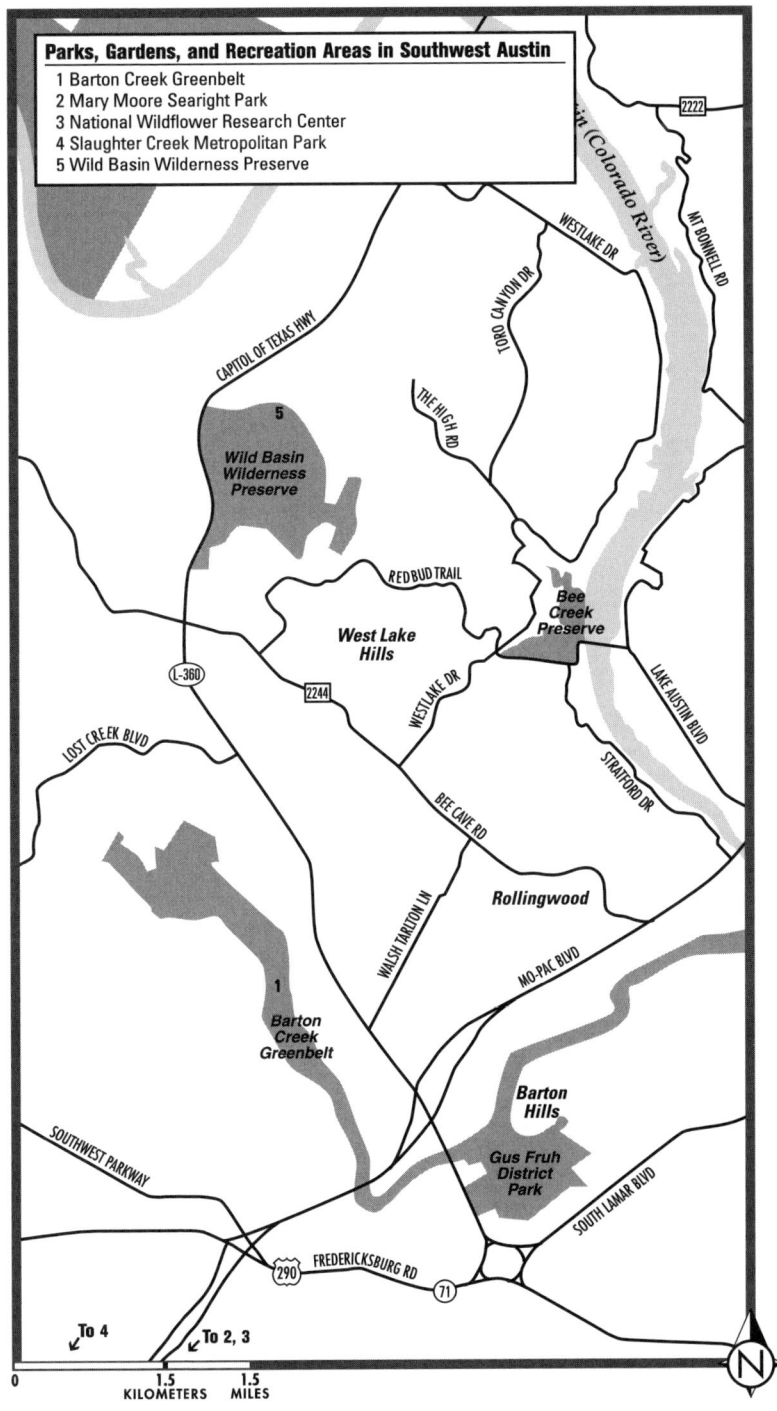

Top Ten Park Activities for Children
By Sally Scott
Texas professional home childcare representative

1. Climb the fire escape at Zilker Park Playscape, Zilker Park.
2. Hike along Shoal Creek.
3. See the owls and walk the nature trail at the Austin Nature and Science Center, 301 Nature Center Dr., 512/327-8180.
4. Play "Frisbee Golf" at Pease Park, W. 24th St.
5. Try fishing at Northwest Park, Shoal Creek at North Park.
6. Climb the rocks by Lakewood Park along Bull Creek.
7. Explore the rocks and the peacocks at Mayfield Park, 3505 W. 35th St., 512/327-5437.
8. Enjoy the view from the top of Mt. Bonnell, 3800 Mount Bonnell Rd.
9. Go to the playscape in Garrison Park in South Austin.
10. Picnic, wade, or enjoy the playscape at the Stacy Park Hike and Bike Trail in South Austin.

airplane field, and a fully accessible fishing pier on Slaughter Creek. Hours: Daily 5 a.m.–10 p.m.

MAYFIELD PARK
3505 W. 35th St., Austin
512/327-5437   NWA
This 22-acre park on Barrow Brook Cove at Lake Austin is also a preserve. Grounds include gardens and lily ponds, peacocks and hens, and trails meander among them through woods and over creek bridges and foot stones. On display is an early 1900s home representative of suburban lake cottage retreats during the turn of the century. Allison Mayfield, both Chairman of the Railroad Commission and Texas Secretary of State, purchased the 23-acre property in 1909 as a summer and weekend retreat for his family. His daughter Mary Frances married University of Texas History Department Chairman Milton Gutsch. The couple designed gardens and received peacocks as gifts from friends. The park was left to the City of Austin in 1972, and descendants of the first peacocks strut through the park today.

MCKINNEY FALLS STATE PARK
7102 Scenic Loop, Austin
512/243-1643   EA
This 641-acre state park is located just 13 miles southeast of the capitol. Activities include a 4.5-mile hike, bike and nature trails (booklet available), and fishing, as well as picnicking, camping, and viewing wildlife such as white-tailed deer, raccoons, squirrels, and armadillos. There's bird watching, too. Hours: Daily 8 a.m.–10 p.m. Admission: $2 per person.

> **TiP** Neighborhood parks are generally close enough to area residents to be accessible by foot or by bicycle. Traditional recreational facilities such as children's playscapes, sports courts, open play areas, swimming pools, and picnicking facilities are usually provided.

MOUNT BONNELL
3800 Mount Bonnell Rd., Austin   NWA
Austin's most romantic park is Mount Bonnell, famed throughout town history for trysts at sunrise and sunset. It's the highest scenic spot (you'll climb 99 steps) for viewing Austin and the surrounding Hill Country. The mountaintop park is 775 feet above sea level, and there's a shade structure and picnic tables on the bluff overlooking Lake Austin. Hours: Daily 5 a.m.–10 p.m.

PEASE PARK
1100 Kingbury St., Austin   NA
Located on Shoal Creek along Lamar Boulevard, Pease was the first city park, dedicated in 1876 by Governor Pease himself. One of the city parks with a picnic area for large groups, it has a 3-mile hike-and-bike trail, swimming pool and wading pool, basketball and volleyball courts, picnic facilities, play equipment, children's playground, and restrooms, and is popular for informal volleyball and softball games. If you need play equipment, it's necessary to reserve. (Austin Parks and Recreation, 200 South Lamar Blvd., 512/499-6700.)

SLAUGHTER CREEK METROPOLITAN PARK
507 W. Slaughter Ln., Austin   SWA
Here are 546 acres ideal for soccer, bicycling, and rollerblading. The park is the headquarters for the Southwest Soccer Complex and the Veloway Bicycle Course. There are also facilities for basketball, volleyball, and picnics, as well as an 18-hole disc golf course, a mile of hike and bike trails, play equipment, and restrooms.

TOWN LAKE METROPOLITAN PARK
**Along the Colorado River
Tom Miller Dam
to U.S. 183 Bridge   DA, SA**
This metropolitan park includes 509 acres of parkland along the banks of the Colorado River from the Tom Miller Dam on Red Bud Trail to the Longhorn Dam. The park contains 10 miles of jogging and bicycle trails surrounded by trees and greenery. An athlete's paradise, Town Lake

Stairway up Mount Bonnell, page 132

SOUTH AUSTIN

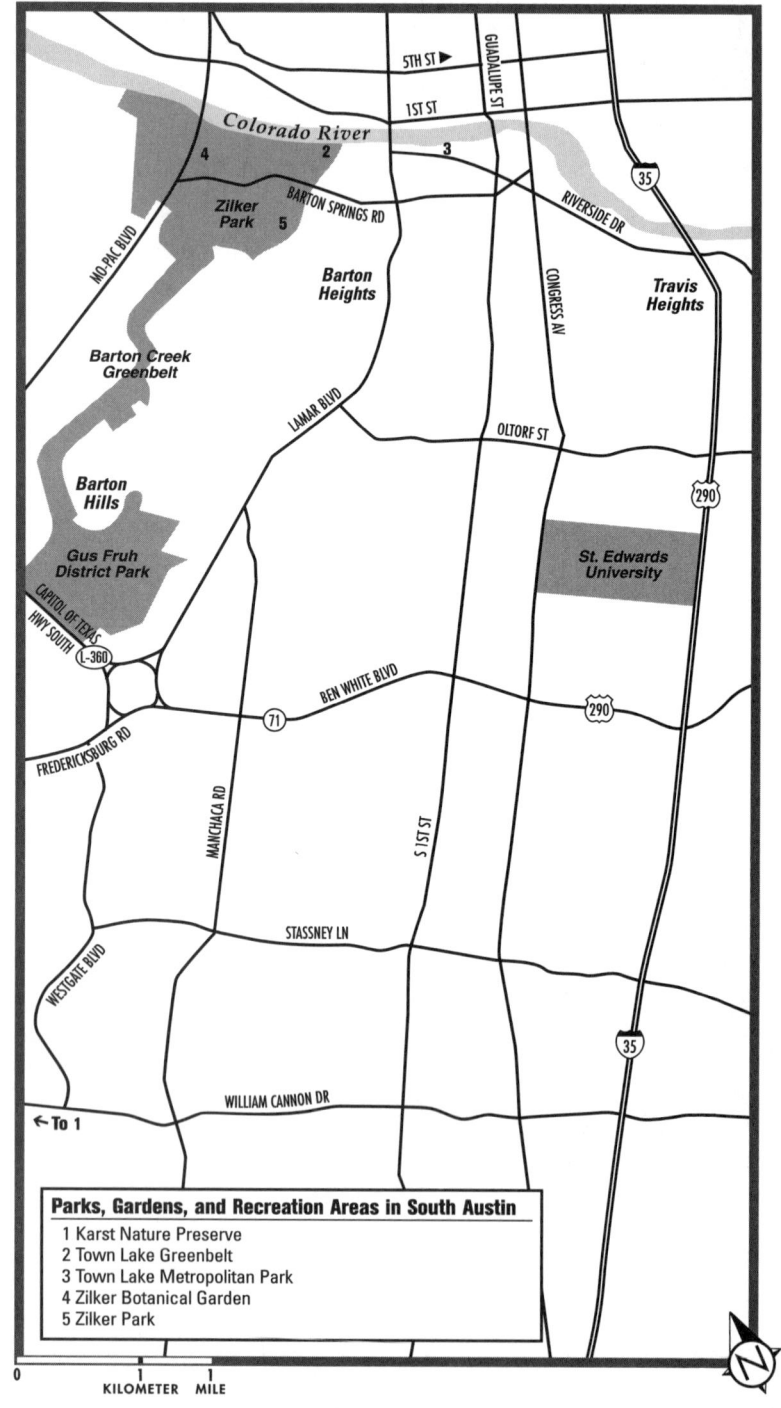

Zilker Botanical Graden, page 139

has 17 ballfields for baseball, football, soccer, and rugby, as well as facilities for both team and performance rowing, and canoeing. Other facilities include a swimming pool, picnic areas, a playscape, and a boat ramp.

**WALNUT CREEK
METROPOLITAN PARK
12138 N. Lamar Blvd., Austin
512/837-4500   NA**
This park is considered an athlete's treat. Home to the Havins Softball Complex, the park features three ballfields, a swimming pool and bathhouse, basketball, volleyball, and multi-use courts, a playscape, and a hike and bike trail along Walnut Creek. The 294-acre park also has concessions.

**WILD BASIN WILDERNESS
PRESERVE
805 N. Capital of Texas Hwy., Austin
512/327-7622   SWA**
These 227 acres of beautiful Hill Country were set aside in the mid-1970s to preserve the land through active management, nature education, and research. Operated with the help of trained volunteers, about 4 miles of trails pass through wood-

> **TRIVIA**
>
> Town Lake Metropolitan Park is also the home of Austin's beloved Auditorium Shores, a terraced amphitheater offering a Summer Concert Series and the Austin Symphony Independence Day Concert. The latter draws thousands, creating quite a traffic jam—the locals have learned to come early to get a place anywhere close to catch the grand Fourth of July finale of Tchaikovsky's booming 1812 Overture and the magnificent fireworks display that immediately follows.

PARKS, GARDENS, AND RECREATION AREAS

 **If the crowd keeps you away from the Fourth of July fireworks at Town Lake Metropolitan Park, you can catch sight of the skyful of rockets and flares from along MoPac (Loop 1) along the lake, and even catch glimpses from the Barton Creek Mall parking lots.**

land, grassland, and streamside habitats. Wild Basin is home to some threatened and endangered species of plants, animals, and birds like the golden-cheeked warbler and the black-capped vireo, as well as hundreds of both common and unique species. Open daily from sunrise to sunset.

WOOLDRIDGE SQUARE
900 Guadalupe St., Austin   DA
This bright green square with a charming white gazebo is set in the middle of downtown on Guadalupe between 9th and 10th Streets. It's one of four parks deeded in the original city plan when Edwin Waller came to survey the city. It has been the scene of countless weddings, political rallies, and sometimes the city council is sworn in here.

ZILKER PARK
2100 Barton Springs Rd., Austin
512/476-9044   SA
Downtown on Town Lake, Zilker is one of Austin's most popular parks. Originally the site of temporary Franciscan missions in 1730, the 349-acre park along the shores of the lake was once used by native Americans as a gathering place. One of its most attractive features is Barton Springs Pool (whose waters were once used by early Austinites as power for several mills). The springs rise from a limestone strata of the Balcones Fault, formed millions of years ago when the Hill Country uplifted to form the Edwards Plateau. The clear springs produce a minimum of 12 million gallons to a maximum of more than 90 million gallons in any 24-hour period. The swimming pool is more than 300 yards long, and the water varies from 66 to 70 degrees, keeping Austinites pretty cool nowadays as a primary recreational facility for the entire city. Zilker Gardens in the park includes the Oriental Garden, a meditation trail, and the famous Rose Garden, as well as a Swedish log cabin dating from the 1840s; there's also a fine Garden Center.

GREENBELTS

Austin has beautiful greenbelts, parks which follow rivers, creeks, and scenic ravines. These are areas of natural beauty, and they provide a diversity of recreation, including walking, hiking, jogging, running, bicycling, and even rock climbing. Greenbelt sizes vary, depending upon the location as well as the size and length of the natural feature— river, creek, ravine—which they follow. They are used by people in adjacent neighborhoods, but also from all areas of the city. Since almost no maintenance is provided for these natural areas, it's important to pack out what you take in, to preserve the beauty of the greenbelts.

GREATER AUSTIN

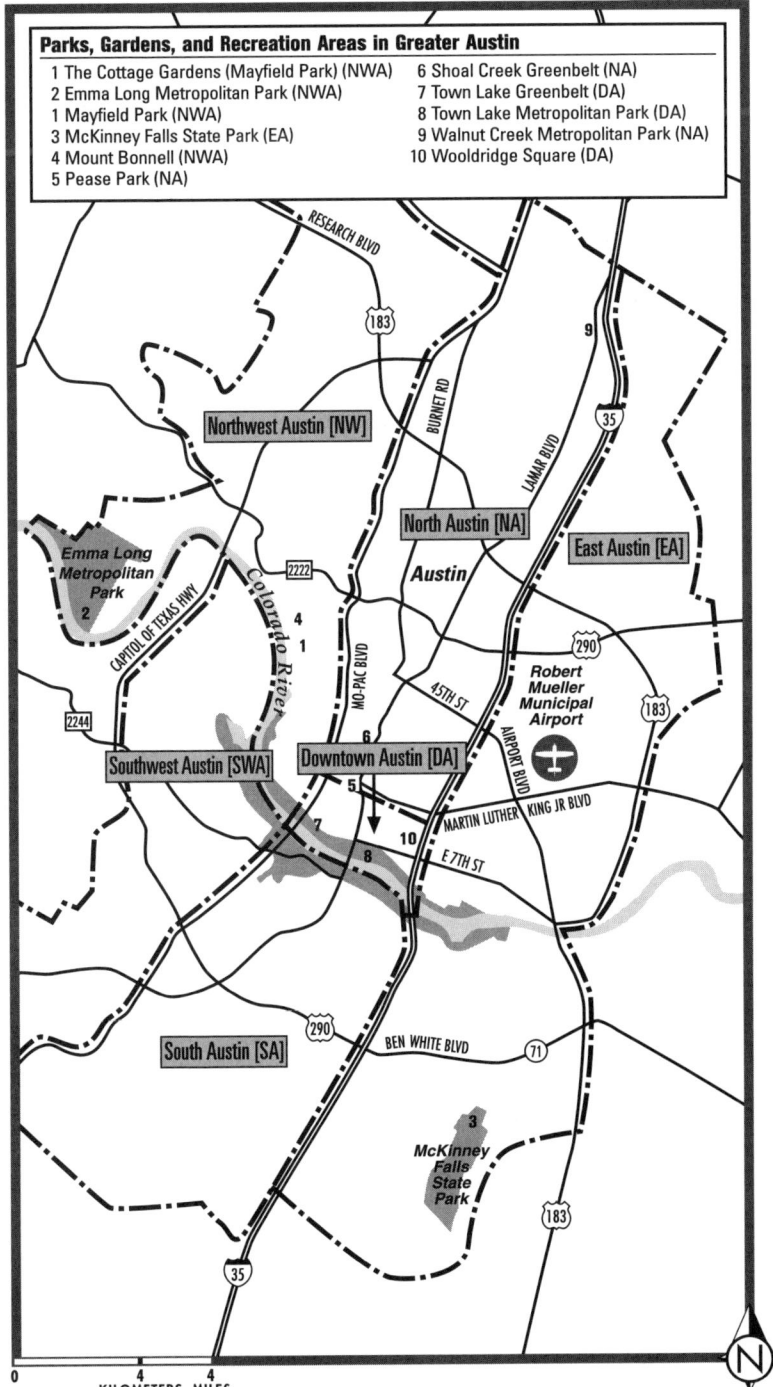

Parks, Gardens, and Recreation Areas in Greater Austin
1 The Cottage Gardens (Mayfield Park) (NWA)
2 Emma Long Metropolitan Park (NWA)
1 Mayfield Park (NWA)
3 McKinney Falls State Park (EA)
4 Mount Bonnell (NWA)
5 Pease Park (NA)
6 Shoal Creek Greenbelt (NA)
7 Town Lake Greenbelt (DA)
8 Town Lake Metropolitan Park (DA)
9 Walnut Creek Metropolitan Park (NA)
10 Wooldridge Square (DA)

TRIVIA

If you want to understand how committed the Austin community is to preserving nature, listen in on a discussion about saving say, the black-capped vireo, the golden cheeked warbler, or a certain rare salamander found in Barton Creek. There's often a fierce battle raging between the environmentalists and the developers, and the former often win.

**BARTON CREEK GREENBELT
Scottish Woods Trail, off Loop 360
(Capitol of Texas Highway),
Austin
512/327-5478 SWA**
Located less than 2 miles from downtown, this single-track trail is Austin's most accessible, and it offers 7 3/4 miles of wooded, beautiful scenery for a quick escape from the daily grind. Access the greenbelt from Scottish Woods Trail, off Loop 360 a mile north of MoPac. The greenbelt also can be accessed from several other locations. The closest to downtown is Zilker Park. Drive south to Barton Springs Road and west to the park. The trailhead is located by Barton Springs Pool. Another access is south of MoPac at Barton Skyway. Exit and drive to the end of the street. Trail access is located across the street from the Stop and Go convenience store. The natural surface is rocky in spots. Be sure to bring water as there are no drinking fountains on the trail. Call for trail conditions in bad weather.

**SHOAL CREEK GREENBELT
North side of Town Lake between Guadalupe St. and Lamar Blvd.,
Austin NA**
This 3-mile granite, crushed limestone, and concrete trail goes north to 38th Street, passing Duncan Park, Pease Park, and Bailey Park, winding up at Seider's Spring Park.

**TOWN LAKE GREENBELT
Loop 1 Bridge to South First St.,
Austin DA, SA**
The scenic shores that line the north and south sides of Town Lake are home to popular trails where Austinites come to walk, jog, and enjoy the beauty of the city. The best view of the downtown skyline can be seen from the south side of Town Lake.

Bluebonnets at one of Austin's many lakes

Austin CVB

Acres and Acres of Developed Park Land

The Operations Division of the Austin Parks and Recreation Department provides maintenance and repair to all parks, recreation facilities, and other city-owned land. More than 3,000 acres of developed parkland are maintained at the present time, and over 14,000 total acres of parkland have been acquired for future development. The Operations Division provides a one-call-does-all number (512/480-3036) to report a problem with any park or facility, as well as to reserve any of the popular park areas for group activities. The Urban Forestry Program provides many public, tree-related activities such as tree planting, maintenance, and horticulture. The Forestry Program also provides both education and suppression techniques in Austin's battle against oak wilt, a plague visited upon the beautiful oaks native to the area. Forestry also trims branches causing traffic problems.

GARDENS

THE COTTAGE GARDENS AT MAYFIELD PARK
2704 Macken, Austin
512/327-5437   NWA

Patterned after the cottage gardens of England, the Cottage Gardens at Mayfield Park are composed of small beds divided by narrow paths. Flowers, vegetables, and herbs are planted in an informal manner and shaded by Mexican plum and peach trees. More than 30 beds of randomly mixed flowers can be seen, each provide color, texture, and fragrance year round. Jonquils, pinks, lilies, roses, and honeysuckle, which require less attention than more exotic flora, are among the hearty plants found at Mayfield Park. Rock gardens, too, sport multitiered flower beds of native plants and wildflowers.

NATIONAL WILDFLOWER RESEARCH CENTER
4801 La Cross Ave., Austin
512/292-4100   SWA

The National Wildflower Research Center is unique in its focus on native plants, resource conservation, and ecologically sensitive design. The center, created by Lady Bird Johnson in 1982 as part of a national beautification project, will give you an eyeful of natural beauty; this is the only institution in the nation dedicated exclusively to conserving and promoting the use of plants native to North America, including 75 species of wildflowers. The 42-acre site includes numerous research display gardens, landscaped areas, theme gardens, preserved woodlands, and natural grasslands. Hours: Tue–Sun 9–5:30. Admission: $3.50 adults; $2 students and seniors; $1 children 18 mos.–5 years.

ZILKER BOTANICAL GARDEN
2220 Barton Springs Rd., Austin
512/477-8672 SA

There are six separate areas to be explored in Zilker Botanical Garden. It all began in October, 1954, when seven Austin Garden Clubs petitioned the City of Austin for permission to build a Garden Center on city property. The City Council allocated space in Zilker Park and today the center is the site of 45 to 50 garden club meetings each month.

Xeriscape Demonstration Garden: In providing a display of more than 50 native and low water-use trees, shrubs, groundcovers, and wildflowers, the garden is a showcase of the seven principles of Xeriscape design. These are soil improvement, use of mulch, limited lawn areas, native and low water-use plants, efficient irrigation, and low maintenance.

Cactus and Succulent Garden: In this collection of mostly native West Texas cactus and succulents, the major blooming period is from mid-April to mid-May. Blooming cactus is a wonderful sight.

Isamu Taniguchi Oriental Garden: The unique garden strikes a delicate balance between water and plant materials which descend in a series of waterfalls, water lily ponds, and handmade oriental lanterns. Cherry trees bloom mid-March to mid-April and water lilies bloom mid-June to October, giving soft color to the garden almost all summer. The garden was contributed to the Botanical Garden by Taniguchi, who worked without salary or restrictions as he spent 18 months transforming 3 acres of rough caliche hillside into this peaceful garden. There is an authentic teahouse in the garden.

Mabel Davis Rose Garden: This is one of the special beauties of the Botanical Garden. You can wander among beds of roses of every color, ranging from the latest All-America Rose Society award winners to the antique shrub roses of the Republic of Texas collection. There are two special blooming times, April to June and again in October.

Herb and Fragrance Garden: Dozens of culinary and fragrant plants are here for visitors to scratch, sniff, and feel the plants among the raised beds.

Hamilton Parr Memorial Azalea Garden: Azaleas bloom in Austin in March and April, and no more brilliantly than here in these beautifully landscaped azalea beds surrounding a shaded flagstone patio. Nearby, a brook bubbles from a small pond.

Douglas Blachly Butterfly Trail: Local flowers and plants which attract numerous species of Texas butterflies have been planted along this trail. Visitors can view Austin's attractive butterflies and migrating species as well.

9

SHOPPING

Vintage clothing to couture, imported coffees to Texas-made crafts, antiques to trendy furniture—no matter what you're seeking, an Austin store undoubtedly offers it.

Many Austin shops reflect the relaxed lifestyle of the city. Downtown, several shopping districts are filled with funky boutiques, used clothing stores, and unique gift emporiums. Modern malls offer high-end and mass market shopping for national brands and designer labels on the fringes of the city limits.

SHOPPING DISTRICTS

Shopping West End (DA)

As 6th Street winds beyond the entertainment district and crosses Lamar Boulevard, the atmosphere moves from funky to fine, evolving from hip T-shirt joints to highbrow fashion establishments and gift boutiques. At the intersection of 6th and Lamar, some of Austin's largest retail operations have recently sprung to life. Further west, the West End offers plenty of excellent shopping in specialty stores sprinkled with a selection of fine restaurants.

BOOKPEOPLE
603 N. Lamar Blvd., Austin
512/472-5050   **DA**
This mega-store calls itself the largest bookstore in the U.S., spanning four floors with over 300,000 titles, 2,000 magazines and news-papers, and plenty of space just to hang out and browse. The third floor is filled with New Age materials, the cornerstone on which the original BookPeople was built. An espresso bar fills the first floor with the scent of fresh brew. Hours: Daily 9 a.m.–11 p.m.

COFFEE EXCHANGE
1200 W. 6th St., Austin

512/474-5300   DA
It's worth a visit here just to enjoy the heavenly scent of the world's best brews. Coffees, along with teas, wines, champagnes, cheese, and chocolates are the specialties of this boutique, which also produces gift baskets. Stop in for an espresso, latté, or just a jolt of java. Sandwiches and bagels also available. Hours: Mon–Sat 6:30–6, Sun 6:30–4.

DEVONSHIRE APOTHECARY
606A Blanco St., Austin
512/477-4301   DA
New Age music plays in the background as shoppers wind their way past cards, stationery, self-help books, teas, and herbs. This shop is filled with items to appeal to those looking for natural and herbal remedies and preventatives. Hours: Mon–Sat 10–6.

EMERALDS
624 Lamar Blvd., Austin
512/476-4496   DA
This high-priced boutique sells jewelry, house gifts, stationery, and women's fashions. Look for New York fashions, footwear, and furnishings for those with discriminating tastes and discretionary income. Hours: Mon–Sat 10–10, Sun noon–7.

FORTNEY'S ARTFUL
HOME FURNISHINGS
1116 W. 6th St., Austin
512/495-6505   DA
Check out the one-of-a-kind furnishings in this eclectic shop that combines lodgepole furniture with traditional, Southwest, and contemporary items. Massive couches and bedsteads are accessorized with imported masks, artist-produced fountains, and sculptures for the home. Hours: Mon–Sat 10–6, Sun 11–4.

NECESSITIES AND TEMPTATIONS
1202-A W. 6th St., Austin
512/473-8334   DA
This shop is a good stop for those looking for a Texas souvenir in the form of Texas trinkets, Southwestern jewelry, coffee cups, or more. Texas games test your knowledge of the Lone Star State. Hours: Mon–Sat 10–6, Sun 11–3.

PECAN STREET EMPORIUM
1122 W. 6th St., Austin
512/477-4900   DA
Fine European imports, from Swiss music boxes to German nutcrackers, fill this charming gift shop. This shop claims to have Austin's largest selection of German collectibles, and you'll also find Christmas decorations year round. You'll also find stationery, stamps, stickers, and more for small gift purchases or just to treat yourself. Hours: Mon–Sat 10–6, Sun 11–4.

TRAVELFEST
1214 W. 6th St., Austin
512/469-7906   DA
The creator of BookStop founded this store that combines travel books, travel gadgets, and a travel agency under one roof. Separate rooms are dedicated to different parts of the globe with videos, guides, and maps to plan any trip. Travel magazines and gadgets designed to do everything from purify water to hide money are located in the front of the store, alongside a full-service travel agency. Hours: Daily 9–9

TRIVIA

Austin's bookstore sales are highest per capita of the U.S.'s 50 largest cities.

NORTH AUSTIN

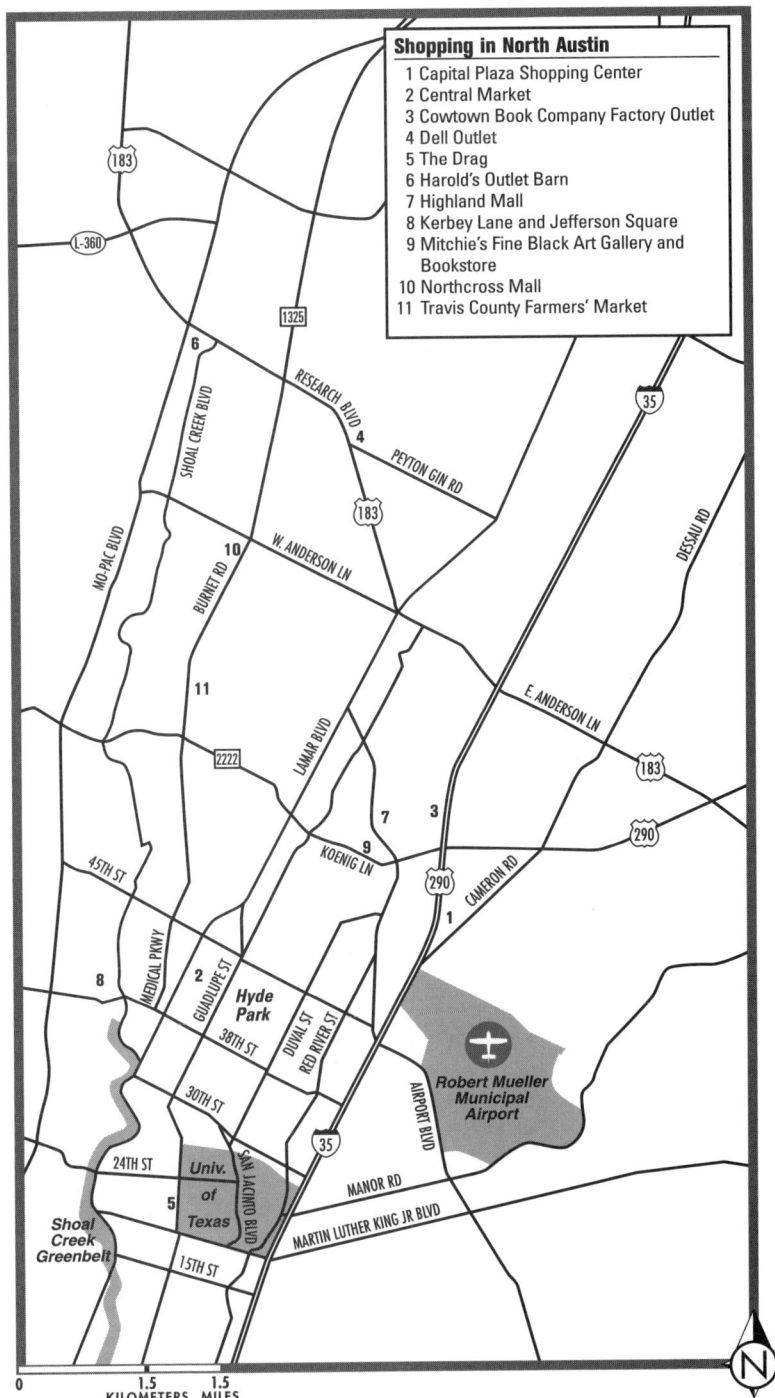

WHIT HANKS ANTIQUES AND DECORATIVE ARTS
1009 W. 6th St., Austin
512/478-2101 DA
Actually a compendium of 50 shops, this dealership offers American, European, and Oriental antiques including furniture, lamps, china, collectibles, and even architectural features such as paneling, leaded glass windows, doors, lighting, and ironwork. This shop is an excellent place to visit if you're looking for an unusual housewarming gift or just some accessories to make your own abode a little different. Just down the street, look for a Whit Hanks consignment shop next to TravelFest. Hours: Mon–Sat 10–6, Sun 1–5.

WHOLE FOODS MARKET
6th St. and Lamar Blvd., Austin
512/476-1206 DA
This funky grocery store is a dream for those seeking health foods, organic produce, and anything herbal, from skin treatments to teas to health remedies. You'll also find a large array of wines and cheeses as well as a good inventory of beers from around the globe. And if you get hungry, you'll find a small cafe ready with healthy sandwiches, soups, snacks, and a juice bar. Hours: Daily 8 a.m.–11 p.m.

WILD ABOUT MUSIC
710 W. 6th St., Austin
512/708-1700 DA
Appropriately located just west of Austin's entertainment district, this shop features everything music related, including jewelry, frames, clothing, books, and artwork with a musical theme. All genres of music are included. Check out the gallery which includes music-related artwork. Hours: Mon–Sat 10–7, closed Sunday.

Shopping the Drag (NA)

For a true Austin shopping experience, consider an afternoon on the Drag, the stretch of Guadalupe Street that runs adjacent to the University of Texas campus. This strip is peppered with shops aimed at the college student, from bookstores to cool clothing outlets.

Unfortunately, the Drag has always had a reputation as a hangout, and runaways from across the nation come to live on its streets. Panhandling is illegal but not unusual.

ANTONE'S RECORD STORE
2928 Guadalupe Blvd., Austin
512/322-0660 NA
Located directly across the street from Antone's (see Nightlife), this mega-music store features a little bit of everything, plus some hard-to-find releases. Work by local musicians makes up part of the inventory. Hours: Mon–Sat 11–11, Sun noon–5.

Central Market, page 151–152

Central Market

Top Ten Antique Stores in Austin
By Elizabeth Huber
Knowledgeable collector of fine antiques

1. Whit Hanks Antiques, 1009 W. 6th St., 512/478-2101.
2. Chantal's Antique and Design, Barton Creek Mall, 2901 Capitol of Texas Hwy., 512/328-6376. Also at Northcross Mall, 2525 W. Anderson Ln., 512/451-5705.
3. 1776 House Antiques, 5530 Burnet Rd., 512/453-6355.
4. Austin Auction Company, 8425 Anderson Mill Rd., 512/258-5479.
5. Attal Galleries, 3310 Red River, 512/476-3634.
6. Antique Marketplace, 5350 Burnet Rd., 512/452-1000.
7. L'Elysee Antiques, 5603 Adams, 512/459-1727.
8. Austin House Antiques, 2041 S. Lamar Blvd., 512/445-2599.
9. Fantastic Finds, Antique Mall of Texas, 1601 S. I-35, Round Rock (15 miles north of Austin), 512/218-4290.
10. The Antique Outlet Center, 4200 I-35 (across from San Marcos Outlet Mall—see Shopping), 800/965-8333.

THE CADEAU
2316 Guadalupe St., Austin
512/477-7276　　　　　　　　**NA**
Look for men's and women's fashions at this trendy store that includes china, crystal, linens, jewelry, home furnishings, and cookware. Often named the top gift store in Austin, this shop has something for everyone. Hours: Mon–Sat 10–6:30.

HALF-PRICE BOOKS
RECORDS MAGAZINES
2110 Guadalupe St., Austin
512/451-4463　　　　　　　　**NA**
Half-Price Books is one of Austin's most tempting places to stop and browse. An Austin institution, this sprawling bookstore carries all types of reading and listening materials. Shop for some new or used books or sell some of your old ones. Hours: Mon–Sat 10–10, Sun noon–9.

NOMADIC NOTIONS
2426 Guadalupe St., Austin
512/478-6200　　　　　　　　**NA**
Beads from around the globe fill this funky store that's a dream come true for those creative enough to produce their own jewelry. This eclectic shop also sells imported fashions and a few home accessories such as statuettes and wall hangings, many from Indonesia. Hours: Mon–Sat 11–7, Sun noon–5.

RENAISSANCE MARKET
23rd and Guadalupe Streets,
Austin　　　　　　　　　　　　**NA**
Tucked right off the Drag, this open air market is filled with the work of

Whole Foods Market, page 144

Austin artisans who sell handmade jewelry, woodcrafts, tie-dyed shirts, glasswork, toys, pottery, and more one-of-a-kind items. This market claims to be Texas' only continuously operated open-air arts and crafts market. The number of artists varies by season, reaching a crescendo in the weeks before the holidays and a low point during the Christmas break when UT students are few and far between. Hours: Daily 8 a.m.–10 p.m.

TOWER RECORDS
2402 Guadalupe St., Austin
512/478-5711   NA
This institution is easy to spot: just look for the two-story mural. New releases, specialty recordings, and local artists are found throughout the store's large inventory. Hours: Daily 9–midnight.

TOY JOY
2900 Guadalupe St., Austin
512/320-0090   NA
Funky playthings for the adult child make this a favorite UT shopping spot. Stickers, stamps, figurines, action heroes, and just plain silly items appeal to kids of all ages. It's not everywhere in Austin you can find toy boxing nuns. Hours: Sun–Thur 10–10, Fri–Sat 10–midnight.

UNIVERSITY CO-OP
2244 Guadalupe St., Austin
512/476-7211   NA
For over 90 years, this bookstore has supplied UT students with all the essentials. Over 70,000 titles, Texas souvenirs and clothing, and more can be found here; a complete camera department on the second floor covers any photographic need. The main floor offers UT and Texas souvenirs, or head upstairs for the popular book collection. Textbooks are located in the basement. Hours: Mon–Fri 8:30–7:30, Sat 9:30–6, Sun 11–5.

URBAN OUTFITTERS
2406 Guadalupe St., Austin
512/472-1621   NA
Clothes with an attitude fill the racks of this trendy two-story shop. Cloth-

Every good shopper knows some of the best bargains come from garage sales, and in Austin every savvy shopper heads to the monthly Austin City-Wide Garage Sale. Records, collectibles, toys, antiques—you name it, you'll find it here somewhere. Held in the City Coliseum off Riverside Drive and Bouldin Street, admission is $3. The event is held every month with Saturday admission from 10 to 5 and Sunday 11 to 5. Call 512/441-2828 for information.

ing and accessories for fashion-conscious Generation Xers are offered along with home accessories ranging from beaded doors to beanbag chairs. Hours: Mon–Sat 10–9, Sun noon–6.

WHEATSVILLE FOOD CO-OP
3101 Guadalupe St., Austin
512/478-2667   NA

Owned by consumers, this co-op carries both traditional and natural foods. A deli offers vegetarian items if all this shopping makes you hungry. Membership in the co-op costs $10 a year. Hours: Daily 9 a.m.–11 p.m., deli closes at 9 p.m.

Shopping Kerbey Lane and Jefferson Square   NA

This charming enclave of boutiques is located just off Austin's medical district on West 35th Street between Kerbey Lane and Jefferson Street. It is lined with homes converted to shops, each filled with unique gift items, collectibles, or fashions. Jefferson Square is a small open-air center with high-priced shops and fine items.

ANDERSON COFFEE COMPANY
Jefferson Square, Austin
512/453-1533   NA

Take a deep breath and enjoy the aroma of the world's finest coffees and teas. Fresh roasted brews are available along with coffee making accessories. Hours: Mon–Sat 8:30–6.

THE GARDEN ROOM
Jefferson Square, Austin
512/458-5407   NA

Fashion conscious Austinites can select from faux reptile bags, silk charmeuse scarves, designer togs, and home accessories in this upscale boutique. Hours: Mon–Sat 10–5:30.

KERBEY LANE DOLL SHOPPE
3706 Kerbey Lane, Austin
512/452-7086   NA

Whether you're looking for a doll as a children's gift or as a collector's investment, you'll find plenty from which to select in this home that's filled with room after room of dolls. Antique and modern dolls fill shelves and display cases, along with doll related accessories and stuffed toys. This shop also buys and repairs dolls. Hours: Mon–Sat 10–5.

KERBEY LANE DOLLHOUSES AND MINIATURES
3503 Kerbey Ln., Austin
512/454-HAUS   NA

You'll feel like Gulliver in this Lilliputian world of tiny furnishings and accessories designed to help collectors design and furnish miniature versions of their dream homes. Hours: Mon–Sat 10–5.

POSSESSIONS GIFT GALLERY
1600 W. 35th St., Austin
512/302-1132 NA
Unique gift items, from glass picture frames to Indonesian ornaments to funky jewelry, fill this shop. Hours: Mon–Fri 10–6, Sat 10–5.

SECOND TIME AROUND
3704 Crawford, Austin
512/451-6845 NA
Recently named the best resale boutique in Austin, this consignment store offers fine fashion and everyday wear at affordable prices just steps from Kerbey Lane. Four rooms filled with seasonal wear make this shop a favorite stop for budget shoppers with an eye for fashion. Hours: Tue–Fri 10–6, Sat 10–5.

TRENDS AND TRADITIONS
3707 Kerbey Ln., Austin
512/450-1121 NA
Owners Cathy and Monte Franzetti create custom jewelry using fine diamonds and gemstones. You'll also find jewelry that's easy on any budget, with silver imports, amber, and more. Hours: Mon–Sat 10–5.

Shopping South Congress Avenue (SA)

Funky collectibles, Mexican imports, out-of-this-world costumes, and a truly flippant Austin atmosphere make this an eclectic district for those looking for something a little different. Park and walk from shop to shop.

ALLEN BOOTS
1525 S. Congress Ave., Austin
512/447-1413 SA
If you want to dress like a cowboy or even an urban version of one, here's your chance. Along with boots, this shop will have you moseying out in a cowboy hat, western shirt, jeans, and, of course, the obligatory western rodeo belt buckle. Hours: Mon–Sat 9–8, Sun noon–6.

ANTIGUA
1508 S. Congress Ave., Austin
512/912-1475 SA
Shop for imported items such as wood carvings, handcarved furniture, primitives, silver, colonial art, santos, tin mirrors, and Mexican antiques at this delightful store. Hours: Tue–Sat 10–6:30, Sun noon–6.

THE ARMADILLO
1712 S. Congress Ave., Austin
512/443-7552 SA
Whatever you're looking for is probably here: the question is will you ever find it? Display cases overflow with antique and imported silver jewelry, walls sag with innumerable displays, tables creak with figurines and collectibles. Hours: Daily 10–5.

LUCY IN DISGUISE WITH DIAMONDS/ELECTRIC LADYLAND
1506 S. Congress Ave., Austin
512/444-2002 SA
This store defines funky with an inventory of vintage clothing and costumes. Dress—for parties or just to portray your personality—in everything from mariachi outfits to French maid uniforms to Seventies disco polyester. Along with rentals, the shop also sells clothing, shoes,

GREATER AUSTIN

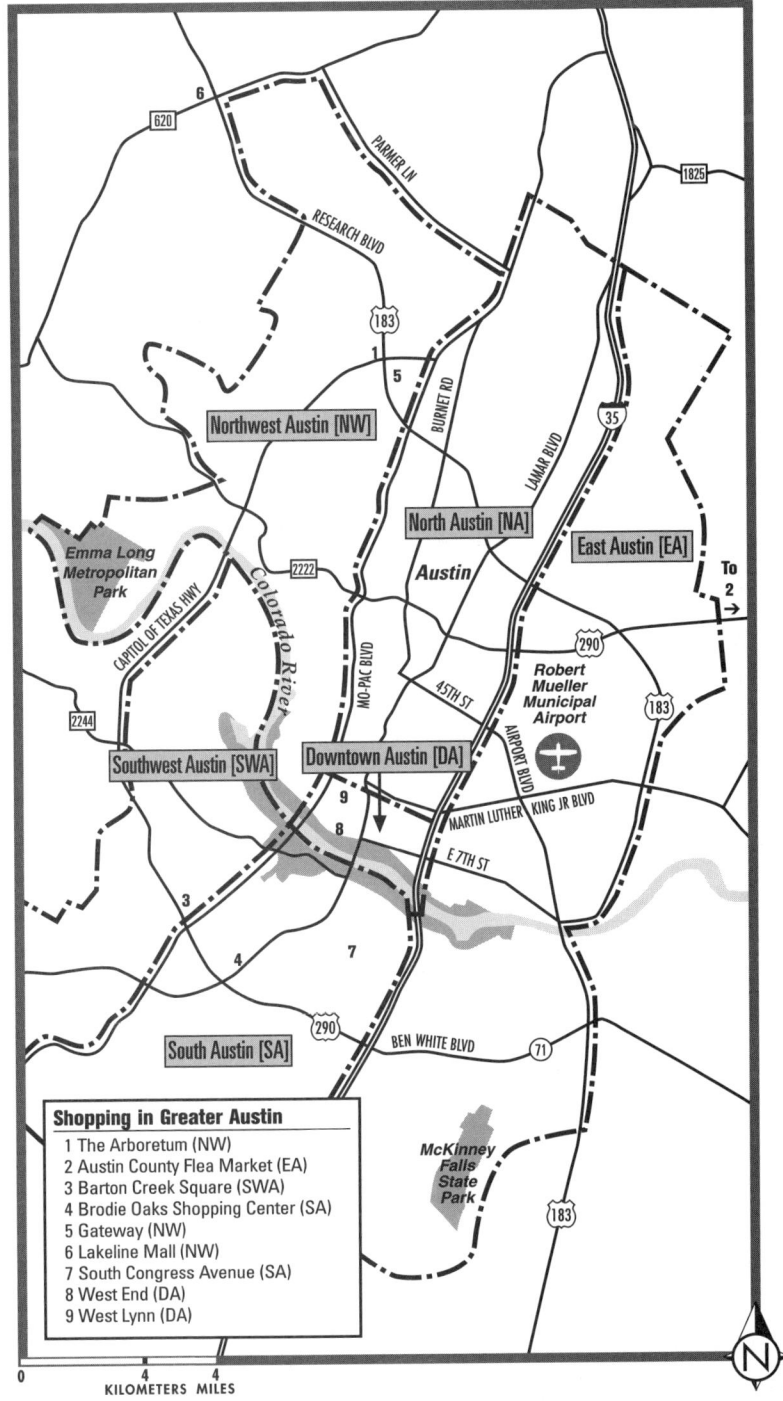

Top Ten Places for Teens to Shop
By Lauren Bigley, Age 15

1. Electric Ladyland, 1506 S. Congress Ave., 512/444-2002.
2. New Bohemia, 5015 Duval St., 512/323-2228.
3. Half-Price Books, 2110 Guadalupe, 512/451-4463.
4. Austin City-Wide Garage Sale, City Coliseum, 512/441-2828.
5. Urban Outfitters, 2406 Guadalupe St., 512/472-1621.
6. Tower Records, 2402 Guadalupe St., 512/478-5711.
7. Old Navy Clothing Co., 9607 Research Blvd., 512/346-1991.
8. Barnes and Noble, 10000 Research Blvd., 512/418-8985.
9. Nomadic Notions, 2426 Guadalupe St., 512/478-6200.
10. Renaissance Market, 23rd and Guadalupe Sts.

hats, unique jewelry, and costume accessories. Hours: Mon–Fri 11–7, Sat 10–7, Sun noon–5.

OFF THE WALL
1704 S. Congress Ave., Austin
512/445-4701 SA
If you're looking for a collectible portraying any animal—from armadillo to zebra—look here first. Ceramics, wooden boxes, wall plaques, and more, all featuring animals, make up much of the shop, along with some antiques, handmade wooden clocks, and home accessories. Hours: Mon–Sat 10–6:30, Sun noon–6.

RUE'S ANTIQUES, INC.
1500 S. Congress Ave., Austin
512/442-1775 SA
Whether you're shopping for an antique movie poster or an oak wardrobe, make a stop at this antiques shop with a varied and changing inventory. Hours: Mon–Sat 10–6, Sun noon–6.

TERRA TOYS
1708 S. Congress Ave., Austin
512/445-4489 SA
This toy shop's motto is "If you can't play with it, why bother?" The multiple rooms of this fun store invite play from shoppers of all ages. Imported dolls, toddlers' indestructible toys, stamps, stickers, gift wrap, books, and more fill the shelves. Hours: Mon–Sat 10–7, Sun noon–6.

TINHORN TRADERS
1608 S. Congress Ave., Austin
512/444-3644 SA
This small store specializes in architectural details and imported housewares. Look at their collection of oversized planters and other purchases to make your home unique. Hours: Tue–Sat 10:30–6.

UNCOMMON OBJECTS
1512 S. Congress Ave., Austin
512/442-4000 SA
Yes, you will find truly uncommon

objects in this shop where you can easily spend an hour or two checking out the architectural details such as old doors and gatelamps, the clothing that harks back to the Forties and Fifties, and antique imports from south of the border. Hours: Mon–Fri 10:30–6, Sat noon–5.

Shopping West Lynn

The quiet mood of the residential neighborhood of West Lynn, west of the capitol, is reflected in the laid-back shops of this district. Enjoy some shopping, then a snack at a genuine drug store fountain.

GARNER AND SMITH ANTIQUES, ETC.
1013 West Lynn, Austin
512/474-1518 DA
Fine home furnishings, china, books, and antiques fill this elegant shop. A home behind the main store houses more casual furniture including tables, wardrobes, dressers, and bookcases. Tue–Sat 11–5:30, Sun 2–4.

EL INTERIOR
1009 West Lynn, Austin
512/474-8680 DA
Look for folk art from the interior of Mexico in this pleasing shop. Items include handpainted wooden animals from Oaxaca, terra-cotta pieces from Puebla and Jalisco, and lacquer work from Guerrero. Hours: Mon–Sat 10–6, Sun noon–5.

NAU'S ENFIELD DRUG
1115 West Lynn, Austin
512/477-8888 DA
This old-fashioned drug store is a favorite with Austinites, whether they're looking for a birthday card or over-the-counter cosmetics. The real draw, though, is the soda fountain, which serves up breakfast and lunch as well as tasty malts and sundaes. Hours: Mon–Fri 7:30 a.m.–9 p.m., Sat 8 a.m.–9 p.m., Sun 10 a.m.–6 p.m.

OTHER NOTABLE STORES

AUSTIN COUNTRY FLEA MARKET
9500 US 290 East, Austin
512/928-2795 EA
If you're into flea markets, here's a mega-market with over 500 booths. You'll find jewelry, clothing, furniture, records, tools, and more at this combination shopping extravaganza and festival. Hours: Sat–Sun 10 a.m.–6 p.m.

BLUEBONNET MARKET PLACE
3rd St. and Neches, Austin
512/476-3484 DA
Located just across 3rd Street from the Convention Center, this mall is a popular stop for convention delegates and a great place to stop to pick up a Texas souvenir. Shop for clothing, furniture, cookbooks, Texas gift foods, toys, and lots more at this downtown market. Hours: Mon–Sat 10–6, Sun 1–5.

CALLAHAN'S GENERAL STORE
501 US 183, Austin
512/385-3452 EA
Like a true general store, this sprawling store has just about everything a person could want. Western wear, saddles, boots, household items, and, yes, even chicks and ducks make up the extensive inventory. Hours: Mon–Sat 8–6.

CENTRAL MARKET
4001 N. Lamar Blvd., Austin
512/206-1000 NA

The Arboretum shopping center, page 154

More than a mere grocery store, Central Market is an international smorgasbord of produce, wines, meats, fish, and seasonings from around the globe. Regularly scheduled cooking classes offer visitors the chance to learn techniques from pros. Hours: Daily 7 a.m.–10 p.m.

CLARKSVILLE POTTERY
4001 N. Lamar Blvd., Austin
512/454-9079 NA
Shop for handmade stoneware, from bowls to goblets to decorative ware, at this fine crafts gallery. Another location in the Arboretum Market is convenient for shoppers in northwest Austin. Hours: Mon–Wed, Fri–Sat 10–6; Thur 10–8; Sun noon–6.

MITCHIE'S FINE BLACK ART GALLERY AND BOOKSTORE
5312 Airport Blvd., Austin
512/323-6901 NA
African-American, Caribbean, and African arts and collectibles fill this eclectic shop, which also sells books and all types of materials related to black art and history. Framing is available here. Hours: Mon–Sat 10–7, Sun 1–6.

TRAVIS COUNTY FARMERS' MARKET
6701 Burnet Rd., Austin
512/454-1002 NA
Look for homegrown produce and homemade products at this 3½-acre market. Start with a walk through the 5,000-square-foot barn for a look at Texas antiques and primitive furnishings, then shop for homegrown fruits and vegetables. Barbecue, tamales, soups, sandwiches and fresh baked goods are also available. Hours: Daily 7 a.m.– 6 p.m.

MAJOR DEPARTMENT STORES

DILLARDS DEPARTMENT STORE
2901 Capitol of Texas Hwy., Austin
512/327-6100 SWA
This extensive store includes clothing, jewelry, perfumes, housewares, gift items, and more. Other locations are found at Highland Mall in far north Austin and Lakeline Mall in northwest Austin. Hours: Mon–Sat 10–9, Sun noon–6.

FOLEY'S DEPARTMENT STORE
4300 Highland Mall, Austin
512/329-2238 NA
Shop for fine housewares, women's and men's fashions, fine and costume jewelry, cosmetics, and more at this Texas-based department store. Hours: Mon–Thur 10–9:30, Fri 10–10, Sat 9 a.m.–10 p.m., Sun 11–7.

MERVYN'S DEPARTMENT STORE
Lakeline Mall, Austin
512/219-0088 NWA
Moderately priced clothing for the

entire family as well as limited housewares, jewelry, and accessories draw shoppers to this two-story department store. Other locations include 4040 South Lamar Boulevard in south Austin and 8000 Research Boulevard in far north Austin. Hours: Mon–Sat 9:30–9:30, Sun 10–8.

MAJOR SHOPPING MALLS

THE ARBORETUM
10000 Research Blvd., Austin
512/338-4437   NWA
Austin's largest collection of exclusive shops is fun for window shopping when you can't afford the lofty price tags. The open-air mall is Austin's most scenic, dotted with oaks and including a sculpture-filled garden that's home to Blues on the Green, a series of free blues concerts every summer. Hours: Mon–Sat 10–6, Sun noon–5.

BARTON CREEK SQUARE
2901 Capitol of Texas Hwy., Austin
512/327-7040   SWA
Austin's largest shopping mall is home to Foleys, JC Penney, Dillards, Montgomery Wards, Sears, and many specialty shops. Hours: Mon–Sat 10–9, Sun noon–6.

BRODIE OAKS SHOPPING CENTER
4115 S. Loop 360, Austin
512/474-9900   SA
This open-air mall is filled with medium-priced stores such as Mervyn's. Hours: Mon–Sat 10–9, Sun noon–6.

CAPITAL PLAZA SHOPPING CENTER
5400 N. I-35, Austin   NA
One of Austin's original malls, built in 1961, this open-air compendium of shops includes Bealls, Office Max, Montgomery Ward, Toys R Us, Weiners, and several discount shops. Hours: Vary by store.

GATEWAY
US 183 North at Loop 360, Austin   NWA
A new addition to the Austin scene, this open-air mall includes Whole Foods, Linen's N Things, Old Navy Clothing Company, TravelFest, CompuUSA, and Marie Callendar's restaurant. Hours: Vary by store.

HIGHLAND MALL
6001 Airport Blvd., Austin
512/454-9656   NA
Over 180 shops in this two-story mall include Foley's, Dillards, and JC Penney as well as specialty shops selling books, houseware, jewelry, music, and sporting goods. A large food court on the second floor offers fast food, salads, and baked goods. Hours: Mon–Sat 10–9, Sun noon–6.

LAKELINE MALL
11200 Lakeline Mall Dr., Austin
512/257-SHOP   NWA
Austin's newest enclosed mall, this two-story compendium of shops includes Foley's, JC Penney, Sears, Montgomery Wards, Dillards, a food court, movie theaters, and Austin's first interactive video arcade. Hours: Mon–Sat 10–9, Sun noon–6.

NORTHCROSS MALL
2525 W. Anderson Ln., Austin
512/451-7466   NA
Perhaps best known as home of Austin's first ice skating rink, this enclosed mall includes Bealls and

Outlet Malls

Two favorite destinations for Austin shoppers are just south of the capital city in the community of San Marcos, south on I-35. Located at exit 200, the San Marcos Factory Shops (800/628-9465) feature over 100 shops that sell direct from the factory. Luggage, shoes, leather goods, outdoor gear, china, kitchen goods, and other specialties are offered for sale. There's even a miniature golf course to distract nonshoppers. Stores are open daily from 11 to 6.

Just across the road, the Tanger Factory Outlet Center (512/396-7444) tempts shoppers with over 30 shops that feature name-brand designers and manufacturers. Housewares, footwear, home furnishings, leather goods, perfumes, and books are offered in Reebok, American Eagle, Levi's, and other outlet shops. Stores are open Monday through Saturday from 9 to 9 and Sunday from 11 to 6.

Oshman's Super Sports, a food court, and several movie theaters. Hours: Mon–Sat 10–9, Sun noon–5:30.

FACTORY OUTLET CENTERS

COWTOWN BOOK COMPANY FACTORY OUTLET
6700 Middle Fiskville, Austin
512/467-7117   NA
Look like a real cowboy after a visit to this boot outlet selling Cowtown Boots at bargain prices. Hours: Mon–Wed, Fri–Sat 10–6; Thur 10–7; Sun noon–5.

DELL OUTLET
8801 Research Blvd., Austin
512/728-5656   NA
Austin's own home-grown computers, designed by Austinite Michael Dell, are offered in this discount outlet. Hours: Mon–Sat 10–6, closed Sun.

HAROLD'S OUTLET BARN
8611 N. Mo-Pac Expwy., Austin
512/794-9036   NA
Harolds, a San Antonio women's fashion store, offers upscale items at outlet prices. Harold's barn-shaped building is located on the east side of MoPac just south of U.S. 183 or Research Boulevard. Hours: open Mon–Fri 10–7, Sat 10–6, Sun noon–6.

NEIMAN MARCUS LAST CALL
4115 S. Capital of Texas Hwy., Austin
512/447-0701   SA
Yes, you can have haute couture on a budget, thanks to this outlet store for the world-famous, Dallas-based Neiman Marcus store. Goods are discounted 40 to 70 percent. Hours: Mon–Tue 10–6, Wed–Sat 10–7:30, Sun noon–6.

© Permenter & Bigley

10
SPORTS AND RECREATION

Austin has plenty for sports lovers to enjoy, both as participants and observers. Fun comes in many forms, from bicycling to bowling, from disc golfing to day hikes. Many of the outdoor activities revolve around the water, with windsurfing, boating, fishing, and other watersports among the most popular.

In the summer months, Austin really lives up to its nickname of "The River City." Austinites beat the heat on Lake Austin and Lake Travis, happily taking to the water to enjoy swimming, scuba diving, skiing, and boating. Weekends on the lake are a central Texas ritual; the activity level of these outings ranges from siesta to fiesta. Note: The map in this chapter shows locations of major sports venues only.

BIKING

Austin offers a network of more than 30 miles of bike trails. Eighteen of them are on well-surfaced scenic paths following natural greenbelts into all areas of the city, making excellent trails available to all. Also, there are an additional 14 miles of natural surface trails to follow, with varied terrain for any level of biker. The hills to the west of Austin are a popular training ground for competitive level cyclists. All trails have a curfew in effect from 10 p.m. to 5 a.m. No motor vehicles are allowed at any time. Dogs must be controlled; Austin has a leash law enforced by the Austin Park Police (Rangers). Note that helmets are required of all bicyclists cycling within the city. For maps of the seven hike-and-bike trails of Austin, contact the Parks and Recreation Department at 512/499-6700 weekdays from 8 a.m. to 5 p.m.

TOWN LAKE GREENBELT
A host of bikers enjoy Town Lake Trail because of the visual beauty of its 10 miles of granite, gravel, and concrete. Loop A, from MoPac

Bike Rentals

Bike rentals are available at these cycling shops:

University Schwinn
2901 N. Lamar Blvd., 512/474-6696

A-1 Bikesmith
4034 Guadalupe St., 512/467-2453

Bicycle Sport Shop
13376 Research Blvd., 512/258-7278

Bicycle Sport Shop
1426 Toomey Rd., 512/477-3472

Bridge to Lamar Boulevard is 2.9 miles; Loop B, MoPac Bridge to South 1st Street is 4.1 miles.

WALLER CREEK WALKWAY
Just east of the main downtown area, Waller Creek Walkway follows the creek from 15th Street to where it flows into Town Lake, 3/4 mile of gravel, concrete, and brick surface. The Waterloo Park area, 15th Street south to 10th street, is 1/4 mile. Lower Waller Creek Development, 10th Street south to Town Lake is 1/2 mile.

BARTON CREEK GREENBELT
Some bikers prefer paths that follow picturesque creeks. Here you'll find 7.5 miles of natural surface both east and west of MoPac (Loop 1).

DUNCAN PARK
8th–10th Sts. along Shoal Creek, Austin   **DA**
The south side of the neighborhood park is outfitted with dirt features to allow motocross riders to jump and perform tricks.

EMMA LONG MOTORCROSS PARK
City Park Rd., Austin   **SWA**
Located just outside the Emma Long Metropolitan Park, this 5-mile motor-cross park offers intermediate and difficult trails for mountain bikers.

VELOWAY
Off Slaughter Ln., Austin
512/480-3032   **SWA**
The Veloway is a 3.1-mile paved asphalt loop used by bicyclists to wind through scenic parkland. Catch the Veloway from behind Bowie High School or from south Loop 1 (MoPac). Hours: Open from dawn until dusk.

BOATING

Motorboats are prohibited on Town Lake, a haven for canoeists and rowers, but watercraft action picks up on Lake Austin. The 22-mile long lake has four public boat launch sites: Emma Long Metropolitan Park, a 1150-acre facility on the north side of the lake; Quinlan County Park; Fritz Hughes Park; and the Walsh Boat Landing, next to Tom Miller Dam. Lake Travis is 65

GREATER AUSTIN

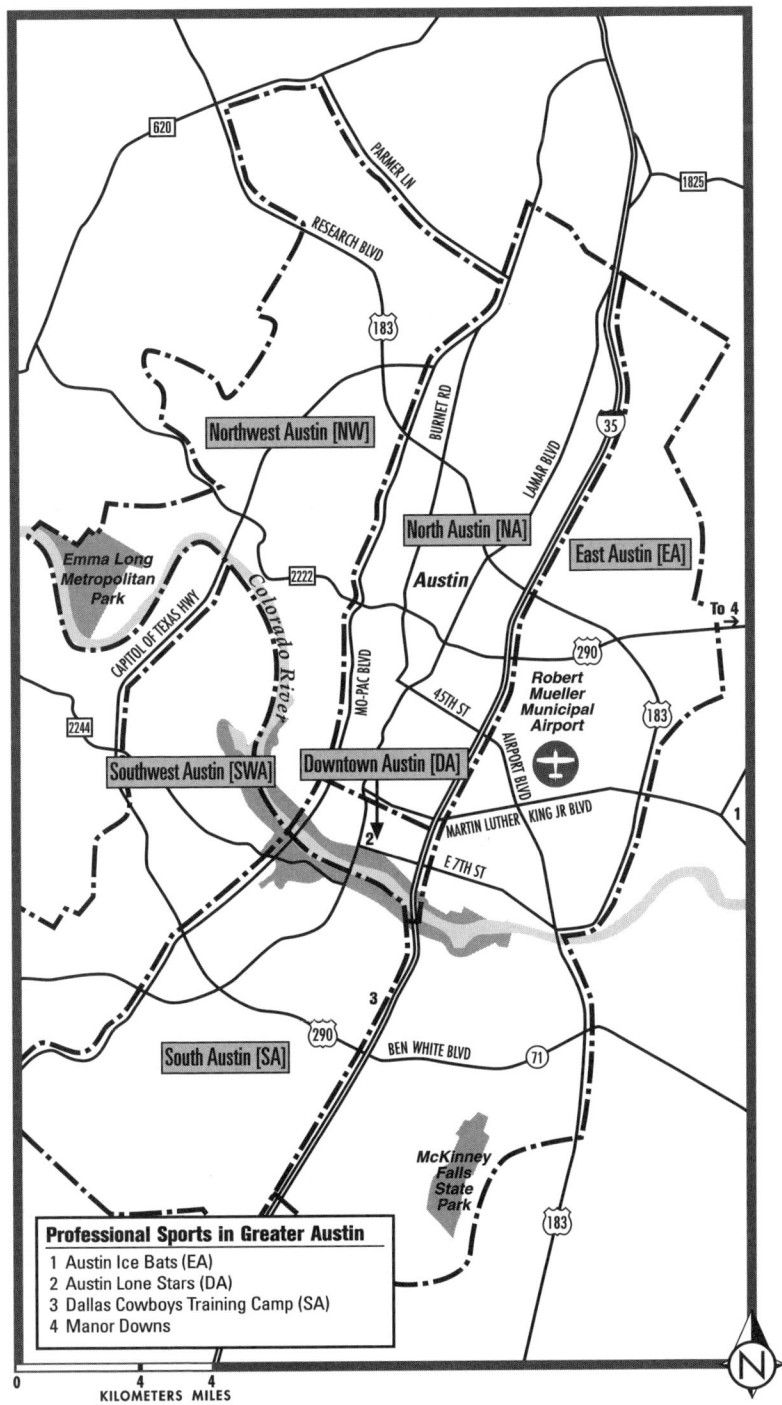

> **TIP**
>
> Capitol Metro buses are equipped with bike racks, so your bike can ride the bus along with you, making it convenient to get to your favorite riding trail. For more information, call 512/474-1200.

miles long, and over 3 miles across in some spots, with literally hundreds of coves and inlets along its snakelike boundaries. Much of the land on Travis' shores is controlled by the Lower Colorado River Authority and remains undeveloped, but there are several excellent public parks. On narrow Lake Austin, boaters are required to stay to the right as they proceed on the lake, unless they're picking up a downed water skier. You must have a Coast Guard–approved personal flotation device for each person on board. Class A and Class 1 motorboat passengers under 13 years of age are required to wear lifejackets.

EMMA LONG METROPOLITAN PARK
City Park Rd., Austin
512/346-1831 SWA
Boat ramps offer easy access into beautiful Lake Austin at this park located 6.2 miles off FM 2222. The park includes a boat dumping station. A 10 p.m. curfew is strictly enforced and gates are locked. Hours: 7 a.m.–10 p.m. daily. Admission: $3 per vehicle Mon–Thur, $5 per vehicle Fri–Sun and holidays.

JUST FOR FUN
6410 Hudson Bend Rd., Austin
512/266-9710 outside map area
Ski boats, jet skis, and pontoon and party boats for groups of up to 150 people are available for rent at this operation at Lake Travis Marina.

LAKE AUSTIN YACHT CLUB
2215 Westlake Dr., Austin
512/327-2110 SWA
This harbor offers ski boats, sailboats, pontoon, fishing, and paddle boats by the hour, half, or full day. Wave runners are also available for rent.

SKIP'S BOAT AND RV RENTALS
4702 Hudson Bend Rd., Austin
512/266-1446 outside map area
Ski boats and pontoon boats are available for hourly, daily, and weekly rental, with discounts available for weekday rentals.

BOWLING

DART BOWL
5700 Grover, Austin
512/452-2518 NA
Hours: Mon–Fri 9 a.m.–11 p.m., Sat–Sun 9–2. Admission: $2.45 before 6 p.m., $2.95 after 6 p.m.; shoe rental $1.60.

HIGHLAND LANES
8909 Burnet Rd., Austin
512/458-1215 NA
Hours: Fri–Sat 9:30 a.m.–1 p.m., Sun–Thur 9:30–11:30. Admission: $2.45 before 6 p.m., $2.95 after 6 p.m.; shoes $1.60.

SHOWPLACE LANES
9514 N. I-35, Austin
512/834-7733 NA
Austin's premier lanes frequently host bowling competitions and tours.

Open 24-hours daily. Admission: $2.10 before 5:30 p.m., $3.25 after 5:30 p.m.

CAMPING/BACKPACKING

**MCKINNEY FALLS STATE PARK
7102 Scenic Loop, Austin
512/243-1643   EA**
Pack up your sleeping bag and enjoy a night among wildlife that includes white-tailed deer, raccoons, and armadillos in this 641-acre state park. Located just 13 miles southeast of the state capitol, the park has 84 tent sites with water and electricity, and six shelters. Tents sites are $12 per night; shelters cost $20 per night. Hours: Daily 8–10. Admission: $2 per person.

CANOEING

**ZILKER PARK CANOE RENTALS
2000 Barton Springs, Austin
512/478-3852   SWA**
Enjoy the quiet beauty of Town Lake as you glide through the water in a canoe. Bring an ID to rent canoes. Hours: 11–dusk. Cost: $6 per hour, $20 per day.

DAY HIKES

You'll find over 25 miles of hiking trails along the major creeks in town. For a free hiking and biking guide, contact Austin Parks and Recreation, 200 S. Lamar Blvd., 512/499-6700. Austin has several hiking groups that offer regularly scheduled hikes and classes. The Colorado River Walkers of Austin offers information on scenic walks; call 512/795-0286 for information. The Sierra Club offers walks around Town Lake every Sunday starting near the Austin High School; call 512/445-6223 for more information. For classes in hiking, contact the University of Texas Recreational Sports department at 512/471-1093.

**BARTON CREEK GREENBELT
3755-B Capital of Texas Hwy.,
Austin   SWA**
Stretching 7 3/4 miles, this greenbelt is a favorite with hikers as well as mountain bikers. The single lane dirt walkway can be accessed from near Barton Springs Pool, MoPac at Barton Skyway or off Loop 360.

**BUTTERMILK BRANCH
GREENBELT
7500 Meador Ave., Austin   EA**
Here you'll find a ballfield and basketball court with play equipment, as well as picnic and barbecue facilities and half-mile hike and bike trail. (Handicap accessible.)

**JOHNSON CREEK GREENBELT
2100 Enfield, Austin   NA**
There is a 1.11-mile concrete trail at this greenbelt.

Town Lake Trail, pages 155–156

Top Ten Places to Hike
By Sheryl Smith-Rodgers
Author of *Weekends Away! Camping and Cooking in Texas State Parks* (Eakin Press)

1. McKinney Falls State Park, 7102 Scenic Loop, 512/243-1643.
2. Mount Bonnell, 3800 Mount Bonnell Rd.
3. Town Lake hike-and-bike trail, MoPac Bridge to S. 1st St.
4. Zilker Park (also Zilker Botanical Gardens and Zilker Nature Preserve), Barton Springs Rd.
5. Mayfield Park and Preserve, 3505 W. 35th St., Austin 512/327-5437.
6. Wild Basin Wilderness Preserve, 805 N. Capital of Texas Hwy., 512/327-7622.
7. Barton Creek Greenbelt, MoPac at Barton Creek.
8. Waller Creek Walkway, 15th St. to Town Lake on Waller Creek.
9. Hamilton Pool Wilderness Preserve, Hwy. 71 30 miles from Austin, 512/264-2740.
10. Westcave Preserve, FM 3238, 210/825-3442.

MARY MOORE SEARIGHT TRAIL
907 Slaughter Lane, Austin   SA
This greenbelt, with 4 miles of hike and bike trails, is in a metropolitan park with a ballfield; an 18-hole disc golf course; two tennis and two volleyball courts; playground, picnic, and barbecue facilities; restrooms; a pavilion, and shelters.

SHOAL CREEK GREENBELT
Town Lake to 38th St., Austin   NA
There are 2.5 miles of hiking and biking trails here, as well as a shelter and picnic facilities.

TOWN LAKE GREENBELT
MoPac Bridge to S. 1st St., Austin   DA, SA
The 10.1-mile hike and bike trail is one of the most popular attractions in Austin. Every day, year-round, you'll find locals and visitors jogging, walking, and biking around Town Lake. The north shore is the least secluded, just a few paces from the road, but when the trail turns south the atmosphere gets quieter.

WALLER CREEK WALKWAY
15th St. to Town Lake, Austin   DA
This greenbelt offers 3 miles of trail on Waller Creek.

WILD BASIN WILDERNESS PRESERVE
805 N. Capital of Texas Hwy. (Loop 360), Austin
512/327-7622   SWA
Several trails over varying degrees of difficulty offer everyone a chance to enjoy the natural side of Austin in this

Dallas Cowboys training camp

227-acre park along Bee Creek. Trails range from an easy-access trail for the mobility impaired with benches every 300 feet, to Triknee Trail (the name says it all), which winds through a rocky incline. No pets, bikes, or motorized vehicles. Hours: Open from light until dark daily.

DISC GOLF

Disc golf, commonly known as "Frisbee golf," is popular with Austin's younger set who are often seen tossing the disc at courses across the city. Disc golf is played similarly to golf but the holes are replaced with metal poles with a chain basket to catch the discs.

BARTHOLOMEW PARK
E. 51st St., Austin   EA
Located just north of Robert Mueller International Airport, this park includes an 18-hole disc course.

PEASE PARK
W. 24th St. off Lamar Blvd.,
Austin   NA
A favorite with UT students, this 12-hole course is always in play.

ZILKER PARK
Barton Springs Rd., Austin   SA
This 9-hole course is located near MoPac Boulevard or Loop 1.

FISHING

Fishermen casting their lines in Lake Austin won't be disappointed by the black bass, catfish, perch, white

TRIVIA

Austin has a grand total of 11,800 acres of greenbelt—uncultivated land preserved for recreational activities: picnics, jogging, hiking and biking, bird-watching, and kite flying, for the entire community.

SPORTS AND RECREATION

Top Spots for Outdoor Sports Enthusiasts

By Warren E. Johnson
Avid and experienced fly fisherman, downhill skier, golfer, waterfowl hunter, and boundary water canoe guide.

1. Fly Fishing Tackle, Equipment, Guide Service: Austin Angler, 312-1/2 Congress Ave., 512/472-4553.
2. Fishing Rod Building and Instruction: Rodmakers, 7739 Northern Dr., 512/452-7637.
3. Trout Unlimited, Guadalupe River Chapter, 207 Finn St., 512/261-4409.
4. Hunting Gear and Equipment: McBride Guns, Inc., 2915 San Gabriel, 512/472-3532
5. Trap, Skeet, Sporting Clays: Capitol City Trap & Skeet Club, 8707 Lindell Ln., 512/272-4707.
6. Golf Equipment, Club Components, Instruction, Apparel: Golfsmiths, 11000 N. I-35, 512/837-4810.
7. Sportswear and Equipment: Oshman's Super Sport, 2525 W. Anderson Ln., 512/459-6541.
8. Archery: Archery Country, 8910 Research Blvd., 512/452-1222.
9. McKinney Falls State Park, 5808 McKinney Falls Pkwy., Austin, 512/243-1643.

bass, and crappie found in these clear waters. The lake is stocked throughout the year.

Licensing

Fishing licenses, required for everyone over the age of 17, are available in most bait and convenience stores. Issued by the Texas Parks and Wildlife Department, the licenses are valid from September 1 to the end of August each year.

A year-round fishing license for a resident of Texas is $13 and is required of anyone who fishes in the public waters. A temporary (14-day) Resident Sportfishing license is available to residents for $10 and is valid for 14 days in a row. A special $6 license if available for any Texas resident who is 65 years of age or who is legally blind.

Out-of-state visitors must obtain a Non-resident Fishing License ($30) or the Temporary Five-day Non-Resident Fishing License ($20). If you are under 17, or 65 years of age or older from Kansas or Louisiana, or 64 years of age or older from Oklahoma, this license is not required. The temporary license is valid for five days in a row for non-residents.

Real fish lovers can obtain a Lifetime Resident Fishing License for $400, valid for the lifetime of a Texas resident. Applications may be obtained from the Texas Parks and Wildlife Department offices or by calling the Department at 800/792-1112 (Mon–Fri, 8–5).

TOM MILLER DAM
Red Bud Tr. at Lake Austin, Austin
800/776-5272   SWA
Tom Miller Dam is just south of the Walsh Boat Landing, with 4 acres for day use only, providing picnicking, boat ramps, and access to Lake Austin. It's illegal to climb on the dam, but you can fish in the lake below the dam. Fishermen park along Red Bud Trail and walk down to the lake shore to cast their lines, hoping to catch catfish and bass.

FITNESS CLUBS

These clubs offer day passes for visitors.

**BIG STEVE'S GYM
AND AEROBICS CENTER**
1126 S. Lamar Blvd., Austin
512/445-2348   SA
Day passes for visitors are $6.

THE HILLS FITNESS CENTER
4615 Bee Caves Rd., Austin
512/327-4881   SWA
This fitness facility covers 12 wooded acres and includes indoor and outdoor pools, racquetball, squash, basketball, an outdoor track, spa services, massage, and a cafe. Day passes are $14 and are good on a come-and-go basis.

GOLF

Austin has boasted some of the top names in golfing including the late Harvey Penick and his protégés Ben Crenshaw and Tom Kite.

BLUEBONNET HILL GOLF COURSE
9100 Decker Ln., Austin
512/272-4228   NA
Greens fees: $12 weekdays, $18 weekends.

BUTLER PARK PITCH & PUTT
201 Lee Barton Dr., Austin
512/477-9025   SA
Greens fees: $3.75 weekdays, $3.25 weekends.

CIRCLE C GOLF CLUB
7401 Texas 45, Austin
512/288-4297   SWA
Located near the south end of MoPac, this private golf course offers daily-fee use. Greens fees: $39 weekdays, $49 weekends, plus tax.

GOLFSMITH
1000 N. I-35, Austin
512/837-4810   NA
Known for their custom golf clubs, this retail store also has practice greens, weekly clinics, and 600 feet of covered tee line.

**JIMMY CLAY-ROY
KYZER GOLF COURSE**
5400 Jimmy Clay Dr., Austin
512/444-0999   EA
Jimmy Clay is an older, traditional golf course dating from the 1960s; the Roy Kyzer course is a two-year-old link-style course. Greens

Austin Recreation Centers

Austin recreation centers offer everything from organized fun to classes. Call the individual centers for a rundown of their facilities and services.

Alamo Recreation Center, 2100 Alamo St., 512/474-2806.
Austin Recreation Center, 1301 Shoal Creek Blvd., 512/476-5662.
Dittmar Recreation Center, 1009 Dittmar, 512/441-4777.
Doris Miller Auditorium, 2300 Rosewood Ave., 512/476-4118.
Dottie Jordan Recreation Center, 2803 Loyola Ln., 512/926-3491.
Dove Springs Recreation Center, 5405 S. Pleasant Valley Rd., 512/447-5875.
Givens Recreation Center, 3811 E. 12th St., 512/928-1982.
Hancock Recreation Center, 811 E. 41st St., 512/453-7765.
Martin Recreation Center, 1601 Haskell, 512/478-8716.
McBeth Recreation Center, 2401-A Columbus Dr., Zilker Park, 512/327-6498; TDD service line, 512/327-6662.
Metz Recreation Center, 2407 Canterbury, 512/478-8716.
Montopolis Recreation Center, 1200 Montopolis, 512/385-5931.
Northwest Recreation Center, 2913 Northland, 512/458-4107.
Pan Am Recreation Center, 2100 E. 3rd St., 512/476-9193.
Parque Zaragoza Recreation Center, 741 Pedernales, 512/472-7142.
Rosewood Recreation Center, 2300 Rosewood Ave., 512/472-6838.
South Austin Recreation Center, 1100 Cumberland Ave., 512/444-6601.

---

fees on Jimmy Clay Mon–Fri $12, weekends $13.50. Greens fees on Roy Kyzer Mon–Thur $17, Fri–Sun $23.

HANCOCK GOLF COURSE
811 E. 41st. St., Austin
512/453-0276 NA
This shady course is the oldest golf course in Texas. It's for walkers; $7.50 for 9 holes and $13 for all 18.

LIONS MUNICIPAL
2910 Enfield Rd., Austin

512/477-6963 SWA
Greens fees: $11 weekdays/$12.50 weekends.

MORRIS WILLIAMS
4300 Manor Rd., Austin
512/926-1298 EA
Greens fees: $11 weekdays, $12.50 weekends.

RIVER PLACE GOLF CLUB
4207 River Place Blvd., Austin
512/346-6784 SW

TRIVIA

You don't need to listen to the nightly news to find out how the Longhorns fared—just have a look at the University of Texas tower. With every win, the top of the tower is illuminated with orange lights. Conference titles earn orange lights all over the building, and when there's a national championship, a number "1" appears in lights down the side of the building.

This private golf club is available for play with a daily fee. Located off FM 2222 close to Lake Austin, the course is not too near the water. Mon–Thur $45, Fri $52, Sat–Sun $57.

RIVERSIDE GOLF COURSE
5712 E. Riverside Dr., Austin
512/389-1070   EA
This 18-hole private course is available for day use with a fee. Greens fees: $12 weekdays, $15.50 weekends.

HORSEBACK RIDING

BLUE STAR RIDING CENTER
9513 S. U.S. 183, Austin
512/243-2583   EA
Trail rides weekends only, over 50 acres in Travis County; indoor and outdoor arenas for lessons in Western, English, hunter-jumper, dressage, and cross-county. Closed Monday.

CAMERON EQUESTRIAN CENTER
13404 Cameron Rd., Austin
512/272-4301   EA
The center offers hour-long rides around a 70-acre ranch. The price is $30 for one person, $25 for two people, and $20 for three or more.

MEDWAY RANCH
13500 Pecan Dr., Austin
512/263-5151   NWA
This 500-acre ranch is considered one of Texas' most beautiful. An hour ride for one person costs $30; two for $25 each; and three or more $20 each. Children 6 and older are permitted to ride the trail, while there are pony rides for children younger than 6.

OL' CACTUS JACK
13433 W. Hwy. 71, Bee Caves, Austin
512/263-2388   SWA
Enjoy a trail ride at this ranch that spans over 300 acres of the Hill Country. An hour's ride costs $20 for one person, $15 for two or more. Children must be 8 years of age or older to ride.

VALLEY CREEK STABLES
8601 Bluff Springs Rd., Austin

Look for a copy of the certificate required by the State of Texas at stables that rent horses. It must be on public display, and should be an assurance that the animals are being treated humanely. Violations can be reported to the Texas Health Department, 512/458-7255.

512/282-6248   SA
There is a regular trail ride here every Wednesday evening at 5:30; other hourly trail rides are by appointment. For three or more persons the charge is $25 per person; $35 per couple or individual. Children as young as six are permitted to ride alone.

JOGGING

CAMP MABRY
West 35th St. and Loop 1 (MoPac), Austin
512/465-5059   NWA
Located on the grounds of historic Camp Mabry, this mile-long jogging trail is a favorite with families on the city's west side. No wheeled vehicles except for strollers are permitted, and leave the pets at home.

TOWN LAKE GREENBELT
MoPac Bridge to S. 1st. St., Austin   DA, SA
Austin's top jogging spot is filled with downtown office workers after 5 p.m. and during the lunch hour. Workout posts offer a chance to do a few chin-ups and stretches as you go; or just enjoy the jog with the best view of the city's skyline. During the spring months, you'll see blooming flowers and scrubs.

ROCK CLIMBING

PSEUDO ROCK
200 Trinity St., Austin
512/474-4376   DA
Whether you're a beginner or an advanced rock climber, you'll find plenty of challenge at this indoor climbing center. Over 5,000 square feet of sculpted climbing surface offer sporting opportunities regardless of the weather. Hours: Mon–Fri 10–10, Sat–Sun 10–8. Admission: $8, $5 equipment rental.

YMCA SOUTHWEST
Oak Hill, Austin
512/891-9622   SWA
This YMCA includes an indoor climbing facility and can offer instruction in climbing techniques. Hours: Mon–Fri 6 a.m.–10 p.m., Sat 8 a.m.–7 p.m., Sun 1 p.m.–7 p.m. Admission: YMCA members only; $99 to join, $40 per month for individual membership.

SAILING

You'll find licensed sailing instruction at several places in the Austin area. Sail and Ski Center offers sail instruction; call 512/258-0733. Texas Sailing Academy, 512/261-6193, offers instruction and rents vessels. Dutchman's Landing, on the north shore of Lake Travis near Volente, offers sailing instruction as well; 512/267-4289. Commander's Point Yacht Basic rents vessels and offers instruction for all levels of sailors; 512/266-2333.

TRIVIA

Test your jogging abilities at the annual Capitol 10,000. One of the nation's largest road races, this event draws about 20,000 participants who start at 15th Street and Congress Avenue and wind along the 10K route to Auditorium Shores. The event is generally scheduled for late March; call 512/445-3598 for information.

Sailboat on Lake Travis

SCUBA DIVING

With its temperate climate, scuba divers find good conditions for year-round diving in Lake Travis, a top Texas dive spot because of good visibility. A popular deep dive is at Mansfield Dam Park. Windy Point is a good access point; others divers enter from the shoreline of Hippie Hollow/MacGregor Park.

AQUATIC ADVENTURES
12129 RR 620 North, Austin
512/219-1220   NWA

DOUBLE D DIVING
8650 Spicewood Springs Rd., Austin
512/331-2199   NWA

GREAT OUTDOORS AQUA SPORTS
4403 Guadalupe St., Austin
512/453-1852   NA

PISCES SCUBA
11401 RR 2222, Austin
512/258-6646   NWA

SEE SEA DIVERS
13376 N. US 183, Austin
512/258-8000   NWA

TOM'S DIVE AND SKI
5909 Burnet Rd., Austin
512/451-3425   NA

SKATING–ICE

Ice-skating was once pretty foreign in Texas, but the increased number of Northern transplants has increased the popularity of this sport. The establishment of Austin's Ice Bats will undoubtedly make ice-skating and hockey a fun diversion for the younger set as well.

AUSTINICE
2525 W. Anderson Ln., Austin
512/451-5102   NA
Located in Northcross Mall, this ice rink offers public skating and lessons. Hours: Daily noon–5, Tue–Thur 7:30 p.m.–9:30 p.m., Fri–Sat 7:45 p.m.–10:15 p.m. Admission: $5 plus $2 skate rental.

CHAPARRAL ICE
14200 N. I-35, Austin
512/252-8500   NA
Public skating, lessons, and birthday parties are available from this new rink. Hours: Mon 1:15–4:45; Tue 1:15–5, 8 p.m.–9:45 p.m.; Wed 1:15–5; Thur 1:15–5, 8 p.m.–9:45 p.m.; Fri 3:30–5, 8:15 p.m.–9:45 p.m.; Sat 1:15–3:45, 7:45 p.m.–10 p.m.; Sun 1:30–4. Admission: $5 plus $2.50 skate rental.

SKATING–ROLLER AND IN-LINE

PLAYLAND SKATING CENTER
8822 McCann, Austin
512/452-1901   NA
Hours: Tue 4–6, 7 p.m.–10 p.m.; Thur 4–6, 7 p.m.–9 p.m.; Sat–Sun 2–5. Admission: $4 including skates.

SKATEWORLD
9514 Anderson Mill Rd., Austin
512/258-8886   NWA
Hours: Wed 3:30–5:30; Fri 7:30 p.m.–11 p.m.; Sat 11–6, 8 p.m.–11 p.m.; Sun 1–5:30. Admission: $3–$5 including skates.

VELOWAY
Off Slaughter Ln., Austin
512/480-3032   SWA
The Veloway is a 3.1 mile paved asphalt loop used by bicyclists as well as in-line skaters to wind through scenic parkland. Located behind Bowie High School. Catch the Veloway from behind Bowie High School or from south Loop 1 (MoPac). Hours: dawn until dusk.

SKIING/JET SKIING

Waterskiing is a popular summer activity on Lake Austin and Lake Travis. Use of jet skis, wet bikes, or similar devices on Lake Austin is prohibited during the holiday weekends of Memorial Day, Labor Day, and July 4. The holiday weekend ban runs from 5 p.m. Friday to 6 a.m. Tuesday. Heavy water traffic during those peak times makes this safety law important.

SWIMMING

With Austin's active population and soaring summer temperatures, it's easy to see that swimming would be a popular pastime. Pools fill with children and adults alike during the summer months, and many locals enjoy a swim in the area lakes. However, swimming is prohibited in Town Lake.

BARTON SPRINGS POOL
2200 Barton Springs Rd., Austin
512/867-3080   SWA
You'll find dedicated swimmers braving the constant 68 degree spring water that makes this one of Texas' most beautiful (and chilliest) year-round swimming holes. Located in Zilker Park, the pool includes a diving board and also a shallow end for children to enjoy, but maintains the look of a natural swimming hole. Restroom and changing facilities available. Hours: Daily 9 a.m.–10 p.m. Admission: $2.50, 25¢ children.

DEEP EDDY POOL
401 Deep Eddy, Austin
512/476-8546   NWA
Swim laps or just hang out at this spring-fed pool. Its cool waters are a favorite with dedicated swimmers and young kids.

STACY POOL
800 E. Live Oak, Austin
no phone   SA

Scuba divers in Lake Travis, page 167

TRIVIA

The Texas Longhorn football team will always hold the last Southwest Conference title.

This spring-fed pool is another beautiful spot to cool off during Austin's long, hot summer. During the cooler months, the warm water of this artesian hole draws dedicated swimmers. Hours: Mon–Fri 6 a.m.–9 a.m. and 11 a.m.–7 p.m., Sun noon–7 p.m., closed Sat. Admission: $2 adults ; 50 cents juniors ; 25 cents children .

TENNIS

Austin has over 15 tennis facilities for a total of over 200 courts—so many, in fact, that Tennis magazine has named the city as the "10th Best U.S. Tennis City in the Nation." Public tennis facilities have a time limit of 1 1/2 hours for singles and two hours for doubles. Cost is $3 for singles and $2.50 per person for double. For information on public courts, call 512/480-3020.

**AUSTIN HIGH
SCHOOL TENNIS CENTER
2001 W. 1st St., Austin
512/477-7802   DA**
After school hours, tennis buffs will find eight courts for play at this high school located just off Town Lake. Hours: Mon–Thur 5 p.m.–10 p.m., Fri 5 p.m.–8 p.m., Sat 8:30 a.m.–6 p.m., Sun 9 a.m.–6 p.m.

**AUSTIN RECREATION CENTER
1301 Shoal Creek Blvd., Austin
512/476-5662   NA**
Four lighted tennis courts are available at this central facility from 7:15 a.m.–10:15 p.m.

**CASWELL TENNIS CENTER
24th St. and Lamar Blvd., Austin
512/478-6268   NA**
Nine lighted courts are available for public play at this center, which also offers lessons and does restringing of rackets. Hours: Mon–Thur 8:30 a.m.–10 p.m., Fri–Sun 8:30 a.m.–9 p.m.

**PHARR TENNIS CENTER
4201 Brookview Dr., Austin
512/477-7773   EA**
This tennis center offers eight lighted courts. Hours: Mon–Thur 8 a.m.–10 p.m., Fri–Sun 8 a.m.–9 p.m.

**SOUTH AUSTIN TENNIS CENTER
1000 Cumberland Dr., Austin
512/442-1466   SA**
Ten lighted courts are available for daily play at this center. Hours: Mon–Fri 8:30 a.m.–10 p.m., Sat–Sun 8:30 a.m.–6:30 p.m.

PROFESSIONAL SPORTS

HORSE RACING

**MANOR DOWNS
512/272-5581   east of map**
Quarter horses race from early March through mid-June at this pari-mutuel track located in the community of Manor, just east of Austin. You can try your luck at the

TRIVIA

Producers found the soccer fields at Zilker Park to be the ideal setting for *The Big Green*, a movie about soccer-playing youths.

simulcast races year-round. Hours: Call for post times.

FOOTBALL

DALLAS COWBOYS TRAINING CAMP
St. Edward's University, Austin
512/416-5858　　　　　　SA

From late July through the opening of football season, the Dallas Cowboys train at Austin's St. Edward's University. Scrimmages and practices are open to the public for free; call for the schedule.

HOCKEY

AUSTIN ICE BATS
512/927-PUCK　　　　　　EA

Austin's first professional sports team is the newly formed Ice Bats, part of the Western Professional Hockey League. The team plays 64 games from mid-October through mid-March and have quickly drawn loyal fans throughout the city eager to learn more about a game new to Austin spectators.

SOCCER

AUSTIN LONE STARS
12th St. and Lamar Blvd., Austin
512/335-0427　　　　　　DA

This semi-pro team plays at House Park Field, at 12th Street and Lamar Boulevard. An average of 1,000 fans frequent every home game.

UNIVERSITY SPORTS

The University of Texas is the closest Austin gets to professional league sports in most fields, and their play is followed closely by fans of the Burnt Orange throughout the city. The Longhorns football team draws huge crowds to Austin with every home game at Darrell K. Royal-Texas Memorial Stadium, formerly Memorial Stadium. During the winter months, both the Lady Longhorns women's and the Runnin' Horns men's basketball teams play at the Frank Erwin Center, the round venue located just off I-35 is also used for Austin's largest indoor concerts. The women's UT volleyball team also serves up a rousing game during the winter months usually at the UT Recreation Sports Center followed in the spring by UT baseball at Disch-Falk Field just east of I-35.

UT BASKETBALL, MEN'S
512/471-3333

UT BASKETBALL, WOMEN'S
512/471-3333

UT BASEBALL
512/471-3333

UT FOOTBALL
512/471-3333

UT VOLLEYBALL, WOMEN'S
512/471-3333

11
THE PERFORMING ARTS

Like so much else in Austin, the arts are thriving. Austin is committed to excellence, supporting the growth of artistic centers which are enriching life in the city by placing a premium on creativity and professionalism. The University of Texas Performing Arts Center hosts music, dance, Broadway, and comedy performances regularly, presenting major stars, great diversity, artistic integrity, and just plain fun. Itzhak Perlman, Pinchas Zukerman, Leontyne Price, Merce Cunningham, Willie Nelson & Friends, Marcel Marceau, and Asleep at the Wheel are some of the nationally and internationally known artists who grace the boards at Bass Concert Hall and Bates Recital Hall and the Paramount Theater. Music runs the gamut from choral to concert, from light opera to classics presenting guest artists.

Austin is so music-happy there are even noonday concerts at four venues. In dance, Ballet Austin and the Sharir Dance Company are joined by other local companies, such as Austin Contemporary Ballet, presenting everything from ballet to jazz to postmodern and innovative dance. Note: The map in this chapter shows locations of major performing arts venues only.

THEATER

AUSTIN CIRCLE OF THEATERS
823 Congress Ave., Austin
512/499-8388   **DA**
This theater alliance is a nonprofit corporation and umbrella organization for theater in Austin, funded in part by the City of Austin and the Austin Arts Commission and by a joint grant from the Texas Commission on the Arts and the National Endowment for the Arts. Call them to find out what's going on about town—theatrically.

AUSTIN MUSICAL THEATER
PARAMOUNT THEATER
713 Congress Ave., Austin
512/499-8388   **DA**

Texas Young Playwrights Festival

To encourage young playwrights-to-be, Austin's annual Texas Young Playwrights Festival, sponsored by the Dougherty Arts Center, the Capitol City Playhouse, and the University of Texas Department of Theater and Dance, invites all Texas writers under the age of 19 to submit plays to be considered for the festival. Submission deadline is in February, and selected works are given public readings and professional performances in the ensuing summer, giving young playwrights the opportunity to work with theater professionals. The program is made possible by a grant from the Texas Commission on the Arts and funds from Austin's City Opportunity for Youth Programs.

Like many others in the past, this new theater company is making its debut as a project sponsored by the Austin Circle of Theaters. The directors of the new company, both professional performers, decided that Austin was ripe for a sophisticated production company of classic musicals. The musicals combine Broadway-caliber leads with Austin's best actors, dancers, and singers.

CAPITOL CITY COMEDY CLUB
8120 Research Blvd., Austin
512/467-2333   NA
Here you'll find live, professional stand-up comedians, like Ellen Degeneres and Bobcat Goldthwait, who have performed on shows like *David Letterman*, the *Tonight Show*, HBO, and Showtime. An evening here can keep you in stitches.

DOUGHERTY ARTS CENTER
1110 Barton Springs Rd., Austin
512/397-1468   SA
This public visual and performing arts center offers theater performances, gallery exhibitions, and affordable arts education to all residents of Austin. The 150-seat proscenium theater, 3,700 square feet, is complete with lighting and sound systems, box office and concession areas, dressing rooms with shower, gallery entrance, and outdoor marquee. There is ample lighted parking for drama, dance, or music events.

TRIVIA

When the English National Opera's production of *War and Peace* came to the U.S., it played in only two venues in the entire country, New York's Metropolitan Opera and Bass Concert Hall at the University of Texas Performing Arts Center, where the facilities, amenities, and audiences are first class.

GREATER AUSTIN

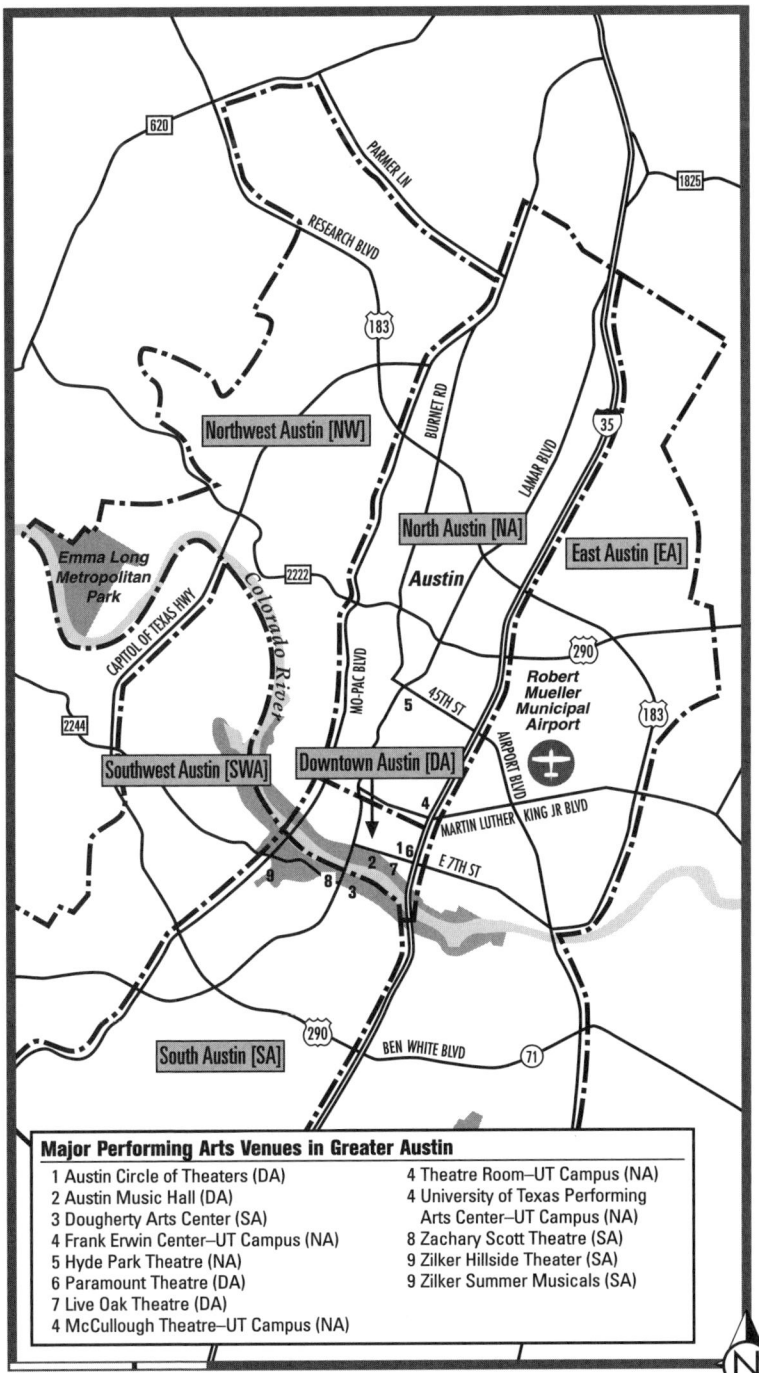

 Get half-price tickets for some venues on the same day as the theatrical performance. Call ahead because the selection varies. Dougherty Arts Center, 1110 Barton Springs Road, Wed–Fri 11:30–1:30 and 4:30–6:30; Sat 11–2. Also at the Visitors Center, 201 E. 2nd Street, Mon–Fri 8:30–5, Sat 9–5, Sun 12–5. To find out what's available, call 512/320-7168 or 512/397-1450.

ESTHER'S POOL
525 E. 6th St., Austin
512/320-0553   DA
Esther's Follies is one of Texas' premier musical and comedy troupes, performing hilarious original and topical satire and musical parody. Both revered and feared for its biting wit, the Follies are a centerpiece of the 6th Street entertainment strip with such buffoonery as "Boris Yeltsin" tap-dancing his way back to health, "Madonna" making Argentina cry, and "Chi Chi LaBomba" picking her man of the year. Not to mention Esther's classics like "Ode to Football Joy" and "The Jalapeño Chorus." Tickets $10 to $14.

**FRONTERA @
HYDE PARK THEATER**
511 W. 43rd St., Austin
512/452-6688   NA
Known for interesting and provocative works, the group Frontera is the resident company of the Hyde Park Theater in the historic Hyde Park neighborhood. The company puts on performances such as one called "the fringe theater event of the Southwest," with playwrights, dancers, and actors mixing media.

HYDE PARK THEATER
511 W. 43rd St., Austin
512/452-6688   NA
Productions range from comedy to tragedy and everything in between in this theater on the northern edge of the city's Hyde Park Historical District.

LIVE OAK THEATER
200 Colorado St., Austin
512/472-5143   DA
The only local professional theater performing on a regular basis and featuring local talent. The theater has more than 15 years of experience behind it and recent performances have included the *Dead Presidents' Club*, *Cabaret*, and *Sweeney Todd*.

**LOUISE T. PETER THEATER
Concordia Lutheran College**
3400 N. I-35, Austin
512/452-7661   NA
Concordia University shows, either premier or popular, are on the program here in the auditorium of the Peter Building. A recent offering was *A Midsummer-Night's Dream*; interesting speakers are featured as well.

**MARY MOODY
NORTHEN THEATRE
St. Edward's University**
3001 S. Congress Ave., Austin
512/448-8484   SA
The University of Texas is not the only drama game in town: St. Edward's University also has a fine drama department. This campus theater is the venue for the drama department's plays, often enhanced by well-known guest directors and stars.

Austin Symphony outdoor concert, page 178

MEXIC-ARTE MUSEUM
419 Congress Ave., Austin
512/480-9373   DA
Director Francisco Jacobi presents three plays a year of cross-cultural performances in the main gallery of this cross-cultural museum. The group within the museum is called Teatro Communitario en Español, and the plays, in Spanish, are works by contemporary Mexican playwrights. Tickets are $5.

McCULLOUGH THEATRE
2400 East Campus Dr.
University of Texas, Austin
512/471-1444   NA
For small operas and dance, call this number for information and tickets about student performances at the College of Fine Arts and for performances at Bass Concert Hall at the Performing Arts Center.

THEATRE ROOM
23rd St. at San Jacinto Blvd.,
Austin
512/471-1444   NA
Call this number for tickets and information about student performances at the College of Fine Arts and the Performing Arts Center. You'll enjoy small University of Texas shows in this cozy room, and you might spot a rising star.

VELVEETA ROOM
521 E. 6th St., Austin
512/469-9116   DA
Down on 6th Street where much of Austin's entertainment happens, visit here for stand-up comedy and cabaret-style selections, and perhaps get into the act on open-mike nights.

VICTORY GRILL/KOVAC THEATRE
1104 E. 11th St., Austin
512/474-4494   EA
This east side cabaret-style venue for small musical and theatrical productions aims to provide cultural and community revival through music. Wednesdays are usually devoted to Harold McMillan's Voodoo Jazz Jam, featuring different performers weekly, but on any given night the club will be open and there will be something

THE PERFORMING ARTS

Zilker Hillside Theatre

The Zilker Hillside Theatre is Austin's oldest performance space, a popular "people place" that has been a showcase for a wide variety of local performing arts groups. The natural grassy hillside can accommodate more than 2,500 people, who bring blankets to enjoy an open-air picnic supper while watching free quality entertainment. The theater is available to both arts groups and individual artists for performance events. Rental fees are reasonable; contact the Special Events office at 512/397-1463.

interesting going on, whether it's older, established musicians or younger, unknown players. Perhaps students will be working together, such as a group of teenage playwrights from the Outreach Program; or there might be dance or even Shakespeare.

**VORTEX THEATER AT
THE PLANET THEATRE
2307 Manor Rd., Austin
512/472-8644   EA**
This repertory company presents a variety of bold, alternative theater. A cutting-edge production of Shakespeare's *Julius Caesar*, for example, alternates with a cybernetic opera such as *Panoptikon*, a trilogy by Ethos. Tickets range from $9 to $12.

**ZACHARY SCOTT THEATRE
1510 Toomey Rd., Austin
512/476-0541   SA**
This professional theater is named for an Austin native turned moviestar. There are two theaters in one: the mainstage in the larger building and the Arena, a theater in the round around the corner. The long season runs from September to the following August, so interested visitors ought to be able to catch something. Productions in this regional theater (using both local and national talent) include musicals, contemporary comedy, and even "hard hitting" drama.

**ZILKER SUMMER MUSICALS
Zilker Park Hillside Theater
512/479-9491   SA**
The Zilker Summer Musical was created in 1959 as a project of the City of Austin Parks and Recreation Department and is funded both by the city and private patrons. Amateur and professional talent combine to provide memorable evenings with full orchestra, innovative sets, costumes, and choreography. The free performances at the Zilker Park Hillside Theater have run the gamut of successful musicals, from *Seventeen* in 1959 to *Once Upon A Mattress* in 1996.

CLASSICAL MUSIC AND OPERA

**AUSTIN CHAMBER
MUSIC ENSEMBLE**

TRIVIA

The Arts in Public Places ordinance sets aside 1 percent of the total construction budget for all new or remodeled public buildings, parks, parking facilities, and decorative commemorative structures for the commission, purchase, and installation of art. The Award of Cultural Contracts is another way the city promotes the arts, and these contracts allow local nonprofit, tax exempt cultural arts organizations to apply for funding from the city. Contract categories include dance, literature, theater, visual arts, mixed art, and music.

512/345-3399
The ensemble meets in private residences of their most devoted fans during their Intimate Concert Series; you'll feel right at home.

AUSTIN CHORAL UNION
512/472-9600
This community group meets in various locations and is open to any Austinite over 16 who has experience as well as musical skills. Typically Austin, it's a very democratic organization and serves as a backup chorus for the University of Texas Opera and presents its own season October to June.

AUSTIN CIVIC CHORUS, INC.
SCOTTISH RITE TEMPLE
18th St. and Lavaca, Austin
512/451-8863   NA
It's tempting to join in after one of these popular choral concerts, presented in various venues around town. The group consists of three entities. The first is composed of an oratorio group of 130 community volunteers, chosen by audition. A major orchestral chorus, they present a season of four concerts by subscription. (Tickets are $36 for the four performances.)

Their second group, the New Austin Singers, presents shorter and more diverse choral works of the sixteenth through the twentieth centuries. (Tickets range from $5 to $10.) The third group is the Summer Musicals for Children, with eight performances during weekends in early August. Past productions include *Snow White*, *Cinderella*, and the *Golden Goose*. Admission is free, with donations welcome at the door.

AUSTIN GILBERT
AND SULLIVAN SOCIETY
2026 Guadalupe, Austin
512/472-4772   NWA
Since 1976 Austin audiences have enjoyed light comic opera, proud to have their own viable Gilbert and Sullivan Society, delighting in the lilting lyrics and score of *The Pirates of Penzance*, the *Mikado,* and *HMS Pinafore* among others. Informal monthly musicals are free and open to the public, held at various homes of society members; more formal productions have been held at the auditorium of St. Stephen's School, and there is a grand annual production at a local theater. The society also takes the performances into the public schools so that youngsters can be exposed to music they might not otherwise have the opportunity to hear.

> **TIP**
>
> There are free screenings at the Texas Union Theater on Tuesday nights, hosted by the Austin Film Society. Take your choice of foreign, classic, or independent cinema by calling 512/322-0145.

AUSTIN LYRIC OPERA
1111 W. 6th St., Austin
512/472-5927   **NA**
For more than ten years this professional company has been performing such works as their signature opera, *The Magic Flute,* as well as other operatic favorites like *La Boheme*. Local artists fill the choir and orchestra, with guests artists such as Leontyne Price from major opera companies all over the world performing. They offer three annual productions, four performances of each, in the University of Texas' Bass Concert Hall. Tickets range from $10 to $80.

AUSTIN SYMPHONY ORCHESTRA
1101 Red River St., Austin
512/476-6064   **NA**
The oldest symphony orchestra in Texas is under the leadership of Maestro Sung Kwak, former assistant conductor of the Cleveland Orchestra. With its high level of performance, the orchestra delights Austin music lovers. The orchestra performs at the University Performing Arts Center, Bass Concert Hall monthly, September through May.

AUSTIN VOCAL ARTS ENSEMBLE
603 N. Lamar Blvd., Austin
512/442-1685   **DA**
The ensemble, formerly the Handel-Haydn Society, has become one of Austin's favorite chamber choirs. Some of the area's most talented singers consistently present quality choral music, both a cappella and with an orchestra.

NOONDAY CONCERT SERIES
512/472-2445   **DA**
For a pleasant lunchtime break, try some noon tunes at one of Austin's noonday concert series chamber music performances. There are several to choose from: Central Presbyterian Church (512/472-2445), Regents' Plaza (512/469-1766), the Texas Medical Association (512/370-1300), and right downtown at 311 Congress Avenue (512/320-7001).

RIVER CITY POPS
MCCALLUM HIGH SCHOOL
U.S. 290 and Cameron Rd., Austin
512/345-7420   **EA**
At these delightful choral concerts, the River City Pops pulls out all the

A performance by Ballet Austin

Austin CVB

stops, in costume and dance, presenting fully staged Broadway and show tunes in two major productions, winter and spring, each year. The chorus of 40 community members performs at McCallum High School, which operates a fine arts academy and provides a handsome auditorium. Tickets are $10 to $13.

UNIVERSITY OF TEXAS OPERA THEATRE
512/471-1444 **NA**

Call this number for information and tickets about student performances at the College of Fine Arts and for performances at Bass Concert Hall at the Performing Arts Center.

DANCE

AUSTIN CONTEMPORARY BALLET
4601 S. Lamar Blvd.
512/892-1298 **DA**

Formed in 1986, this is Austin's second-largest ballet company. The ballet maintains a professional academy with workshops taught by professionals from such companies as Alvin Ailey American Dance Theater, Atlanta Ballet, Lar Lubouvitch Dance Company, and the Royal Winnepeg Ballet. The company usually performs at the Paramount Theater.

BALLET AUSTIN
3002 Guadalupe St., Austin
512/476-2163 **NA**

Austin's first professional ballet company, formed under the direction of Eugene Slavin and Alexandra Nadal (like the Austin Civic Ballet), presents both classical and contemporary works during its fall to spring season. The company keeps getting better and better, testing itself constantly with new material and blending ballet with other forms of dance, such as tap dancing and tango combined with more classical plies and battements. But the annual offering, the classic reliable *Nutcracker,* is still performed every December to the delight of Austin and area children of all ages.

FLAMENCO AUSTIN
2110 B. South Congress Ave., Austin
512/397-1453 **SA**

Here you'll find lively Spanish dance in colorful cultural productions.

LOZANO'S ROY BALLET FOLKLORICA
1928 Gaston Place Dr., Austin
512/928-1111

This folklorica dance company has a fine reputation for authentic dances from south of the border, those from the states of Jalisco, Nayarit, Nuevo Leon, and others. Formed in 1982, they perform professionally at the Paramount Theater (adults $12, children and seniors $7) as well as at the Zilker Hillside

Austin's Annual Festival of Dance, which takes place every March, features local, national, and international dance companies. A sampling of what might await you: the San Francisco Ballet and the Dallas Black Dance Company among others. Call 512/406-6401 for festival information.

THE PERFORMING ARTS   179

Dial up Danceline, 512/474-1766, for a full listing of upcoming dance performances.

Theater free open-air concerts, in local hotels, and in the Austin Convention Center. They also perform in the Capitol Rotunda, and not too long ago their audience there was no less than the Queen of England.

SHARIR DANCE COMPANY
College of Fine Arts
The University of Texas at Austin, Austin
512/458-8158   **NA**
The Sharir Dance Company was organized in 1982 as the professional dance company in residence at the University of Texas College of Fine Arts. Led by award-winning choreographers Yacov Sharir and Jose Luis Bustamante, it has become the leading innovative postmodern dance company in Texas. The company produces three to four home season productions in addition to touring nationally and internationally.

TAPESTRY DANCE COMPANY
2521 Rutland Dr., Austin
512/837-8909   **NA**
All forms of rhythm and motion are combined in the diverse style of this company. This local touring company, directed by Deirdre Strand and Acia Gray, weave modern dance, jazz, ballet, tap, and rhythm into performances by the 12 members, three full-time dancers, and four apprentices. The company performs in Austin three times a year at the Paramount Theater. Tickets range from $15 to $18.

UNIVERSITY OF TEXAS DANCE REPERTORY THEATRE
512/471-1444   **NA**
Call this number for tickets and information about student performances at the College of Fine Arts and for performances at Bass Concert Hall at the Performing Arts Center.

CONCERT VENUES

AUSTIN MUSIC HALL
208 Nueces St., Austin
512/495-9962   **DA**
The roomy music hall hosts concerts running the gamut from rock to country, gospel to reggae.

FRANK ERWIN CENTER
University of Texas Campus
Off Red River and 15th St., Austin
512/477-6060   **NA**
The Frank Erwin Center is one of the largest live music venues in Austin. The 17,871-seat arena hosts a myriad of musical events and professional performances, often hosting concerts by touring mega-stars.

PARAMOUNT THEATRE
713 Congress Ave., Austin
512/472-5411   **DA**
Built in 1915, the Paramount is one of those ornate beauties left over from vaudeville days. Now beautifully restored, it's considered one of the country's most beautifully detailed historic theaters, and it shines for both classic movies on a

Austin Lyric Opera, page 178

big screen and local and national touring artists.

SOUTHPARK MEADOWS
9600 S. I-35, Austin
512/280-8771   **SA**

National touring acts love to play at Austin's largest outdoor concert venue. Spring and summer the sounds are mostly alternative music to heavy rock and country western, with such groups as the Steve Miller Band, Hootie and the Blowfish, Def Leopard, Jimmy Buffett, Sting, and the Horde Festival performing. Bring a blanket and sit on the lawn, or pay some more and have a reserved seat up front.

UNIVERSITY OF TEXAS PERFORMING ARTS CENTER
23rd St. at East Campus Drive, Austin
512/471-1444 or 800/687-6010   **NA**

Constructed in 1981, with no expense spared in building and equipping the center with state-of-the-art facilities, the Performing Arts Center is actually a complex consisting of five buildings. The acoustics are ideal at all of them. Bass Concert Hall is a 3,000-seat venue large enough to host the world's most renowned performers in touring Broadway shows or symphony orchestras. The lighting is controlled by computer and the orchestra pit can be raised and lowered. The smaller Bates Recital Hall is designed for smaller ensembles and for soloists. It contains one of the world's largest organs. The Opera Lab Theater is reserved for chamber

 All University of Texas student recitals are free; they take place at four locations: Bates Recital Hall, Jessen Auditorium, McCullough Theater, or the Recital Studios. Call the Music Department's hotline: 512/471-5401.

operas, dance programs, and productions of the university's drama department. The Center has hosted everyone from schoolchildren to princes and presidents; thousands visit the theater each year, which accomplishes the university's main aim: To bring people together to witness the marvels of the arts, to view exhibits, and to share ideas.

ZILKER HILLSIDE THEATER
Zilker Park, Austin
512/479-9491 SA
This is a free entertainment venue out under the stars in Austin's favorite downtown park. Pack a picnic to savor while you enjoy live music, a lively musical, or some very fine dance. For music under the stars, summer musicals feature local Austin performers mid-July to mid-August. The Bard under the stars is featured here in the park September through October; call 512/454-2273.

BUYING TICKETS

TICKET SERVICES
Austin Circle of Theaters Hotline
512/320-7168
This is a service provided by Austin's theaters, updated every Monday and Thursday mornings, giving theater listings, ticket availability, information on box offices, and half-price tickets where available.

AUSTIX
512/397-1450
Another ticket service, giving information on both half-price "day of performance" tickets and full service theater tickets for theater, dance, and performing arts events, depending upon availability. AusTix is located at both Book People (603 N. Lamar) and the Austin Visitors Center (2nd and San Jacinto).

PAC (PERFORMING ARTS CENTER, UNIVERSITY OF TEXAS)
512/471-1444 NA (on campus)
For events at the UT Performing Arts Center (Bass Hall, Bates Recital Hall, McCullough Theatre). Many but not all of the PAC events sell tickets through UTTM, 512/477-6060—see below.

THE BOX OFFICE
603 N. Lamar Blvd. (Inside Book People)
512/499-8497 DA
The Box Office is a full-price ticket service for smaller companies, offering sales over the phone via MasterCard/Visa as well as information.

STAR TICKETS
512/469-7469 or 800/966-7469
Handles touring acts and local concerts by phone and through a dozen locations in the central Texas area.

UTTM
in Texas Union Building
512/477-6060 NA
University of Texas TicketMaster handles sales for the Erwin Center and other UT facilities as well as some Paramount Theatre events and sports events. Outlets are all central Texas H.E.B. grocery stores.

12
NIGHTLIFE

Austin is especially noted for its music scene. Over 100 clubs have helped Austin earn the title as "The Live Music Capital of the World" and any type of music can be heard nightly from local and internationally known talents.

Much of the music takes place in the downtown entertainment district, 6th Street. This historic seven block area, which is sometimes compared to New Orleans' Bourbon Street, is home to many nightclubs and restaurants, as well as eclectic shops open during the day. Here the music starts late and the fun lasts until the early hours of the morning. All types of music are represented along this bustling boulevard where Austinites and visitors can enjoy an evening of club-hopping any night of the week.

Outside of 6th Street, the beat continues in clubs near the UT campus, at special events in venues ranging from the shores of Town Lake to high-tech concert halls, and at restaurants and bars throughout the city. The Austin Chronicle, *a free publication that's distributed at bookstores and grocery stores throughout town, gives an excellent rundown of who's playing where so that you can plan your night on the town. The* XLent *section of the* Austin American-Statesman *also offers a good look at the happenings in town every Thursday.*

Many nightclubs enforce a "21 and over" age restriction. Those permitting youth admission are noted in the text.

DOWNTOWN AUSTIN

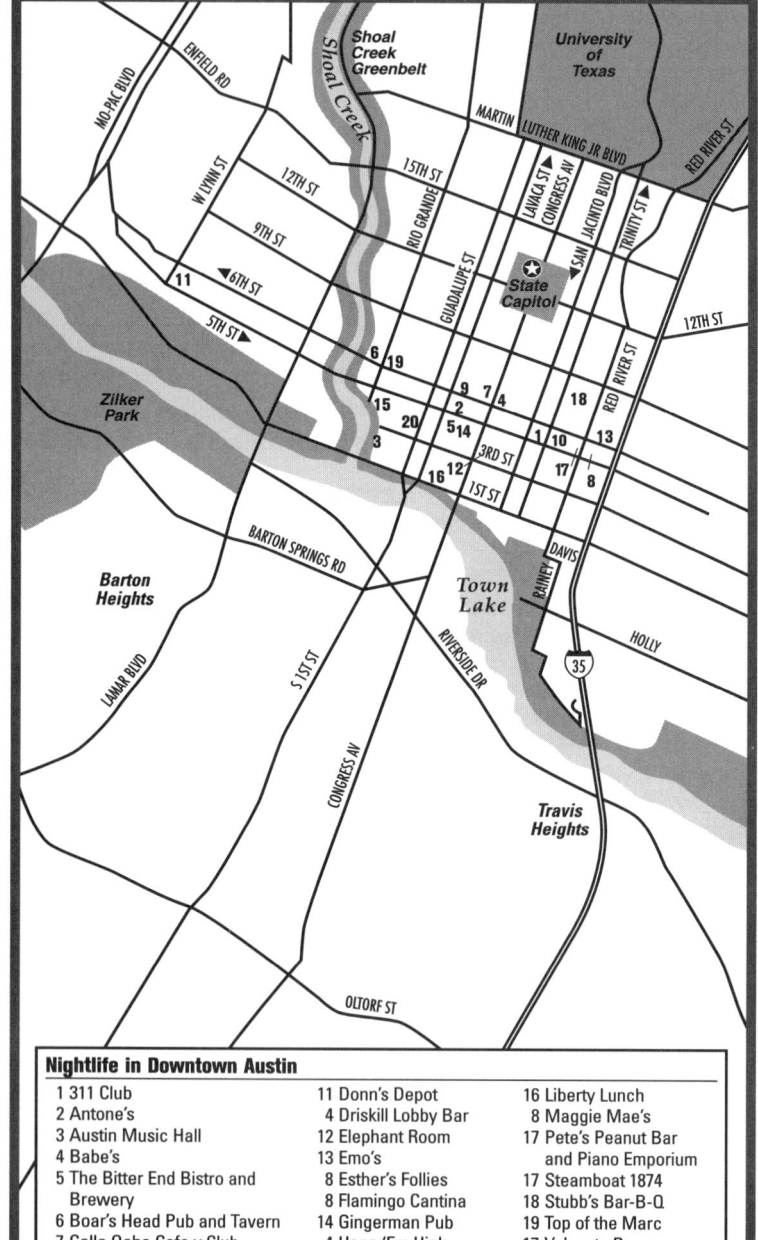

TRIVIA

Some top names on the Austin scene past and present include Rick Trevino, Ian Moore, Nanci Griffith, Tish Hinojosa, Butch Hancock, Joe Ely, Marcia Ball, the late Stevie Ray Vaughan, Willie Nelson, and Jerry Jeff Walker.

DANCE CLUBS

CALLE OCHO CAFE Y CLUB
706 Congress Ave., Austin
512/474-6605 **DA**
Feel the Latin rhythm of salsa or merengue at this pulsating dance club. Stop by early for a lesson then head out on the dance floor. Hours: Monday–Thursday 7 a.m.–9 p.m., Friday 7 a.m.– midnight, Saturday 8 a.m.–midnight. Free.

DANCE ACROSS TEXAS
2201 E. Ben White Blvd., Austin
512/441-9101 **EA**
Dance to live or DJ music with a country beat. Wednesday is ladies' night with no cover for ladies, a $2 buffet from 5–8, and $1 drinks from 8–11. This club claims to have the largest dance floor in Austin. Hours: Wednesday–Saturday 6 p.m.–2 a.m. Cover: $3–$7.

RUMORS
13233 Pond Springs Rd., Austin
512/258-9717 **NWA**
Shuffle to country and western tunes in this neighborhood bar and dance hall. Live bands are scheduled on Friday and Saturday nights with karaoke on Tuesday. Pool, shuffleboard, darts, and a large-screen TV keep things lively. Hours: Saturday 10:30 a.m.–1 a.m., Sunday noon–1 a.m., Monday–Thursday 10:30 a.m.–midnight.

TANGERINE'S
9721 Arboretum Blvd., Austin
512/343-2626 **NWA**
Part of the Renaissance Hotel but with a separate entrance, this dance club moves to the sound of current faves. Hours: Mon–Wed 4 p.m.–midnight, Thursday–Friday 4 p.m.–2 a.m., Saturday 8 p.m.–2 a.m. Cover: $8 Friday–Saturday.

MUSIC CLUBS

Jazz

CEDAR STREET
208 W. 4th St., Austin
512/708-8811 **DA**
Shaken, not stirred could well be the motto of this popular nightspot that's known for its martinis. Over 30 vodkas and 20 gins stock the bar with enough spirits to keep even the choosiest drinker happy. The bar is also home to Giganté, a cedar-lined humidor with some of the world's finest cigars. Hours: Mon–Fri 4 p.m.–2 a.m., Sat–Sun 6 p.m.–2 a.m. Cover: $3–$5 Sat–Sun.

DRISKILL LOBBY BAR
604 Brazos St., Austin
512/474-5911 **DA**
The quiet ambiance of the elegant Driskill Hotel makes this lobby bar the perfect place for a quiet drink and

Velveeta Room, page 197

a chat. Hours: Mon–Thur 11 a.m.–midnight. Free.

ELEPHANT ROOM
315 E. Congress Ave., Austin
512/473-2279 DA
Jazz lovers are well acquainted with this basement club. Very popular with the cool cats, the club is at the top of the list for true jazz buffs. Hours: Mon–Fri 4 p.m.–2 a.m., Sat–Sun 8 p.m.–2 a.m. Cover: $4 Fri–Sat.

JAZZ OF 6TH STREET
212 E. 6th St., Austin
512/479-0474 DA
Listen to the sounds of jazz at this lively 6th Street bar and restaurant. Hours: Sun–Tue 11 a.m.–midnight, Wed–Thur 11 a.m.–1 a.m., Fri–Sat 11 a.m.–2 a.m. Cover: Adds 50 cents to orders while bands are playing.

TOP OF THE MARC
618 W. 6th St., Austin
512/472-9849 DA
Located on the second floor above Katz's Deli (see Restaurants), this rooftop club hosts names like the Guy Forsythe Band. Jazz happy hour shows start the evening off right.

Hours: Varies with performance; call ahead. Cover: $6 Fri–Sat.

**PETE'S PEANUT BAR
AND PIANO EMPORIUM**
421 E. 6th St., Austin
512/472-PETE DA
Jazz and piano tunes keep the crowds happy at this centrally located bar. Hours: Tue–Thur 8–2, Fri–Sat 7–2. Cover: Free.

VICTORY GRILL/KOVAC THEATER
1104 E. 11th St., Austin
512/474-4494 EA
Musical and theatrical acts are usual fare, but on Wednesdays check out Harold McMillan's Voodoo Jazz Jam, featuring different performers weekly. Hours: Mon–Thur 9 p.m.–midnight, Fri–Sun 9 p.m.–2 a.m. Cover: $3–$7 occasionally.

Blues

311 CLUB
311 E. 6th St., Austin
512/477-1630 DA
You don't have to worry about remembering the address for this club, located at 311 E. 6th St. The smoke-

TIP

You'll find free blues concerts every week during summer months at Blues on the Green, a concert series held at the Arboretum in far north Austin at the intersection of U.S. 183 and U.S. 360.

---

filled club is small and nothing fancy, but offers some of the best blues licks in the city. Hours: Daily 8 p.m.–2 a.m.. Cover: Free.

ANTONE'S
2915 Guadalupe St., Austin
512/474-5314   DA
Known as "Austin's Home of the Blues," this legendary nightspot on the north end of the Drag has entertained audiences for over two decades. Since 1975, Clifford Antone has been drawing music lovers with some of the best blues names in the country. All ages welcomed. Hours: Wed–Mon 8:30 p.m.–2 a.m., closed Tue. Cover: $5–$15.

CATFISH STATION
408 E. 6th St., Austin
512/477-8875   DA
Look for musicians like Blues Boy Hubbard and the Jets at this soulful bar and restaurant. Chase away the blues with a plate of catfish and all the fixin's. Hours: Tue–Fri 11 a.m.–2 p.m., Tue–Wed 5:30 p.m.–11:30 p.m., Thur–Sat 5:30 p.m.–2 a.m. Cover: $3–$5 Fri–Sat after 10.

PEARL'S OYSTER BAR
9033 Research Blvd., Austin
512/339-7444   NA
This club may be located in a strip center along busy U.S. 183, but the atmosphere is pure N'awlins. After a Cajun meal, enjoy live blues in the late-night hours in this eatery

decorated with trendy black tiles and glass blocks. Hours: Sun–Wed 11 a.m.–midnight, Thur–Sat 11 a.m.–2 a.m. Cover: $3 Fri–Sat.

STUBB'S BAR-B-Q
801 Red River, Austin
512/480-8341   DA
Barbecue, beer, and blues. Stubbs has it all. The late Charles "Stubb" Stubblefield of Lubbock opened this popular joint that smokes with meat and music. A Sunday gospel brunch is scheduled weekly at 11:30 and 1:30. Happy hour shows at 5 p.m. Tuesday through Friday are followed by headliners. Open until 2 a.m.

Rock

BABE'S
208 E. 6th St., Austin
512/473-2262   DA
Rock as well as blues and country music keep Babe's hoppin'. Check out the itinerary for both the restaurant (which serves up burgers along with the blues) and at the stage. Hours: Sun–Wed 11 a.m.–midnight, Thur–Sat 11 a.m.–2 a.m. Occasional cover on weekends.

BACK ROOM
2015 E. Riverside Dr., Austin
512/444-ROCK   EA
This venue calls itself "The Home of Rock 'n Roll." Games and music keep the action moving. Hours:

NORTH AUSTIN

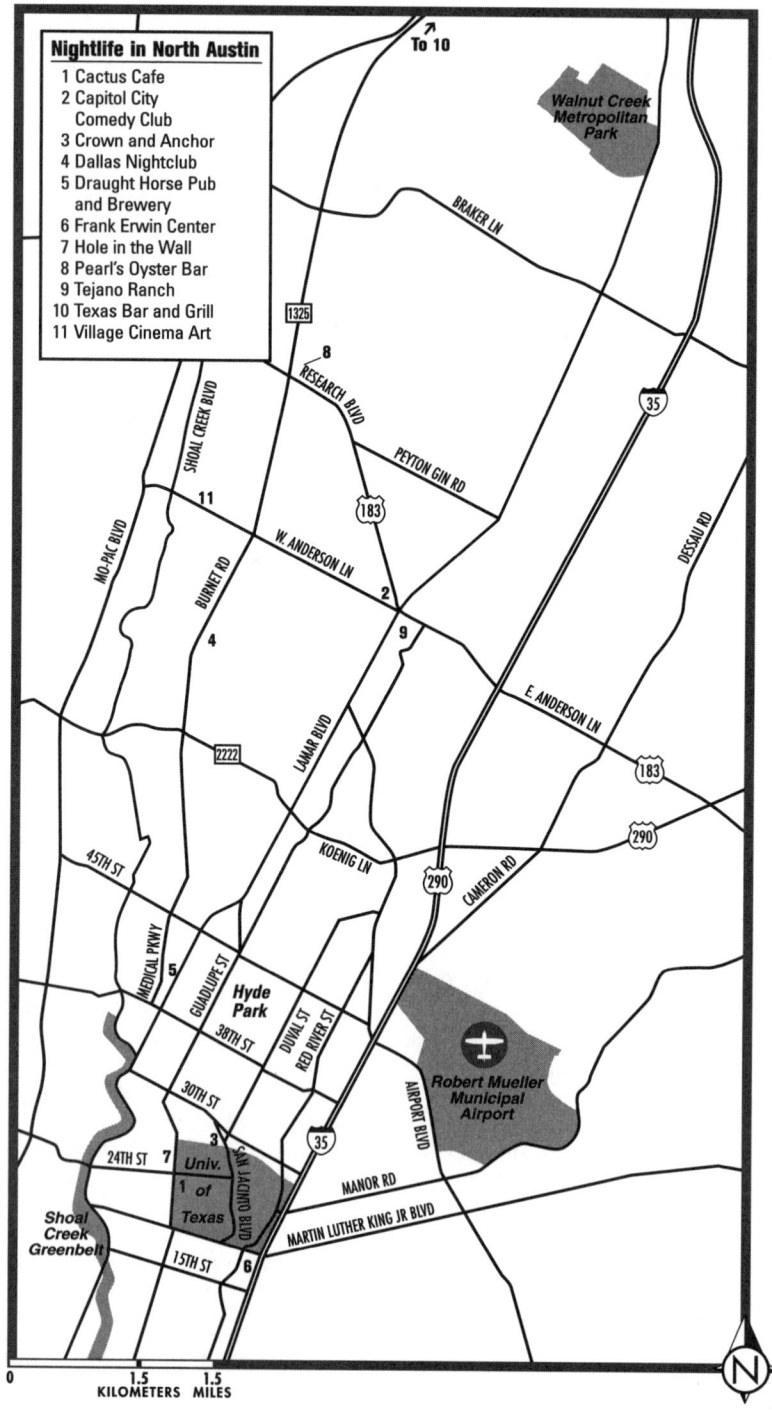

Daily noon–2 a.m. Cover:$3–$5 occasionally.

CONTINENTAL CLUB
1315 S. Congress Ave., Austin
512/441-2444 SA
Enter through doors that look like they belong on a Fifties diner, then enjoy a happy hour show from 6:30 to 8:30 or a headliner act during late evening. Advance tickets are available for some performers. Hours: Tue–Fri 4:30 p.m.–2 a.m., Sat–Sun 9 p.m.–2 a.m., closed Monday. Cover: Varies with show.

EMO'S
603 Red River St., Austin
512/477-3667 DA
Emo's is well known as the place to go in Austin to hear music when the funds run low. Enjoy national acts as well as local names at this alternative lounging club that has some of the lowest cover prices in town. All ages welcomed for all shows. Hours:

Guitar player at one of Austin's many music clubs

Austin CVB

7 p.m.–2 a.m. daily. Cover: $2 adults, $1 children; on weekends no cover before 10 p.m. for 21 and over.

FLAMINGO CANTINA
515 E. 6th St., Austin
512/474-9336 DA
Enjoy rock, reggae, and ska at this downtown club. Names like the Killer Bees headline here. Age 18 and older welcome. Hours: Open 8 p.m., no cover between 8-10 p.m. Show starts at 11:15 p.m. Cover: Varies.

HOLE IN THE WALL
2538 Guadalupe St., Austin
512/472-5599 NA
Located on the north end of the Drag, this joint truly does look like a "hole in the wall." For over two decades, fans have come here to enjoy local alternative bands. Don't come here for comfort, but for some of Austin's best sounds. Hours: Mon–Fri 11 a.m.–2 a.m., Sat–Sun noon–2 a.m. Cover: $3–$5 Tue–Sat.

LA ZONA ROSA
4th St. and Rio Grande, Austin
512/472-9075 DA
Dine on Tex-Mex either indoors or outdoors then enjoy the show. Early dinner shows feature Austin singer/songwriters. A Sunday gospel brunch and all you can eat buffet is scheduled from 11 a.m.–3 p.m. Hours: Fri–Sat 4 p.m.–2 a.m., Tue–Thur 5 p.m.–2 a.m. (kitchen closes at midnight), Sun 11 a.m.–11 p.m., closed Mon. Cover: $5–$10.

LIBERTY LUNCH
405 W. 2nd St., Austin
512/477-0461 DA
One of Austin's best-known clubs, this place is especially popular with touring bands. The large venue holds over 1,000 music lovers.

Austin City Limits

Many television viewers around the world get their first glimpse of the capital city through Austin City Limits, a public television program produced in a television studio on the University of Texas campus. Over 300 markets carry the popular show which spotlights Texas music, especially Austin performers. Past productions have included Willie Nelson, Guy Clark, Gary P. Nunn, Jerry Lee Lewis, Bonnie Raitt, and Austin's own guitarist, the late Stevie Ray Vaughan.

Tickets to the taping of the show are free, but difficult to obtain. Call the KLRU hotline at 512/475-9077 and listen for the artist, taping date, time, and the radio stations that will be handling ticket distribution. Radio stations will announce the time the tickets will be given away. Once the radio announcement is made, go to the KLRU offices in Communications Building "B" at the corner of 26th Street and Guadalupe Street on the UT campus. Two tickets per person are given away, but be warned—they often disappear within five minutes of the radio announcement. And once you have a ticket, you don't have a guaranteed seat at the taping. To ensure a full house, the staff distributes more tickets than there are available seats. Get there early the night of the show.

Even if you don't get to see the taping of the show, you can schedule a look at the Austin City Limits studio. Call 512/471-4811 to arrange a visit.

MAGGIE MAE'S
512 Trinity St., Austin
512/478-8541   DA
Located at the corner of Sixth and Trinity Streets, this club is always popular. Along with the bar, a party deck on the roof overlooking Sixth Street makes this a popular stop for live music. Hours: Daily 4 p.m.–2 a.m. Cover: $2 weekends.

STEAMBOAT 1874
403 E. 6th St., Austin
512/478-2912   DA
Steamboat has rocked with names like the Will Sexton Band, Ian Moore, Chris Duarte, and the Red Hot Chili Peppers. Opened in 1978, its first band was Christopher Cross. Today it's a favorite for those enjoying original live music. Beatles fans will find an entire wall of Beatles artwork and on October 9th the club always celebrates the birthday of John Lennon with a special show when Austin musicians perform the late singer's tunes. Hours: 8 p.m.–2 a.m. Cover: $3–$5.

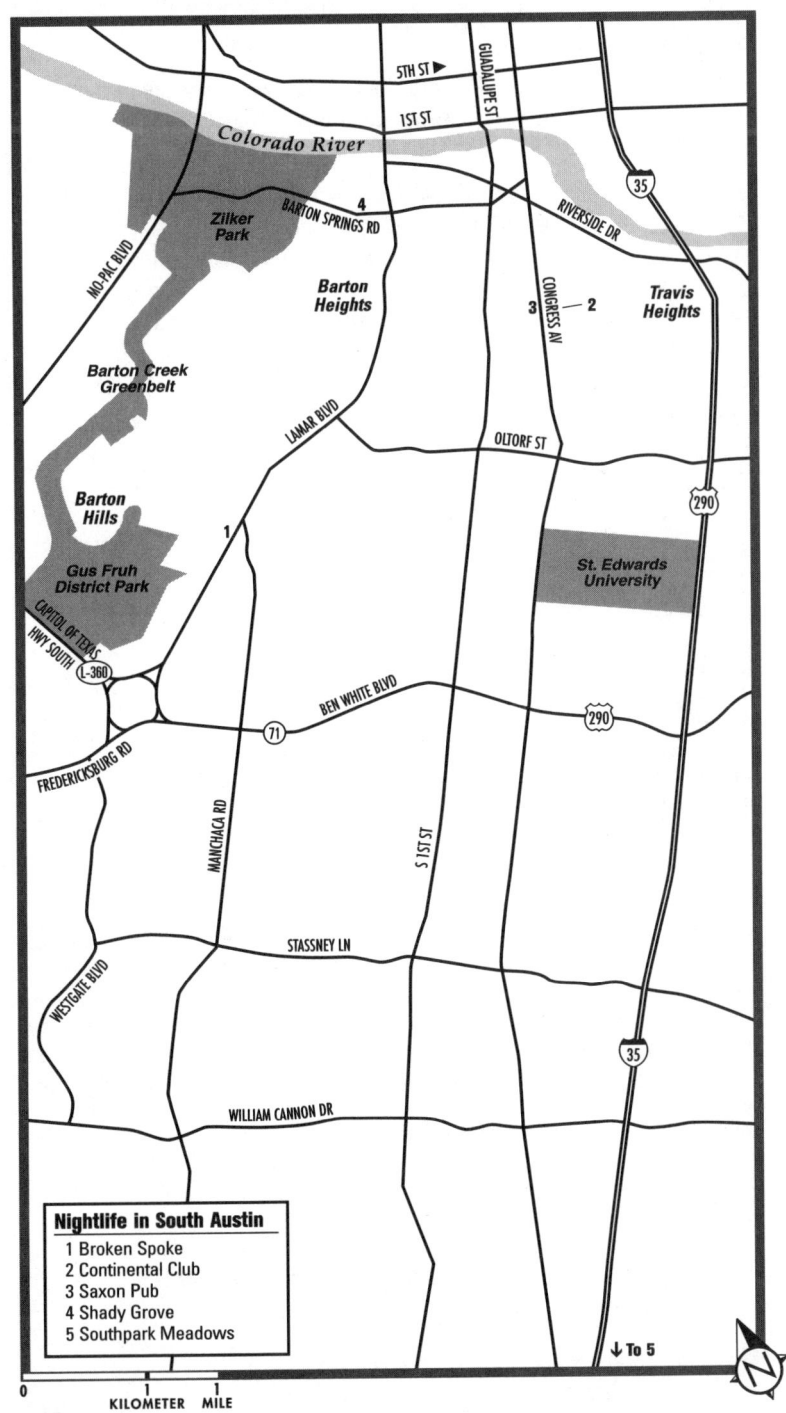

Top Ten Country and Western Songs Recorded in Austin

By Bob Cole
Host of *The Morning Call-In Show* and station manager of KASE 101, Continuous Country Music, KVET 1300 AM News/Talk, and KVET 98.1 FM.

1. "Amy's Back in Austin," Little Texas (reference to a famous Tex-Mex restaurant/live music club).
2. "Margaritaville," Jimmy Buffett (classic song written while artist was in Austin).
3. "Doctor Time," Rick Trevino (artist resides in Austin).
4. "Help, I'm White and I Can't Get Down," The Geezinslaws (artists reside in Austin; Sammy Alred is local radio legend).
5. "Pancho and Lefty," Townes Van Zandt (recorded and performed by Willie Nelson, written by an artist who is part of a group of legendary Lubbock songwriters that reside in Austin).
6. "Hey Baby, Que Paso," Texas Tornados (legendary musical artists who reside in Austin).
7. "Boogie Back to Texas," Asleep at the Wheel (Grammy Award–Winning artists reside in Austin).
8. "Highway Patrol," Junior Brown (artist resides in Austin).
9. "Hill Country Rain," Jerry Jeff Walker (legendary singer-songwriter resides in Austin).
10. "London Homesick Blues," Gary P. Nunn ("I Want to Go Home with the Armadillo," theme song to PBS music program *Austin City Limits*).

Country and Western

BROKEN SPOKE
3201 S. Lamar Blvd., Austin
512/442-6189   SA

The Broken Spoke is a real country dancehall—even though it's also a restaurant, with chicken-fried steak a big item on the menu. The Broken Spoke is famous for being the spot where Willie Nelson came to fame, and you're likely to find a cross section of Austinites here two-steppin' and boot-scootin' around the dance floor to the music of Don Walser or the Geezinslaws, or even sometimes Jerry Jeff Walker. The dance hall is closed Sunday and Monday. Hours: Tue 10:30 a.m.–11 p.m., Wed–Thur 10:30 a.m.–midnight, Fri 10:30 a.m.– 1 a.m., Sat 11 a.m.–1:30 a.m. Dance hall opens nightly at 8. Cover: $4 Wed–Thur , $6 Fri–Sat.

DALLAS NIGHTCLUB
7113 Burnet Rd., Austin

Keeping Up With the Austin Music Scene

The Austin Music Network offers music videos and footage shot at live performances with an emphasis on Austin and Texas musicians. This 24-hour channel broadcasts on Austin CableVision Channel 15 as well as on local broadcast Channel KVR-9 (Texas Student Television). Since 1994, this noncommercial channel has kept viewers up-to-date on the latest Austin releases.

The Austin Music Network offices are located in the basement of the City Annex (just west of City Council Chambers). Office hours are Monday–Friday 9–5. For requests, call 512/499-1810.

512/452-2801   **NA**
They say they're "a two-step above the rest." For almost two decades this nightclub has featured country and contemporary tunes. Hours: Daily 7 p.m.–2 a.m. Cover: Varies, averages $3.

DONN'S DEPOT
1600 5th St., Austin
512/478-0336   **DA**
Styled like an old railroad depot, Donn's is a favorite with Austinites looking for the 6th Street atmosphere without the parking hassles found in the busy entertainment district. The saloon includes a live band and dancing nightly featuring Fifties tunes, country, and easy listening. Hours: Donn's Depot is open Mon–Sat 2 p.m.–2 a.m., closed Sun. Cover: $3 Fri–Sat.

HANG 'EM HIGH SALOON
201 E. 6th St., Austin
512/322-0382   **DA**
Located right in the heart of the entertainment district, this dance club looks like an old-fashioned, Wild West saloon. Hours: Tue–Sat 4 p.m.–2 a.m., closed Sun–Mon. Cover: $5 Thur, $3 Fri–Sat.

TEXAS BAR AND GRILL
14611 Burnet Rd., Austin
512/255-1300   **NA**
This casual bar sports an open mike weekly as well as scheduled performers several times a week. Hours: Daily 11 a.m.–2 a.m. Cover: Free.

Other Great Music Spots

CACTUS CAFE
24th and Guadalupe Sts., Austin
512/475-6515   **NA**
Located in the Texas Union, the student union building on the University of Texas campus, this café features folk and acoustic performances in a smoke-free environment. Hours and cover vary with preformer.

SAXON PUB
1320 S. Lamar Blvd., Austin
512/448-2552   **SA**
Singer-songwriter performances by artists like James McMurtry and W.C. Clark make this pub a popular stop. Hours: Daily 10:30 a.m.–2 a.m. Cover: $3–$5.

SHADY GROVE
1624 Barton Springs Rd., Austin
512/474-9991   **SA**

GREATER AUSTIN

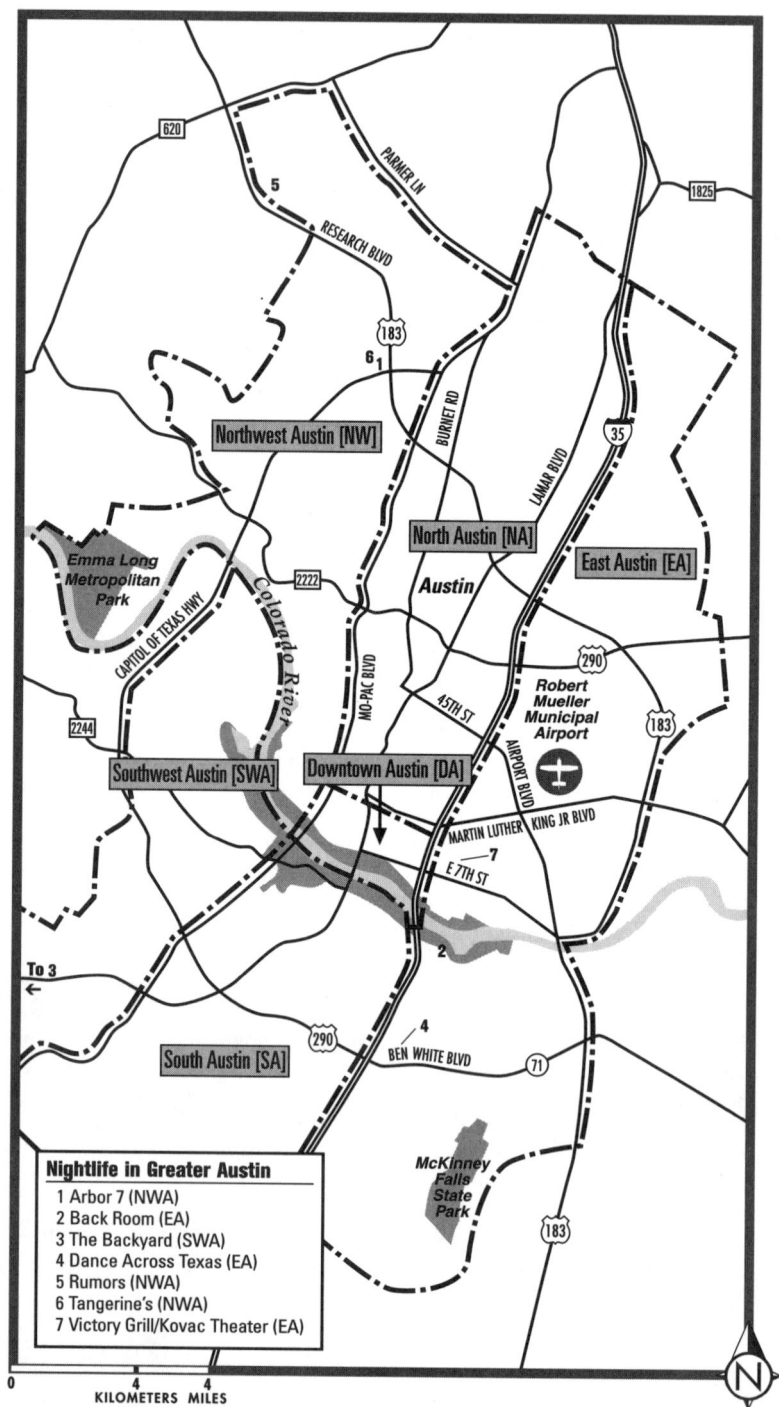

SXSW

The South by Southwest Music and Media Conference, better known as SXSW, attracts over 15,000 music buffs—including professional critics, musicians, and fans—to the capital city for music seminars and nighttime entertainment. Held in mid-March, over 600 acts perform at 42 clubs throughout town during the four-day festival. Wristbands permit music lovers to take in show after show, from rock to blues to Cajun music. The activities begin with the Austin Music Awards. For information, call 512/467-7979.

Acoustic and singer-songwriter sets, along with an excellent menu, bring Austinites to this funky eatery near Zilker Park. Tucked beneath tall pecan trees, enjoy music on Thursday nights with local talent like Asleep At the Wheel, Bad Livers, and such. Hours: Sun–Thur 11 a.m.–10 p.m., Fri–Sat 11 a.m.–10:30 p.m. Cover: Free.

TEJANO RANCH
7601 N. Lamar Blvd., Austin
512/453-6616   NA
Dance to sounds of Tejano and conjunto, a pop twist with a Tex-Mex beat. Live bands on Sunday, Tuesday, and Thursday. Tue–Fri 5 p.m.–2 a.m., Sat–Sun 7 p.m.–2 a.m., closed Mon. Cover: $3–$12.

PUBS AND BARS

THE BITTER END
BISTRO AND BREWERY
311 Colorado St., Austin
512/478-2337   DA
Enjoy fine dining at this brew pub (see Restaurants) or just come in for a taste of some of Austin's best brews. Hours: Mon–Thur 11:30 a.m.– 1 a.m., Fri 11:30 a.m.–2 a.m., Sat 5 p.m.–2 a.m., Sun 5 p.m.–midnight.

BOAR'S HEAD PUB AND TAVERN
700 W. 6th St., Austin
512/472-2739   DA
Select from 38 different varieties of beer at this charming pub, located on the west end of 6th Street. Pub grub, from grilled turkey sandwiches to seven-layer taco salads to chicken-fried steak, is offered. Hours: Mon–Fri 11 a.m.–2 a.m., Sat–Sun noon–2 a.m.

COPPER TANK BREWING CO.
504 Trinity St., Austin
512/478-8444   DA
Brick walls and wood floors give this pub the warm atmosphere of a restored warehouse. Favorite brews here include Big Dog Brown Ale, River City Raspberry Ale, Fire House Stout, and White Tail Pale Ale. Hours: Daily 3 p.m.–2 a.m.

CROWN AND ANCHOR
2911 San Jacinto, Austin
512/322-9168   NA
This bar boasts that it has the longest happy hour in town, extending from 2 p.m. to 7 p.m. The fun here includes

Austin's Best Brews

Brew pubs quickly sprouted up in downtown Austin when the state law regarding breweries was changed. Here Luis Ayala, a brew aficionado and home brewmaster, selects the best Austin-made brews and pubs.

Says Ayala, "Whether you are a beer connoisseur or just a beer lover, Austin is sure to have a brew just for you! Following is a list of selected local breweries and a few of the beers they make. Please note that not all breweries sell beer on their premises, and that not all of these beers are sold bottled outside the breweries."

- **Bitter End Bistro and Brewery**, *311 Colorado St., 512/478-2337. A very good selection of house beers and a complete food menu.*
- **Celis Brewery, Inc**, *2431 Forbes Dr., 512/835-0884. Tours available, no food, sold in stores. Try Celis White or Celis Grand Cru.*
- **Copper Tank Brewing Company**, *504 Trinity St., 512/478-8444. Full food menu most of the day. Try Cliffhanger Alt or Altbiers Big Dog Brown Ale.*
- **Draught Horse Pub And Brewery**, *4112 Medical Pkwy., 512/452-6258. Limited food menu. Seasonal house beers and a good selection of imported beers.*
- **Hill Country Brewing Company**, *730 Shady Ln., 512/385-9111. Available in stores only. Try Red Granite Pale Malt.*
- **Waterloo Brewing Company and American Grill**, *401 Guadalupe, 512/477-1836. Texas' oldest brewpub offers a full food menu, some beers bottled to go. Try Sam Houston Austin Lager or Viena Lager's O. Henry's Porter.*

pool tables and darts. Hours: Daily 11 a.m.–2 a.m.

DRAUGHT HORSE PUB AND BREWERY
4112 Medical Pkwy., Austin
512/452-6258 NA
This German-style pub lies tucked in a quiet residential neighborhood near Austin's medical center. Sample brews from around the globe, and on warm evenings enjoy a brew and a bratwurst at outdoor picnic tables. Live entertainment scheduled regularly. Hours: Mon–Sat 3 p.m.–2 a.m., Sun 3 p.m.–midnight.

GINGERMAN PUB
304 W. 4th St., Austin
512/473-8801 DA
Located directly next door to Waterloo Brewing Company, choose from

Coppertank Brewing Co., page 195

a wide variety of brews at this pub. Hours: Mon–Fri 2 p.m.–2 a.m., Sat–Sun 1 p.m.–2 a.m.

WATERLOO BREWING COMPANY AND AMERICAN GRILL
401 Guadalupe, Austin
512/477-1836　　　　　　　　**DA**
Come with a thirst to this brew pub. Some specialties of the house include Ed's Best Bitter; Clara's Clara, a golden ale named for Clara Driskoll; O. Henry's Porter; and Guytown I.P.A, an India Pale Ale. The pub is a popular lunchtime eatery as well, with plenty of pub grub including burgers and sandwiches as well as pasta, tacos, salads, and daily specials that include everything from pecan-crusted trout to veal parmigiana to pork empañadas. Hours: Mon–Sat 11 a.m.– 2 a.m., Sun noon–midnight.

COMEDY CLUBS

CAPITOL CITY COMEDY CLUB
8120 Research Blvd., Austin
512/467-2333　　　　　　　　**NA**
Get ready to laugh at this club tucked in a strip center along busy U.S. 183. Top names like Ellen Degeneres and Bobcat Goldthwait have entertained audiences here, as have up-and-coming comedians. Hours: Shows Sun–Thur 8 p.m., Fri–Sat 8 p.m. and 10:30 p.m. Cover: $10 Fri–Sat; $7 Sun, Wed, Thur; $3.50 Mon.

ESTHER'S FOLLIES
525 E. 6th St., Austin
512/320-0553　　　　　　　　**DA**
Since 1977, Esther's Follies has been satirizing Texas politics, parodying musical styles, and just tickling the funny bone of those lucky enough to take in a show. All ages welcome. Seating is on a first come, first seated basis, so it's recommended that you arrive at least a half hour ahead of showtime. Hours: Thur show at 8, Fri–Sat shows at 8 and 10. Cover: $14, $10 students.

VELVEETA ROOM
521 E. 6th St., Austin
512/469-9116　　　　　　　　**DA**
Down on 6th Street where much of Austin's entertainment happens, visit here for stand-up comedy and cabaret-style selections, and perhaps get into the act on open-mike nights.

CONCERT VENUES

AUSTIN MUSIC HALL
208 Nueces St., Austin
512/495-9962　　　　　　　　**DA**
Just west of the entertainment district, this renovated green warehouse has hosted performers such as Eric Clapton, Bonnie Raitt, Robert Earl Keen, and Sheryl Crow.

THE BACKYARD
13101 W. Hwy. 71, Austin
512/263-4146 SWA

On the west side of town, relax beneath shady oaks and enjoy an open-air concert at The Backyard. With rock walls, some picnic tables, and a casual atmosphere, the venue lives up to its name. National acts including Joni Mitchell and The Band have played here.

SOUTHPARK MEADOWS
9600 S. I-35, Austin
512/280-8771 SA

Bring along a blanket and stretch out to enjoy a top act at this outdoor venue. Some of Austin's largest concerts are held at this South Austin meadow located just off I-35. Sting, Hootie and the Blowfish, and R.E.M. have drawn crowds to this open-air venue.

FRANK ERWIN CENTER
University of Texas Campus
Off Red River and 15th St., Austin
512/477-6060 NA

Saxophone player at an Austin music club

Austin CVB

TRIVIA
Austin has more movie screens per capita than any other American city.

Also the home of Longhorn basketball, this 17,871-seat circular auditorium hosts nationally recognized touring acts. Concert goers enjoy concessions and reserved theater-style seats in this venue.

MOVIE HOUSES OF NOTE

Austin is sprinkled with movie houses. With its young, movie-going population, the city is often selected as a test market for flicks, so check for "sneak preview" listings in the movie ads.

ARBOR 7
10000 Research Blvd., Austin
512/346-6937 NWA

Located in the Arboretum, this cinema features seven screens, serves bottled water at the concession stand, and even has a high-tech lightning and thunder show every few minutes that flickers across the lobby ceiling. Admission: $3.50 before 6 p.m.; $6.50 for adults, $3.50 for seniors and children after 6 p.m.

VILLAGE CINEMA ART
2700 W. Anderson Ln., Austin
512/451-8352 NA

In this day of multiscreen movieplexes, the Village has one screen that's dedicated to the artsy films that rarely make it to the mall screens. Admission: $3.50 before 6 p.m., $5.50 after 6 p.m.

13
DAY TRIPS FROM AUSTIN

DAY TRIP: Fredericksburg and Enchanted Rock State Park

Distance from Austin: one hour

This Hill Country town of just over 7,000 residents located southwest of Austin bulges with visitors every weekend as travelers seek its small town hospitality and distinct German atmosphere. Whether your idea of a weekend getaway is curling up in front of a fireplace in a secluded log cabin, shopping for antiques, or touring historic sites, Fredericksburg's the spot for you.

Fredericksburg also has plenty of historic attractions, including the **Admiral Nimitz State Historical Park**, 340 E. Main Street, where the contributions of Fredericksburg native Admiral Chester Nimitz, World War II Commander-in-Chief of the Pacific (CinCPac), are recalled through museum displays. Behind the museum lies the Garden of Peace, a gift from the people of Japan. Follow the signs from the Garden of Peace for one block to the Pacific History Walk filled with a collection of military artifacts.

For a look at early Fredericksburg, visit the **Pioneer Museum Complex** at 309 W. Main Street. Or travel two miles east of town on U.S. 290, the **Fort Martin Scott Historic Site** was the first frontier military fort in Texas. Today the original stockade, a guardhouse, and a visitors center are open to tour, and historic reenactments keep the history lesson lively.

Fredericksburg is the capital city of Texas bed-and-breakfast inns. Give Gastehaus Schmidt a call at 210/997-5612 to learn about more than 100 properties, including cottages, log cabins, and a 125-year-old rock barn.

DAY TRIPS FROM AUSTIN

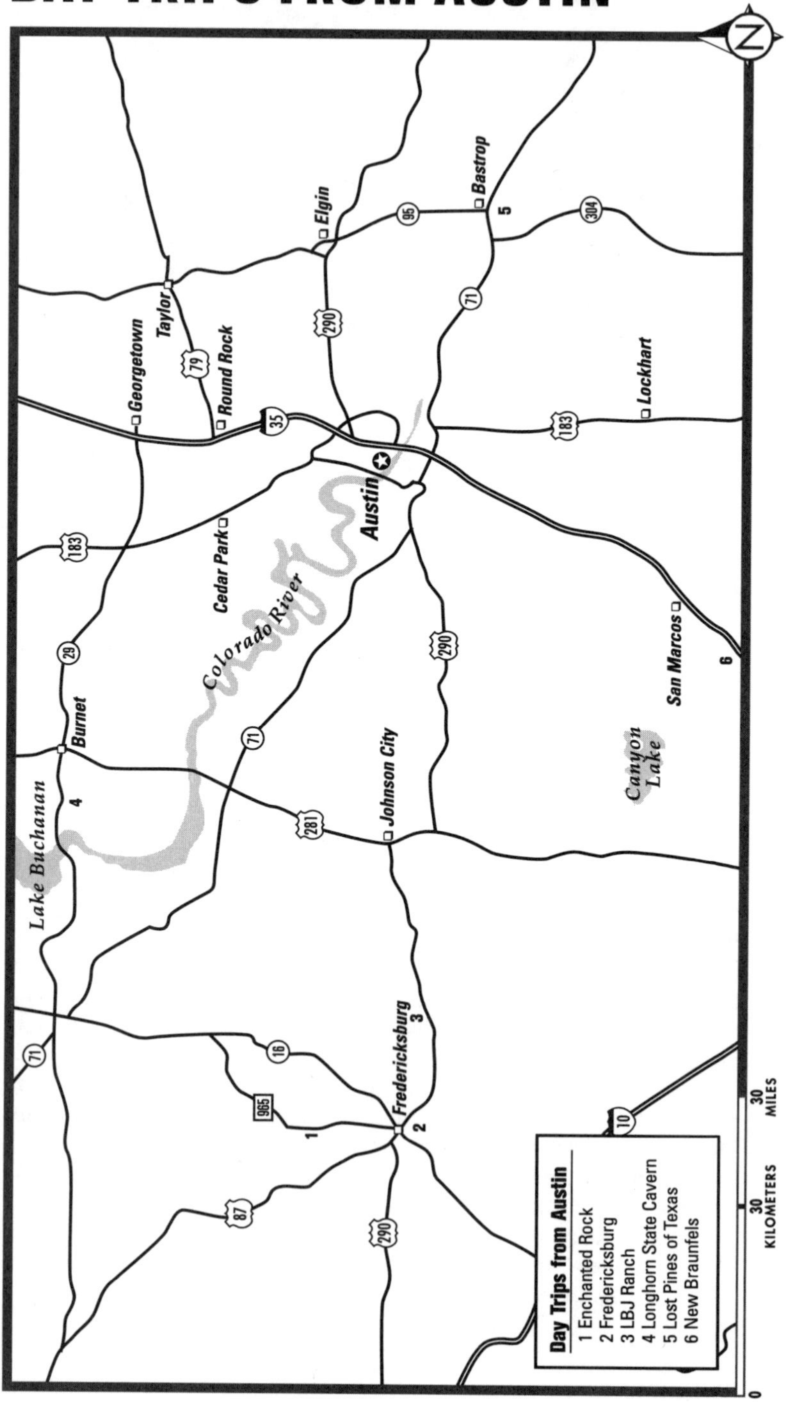

N
Day Trips from Austin
1 Enchanted Rock
2 Fredericksburg
3 LBJ Ranch
4 Longhorn State Cavern
5 Lost Pines of Texas
6 New Braunfels
Austin
Bastrop
Elgin
Taylor
Georgetown
Round Rock
Lockhart
Cedar Park
Colorado River
San Marcos
Canyon Lake
Burnet
Lake Buchanan
Johnson City
Fredericksburg
0
30 MILES
30 KILOMETERS

Enchanted Rock looms over the Texas hillside like a massive bald mountain, an enormous dome of pink granite that rises 325 feet above the small stream flowing at its base. Covering over a square mile, the formation is second in size only to Georgia's Stone Mountain.

See the granite for yourself with a walk up the dome. Bring your best walking shoes for the trek. Except when wet or icy, it is a fairly easy climb, though, and the view is worth the effort. Experienced climbers can scale the smaller formations located adjacent to the main dome. These bare rocks are steep and dotted with boulders and crevices, and their ascent requires special equipment.

If you'd like to extend your stay at the park, tent camping and primitive backpack camping is available.

For more information on Fredericksburg, call the Convention and Visitors Bureau at 830/997-6523. For more information on Enchanted Rock State Park, call 915/247-3903.

Getting There: Take U.S. 290 for 48 miles to the town of Johnson City; continue west for 30 miles to Fredericksburg. he park is located 18 miles north of Fredericksburg on RR 965.

DAY TRIP: LBJ Ranch

Distance from Austin: 50 minutes
If you're looking for a day of history and heritage, head to Johnson City. This is the land that President Lyndon Baines Johnson called home, just as his ancestors had years before when Texas was first being settled.

Start your visit in downtown Johnson City at the **LBJ National Historic Park** (U.S. 290 and 9th Street). Stop by the new Visitors Center for brochures and a look at some exhibits on the late president's family, then walk to the president's Boyhood Home and the Johnson Settlement, a restoration of the cabin and buildings which belonged to Sam Ealy Johnson, Sr., LBJ's grandfather. It's just a short drive to the **LBJ State Historical Park**, the home of the late president. Leave Johnson City on U.S. 290 to Stonewall, then turn on Ranch Road 1 to the park entrance. When LBJ was alive, much of this area comprised his private ranch. Security was very tight, and Secret Service men guarded the grounds.

Today, however, the National Park Service conducts tours of the LBJ ranch. Your visit to the park begins at the visitors center, a building of native rock constructed in a typical Texas style. Displays of LBJ's family, the ranch, and the Hill Country can show you what life was like during the pioneer times, as well as the hectic days when LBJ was president. A short walk away from the building are pens of huge buffalo, native white-tailed deer and wild turkeys.

While you're in the visitors center, sign up for a guided tour of the ranch. An air-conditioned bus, with a guide, will take you on a drive around the ranch and the back pastures. Along with featuring landmarks such as the **Texas White House**, the tour includes a look at this working ranch and offers visitors a peek at central Texas ranch life. Cattle graze lazily over the many pastures; ranch hands cut hay; workers clean the stockbarn used for cattle sales.

Getting There: From Austin: follow U.S. 290 west for 42 miles to the intersection of U.S. 281. Turn north and continue for six miles to Johnson City. The LBJ Ranch is located about 15 miles west of Johnson City on U.S. 290.

DAY TRIP: Longhorn State Cavern

Distance from Austin: 90 minutes

The area west of Austin is riddled with caverns, but the granddaddy of all Hill Country caves is Longhorn Cavern, near Burnet. Longhorn boasts an extensive history from prehistoric day through the early years of this century.

The earliest use of the cavern was by prehistoric man, but the most interesting events occurred since the 1800s. Comanches once kidnapped a young woman named Mariel King and brought her back to the cavern. The Indians did not realize they were followed by three Texas Rangers. When the Indians prepared a campfire, the Rangers fired upon them, grabbed Mariel King, and raced for the entrance. Meanwhile, the surviving Comanches regrouped and began their counterattack, falling upon the Rangers before they reached the cavern entrance. A desperate hand-to-hand battle took place, with the Rangers finally escaping with Mariel King. Ending the story with a fairy tale flourish, Miss King later married one of her rescuers, Logan Van Deveer and the couple made their home in Burnet.

Years later, Confederate soldiers used the cave's main room as a munitions factory. Bat guano from the cave was an ingredient in the manufacture of gunpowder. Additional small rooms in the back reaches of the cavern were used as storerooms for the gunpowder.

Enchanted Rock, page 201

The cave went unused for several decades until the Gay Twenties. A local businessman opened a dance hall in the largest room of the cave, building a wooden dance floor several feet above the limestone. When it proved successful, he then opened a restaurant in the next room, lowering food through a hole in the cavern ceiling. Next, an area minister decided to take advantage of the cool temperature and built bleachers to accommodate crowds for Sunday services. When the Depression struck, business declined. The private owners were forced to sell the cave. It was purchased by the state and opened as Longhorn Cavern State Park in 1932.

Burnet is also home to several other natural attractions. The **Vanishing Texas River Cruise** tours Lake Buchanan then heads up the cliff lined passages of the Colorado River. During the winter months, this cruise is popular with bird-watchers who come to sight the American bald eagles that nest along the shores. Campers enjoy Inks Lake State Park on TX 29, a 2,000 acre park with camping, lakeside picnicking, swimming, and a golf course.

For more information on Burnet area attractions, call Chamber of Commerce at 512/756-4297.

Getting There: From Austin, travel U.S. 183 north to the intersection of TX 29. Drive west on TX 29 for 22 miles to Burnet. Longhorn Cavern State Park is located on Park Road 4 off TX 29.

DAY TRIP: Lost Pines of Texas

Distance from Austin: 25 minutes
According to legend, the Lost Pines of Bastrop were a gift from an Indian brave to his new bride, homesick for East Texas. Scientists provide a less romantic explanation: the coniferous trees were left in central Texas when a shallow sea receded 80 million years ago. A prehistoric forest thrived across much of the state, but when conditions changed only an island of loblolly pines remained.

Regardless of the explanation, one thing's for certain: the Lost Pines are far from lost. This forest enclave southeast of Austin is found by over 600,000 guests annually. Today Bastrop State Park is one of the most visited parks in the Lone Star state.

Some of the most popular features of the park are the cabins, built by the Civilian Conservation Corps in the late 1930s. Two work companies came to the newly created park to plant pine seedlings and to construct buildings using native red sandstone. Paid about one dollar a day, these skilled craftsmen left a legacy of rustic style cabins furnished with hand crafted tables and carved fireplace mantels. Bastrop State Park also boasts a 365,000-gallon swimming pool, and a nine-hole golf course that's consistently cited as one of the top two public courses in the state.

But the popularity of this park has not infringed on the small town atmosphere of Bastrop. With a population of just 4,000 within the city limits and 20,000 in the community, this historic town holds onto its small town roots.

Bastrop dates back to 1829, the first in Stephen F. Austin's "little colony," located where the Camino Real, or King's Highway, crossed the Colorado River. Bastrop holds the honor as one of the oldest settlements in the state. Settlers came by the wagonload from around the country to claim a share of this fertile land and to establish a home in this dangerous territory. Even as homes were being erected, Indian raids continued in this area for many years.

Stop by the **Bastrop Chamber of Commerce** (927 Main Street) for a copy of "A Walking Tour of Historic Bastrop." The tour takes you past the 1883 Courthouse, the Old Colorado River Bridge, and many downtown businesses and homes.

Contact the Bastrop Chamber of Commerce at 512/321-2419) for brochures on lodging, shopping, or historic attractions. For reservations at Bastrop State Park, call (512) 389-8900. For general information on Bastrop State Park, call (512) 321-2101 or write Park Superintendent, Bastrop State Park, Box 518, Bastrop, TX 78602.

Getting There: Bastrop is located about 35 minutes southeast of Austin on TX 71.

DAY TRIPS: New Braunfels

Distance from Austin: 45 minutes

Grab your lederhosen and run, don't walk, to New Braunfels. No matter what time of year you visit, you'll find that this community (known as the antique capital of Texas) greets visitors with a warm Wilkommen.

Founded by a group of immigrant farmers from the Solms-Braunfels region of Germany, this city of 25,000 has never forgotten these ties to the old country. German is the main language in many local homes, and every fall the town hosts Wurstfest, one of the largest German festivals in the country.

Warm weather means outdoor activities in this community, many along the banks of the Comal River, at only two miles long holding the title as the world's shortest river. The river flows through **Landa Park**, a 300-acre center for family picnics and gatherings. New Braunfels' other river is the Guadalupe, where you can drift downriver in an inner tube beneath the tall cypress trees for hours. Outfitters will meet you at a pre-decided point and pick you up at the end of your journey. White water rafting and canoeing enthusiasts will also find plenty of activity on the Guadalupe.

Water lovers can't miss **Schlitterbahn**, the state's largest water park. With a German theme, the park offers stomach-churning thrill rides with names like Der Bahn. For those looking for a slower pace, there's a huge hot tub and paddleboats. You're welcome to bring a picnic lunch to enjoy along the riverbanks.

The rivers are just part of New Braunfels natural attractions. Drive out to Texas' largest cave, **Natural Bridge Caverns**, for a look at what lies beneath the Hill Country. Natural Bridge is a limestone cave, formed by underground waters. It's a showcase of glittery stalactites and stalagmites, with huge flowstones and rooms larger than football fields.

Just next door, animals are the star attractions at **Natural Bridge**

Admiral Nimitz Museum, page 199

Wildlife Park. This drive-through park is filled with both native and exotic species, ranging from some very pushy ostriches to excited zebras. You'll receive a bucket of food when you arrive, and the animals come right up to the car (and inside the vehicle if you leave your window down!)

It's easy to see why this town earned the title of antique capital of Texas. There are antique malls with dozens of vendors, small one room stores and warehouses of antiques for sale all over town. Another top attraction is the **Hummel Museum**, which chronicles the life of German nun Sister Maria Innocentia Hummel through her sketches, paintings, and personal diaries. It's filled with 350 original paintings and early sketches that spawned the popular Hummel figurines, plates, and other collectibles.

For more information on New Braunfels attractions, call the New Braunfels Chamber of Commerce at (800) 572-2626.

Getting There: New Braunfels is located south of Austin on I-35. The journey takes about an hour.

APPENDIX: CITY·SMART BASICS

IMPORTANT PHONE NUMBERS

Ambulance, Police, Fire 911
Fire Department Headquarters 512/477-5784
Police Administration 512/480-2922

MAJOR HOSPITALS & EMERGENCY MEDICAL SERVICE

Austin Diagnostic Medical Center, 901-1000
Brackenridge Hospital, 512/476-6461
Children's Hospital of Austin at Brackenridge, 512/480-1818
Pro Medical Emergency Center
North 512/459-4367
South 512/447-9661
Round Rock Hospital, 512/255-6066
St. David's Hospital, 512/476-7111
Seton Medical Center, 512/323-1000
South Austin Medical Center, 512/447-2211

VISITOR INFORMATION

Austin Convention & Visitors Bureau, 800-926-2282; Events Line, 800/888-8287
Austin Visitors Center, 478-0098 1-800-926-2282
Better Business Bureau, 445-2911
Citizen Information/Help Center, 512/480-0370 and 499-CITY
Greater Austin Chamber of Commerce, 478-9383

CITY TOURS

Around Austin, 512/328-6690
Austin Adventure Company, 512/451-3719 and 1-800-326-2264.
Central Texas Tours, 512/376-5000
Clark Travel & Tours, 512/272-5568
Gray Line Austin, 512/345-6789 and 1-800-950-8285
Heart of Texas Tours, 512/345-2043
Sjo-Pro Tours, Inc., 512/467-2345 and 1-800-776-4126
Unique Tour and Travel, 512/882-3791

CAR RENTAL

Advantage Rent-A-Car 512/388-3377 or 1-800-777-5500
Alamo Rent-A-Car 1-800-327-9633
Avis Rent-A-Car, 512/476-6137 or 1-800-831-2847
Budget Rent-A-Car, 512/474-6437 1-800-527-0700
Capps Van and Car Rental, 512/323-0003
Dollar Rent a Car, 512/323-9881
Enterprise Rent-A-Car, 1-800-325-8007
Federal Rent-A-Car, 512/255-1314
Hertz Rent-A-Car, 512/478-9321
National Car Rental, 512/476-6189
Payless Car Rental, 1-800-729-5377
Thrifty Car Rental, 512/474-2985

BABYSITTING/DAYCARE

Austin Families, Inc. (512/834-0342 or 834-0748) and **Kid Care Locators** (512/892-3135) help parents locate available child care. To verify that a facility is licensed, call the **Texas Department of Protective and**

Regulatory Services (512/834-0162) and ask for childcare licensing.

DISABLED ACCESS INFORMATION

ADAPT of Texas (Services for the Disabled) 512/442-0252
Services for the Deaf
Relay Texas, TDD, 800-735-2989
Relay Texas, Voice, 800-735-2988

MULTICULTURAL RESOURCES

Asian Chamber of Commerce, 472-7262
Capital City Chamber of Commerce (African-American Chamber) 459-1181
Hispanic Chamber of Commerce, 476-7502
Women's Chamber of Commerce of Texas, 346-2676
Austin Latino/a Lesbian Gay Organization, 472-2001
Austin Stonewall Chamber of Commerce, social and educational group for professional gays and lesbians, 707-3794
Metropolitan Community Church of Austin, church group supportive of gay and lesbian relationships, 708-8002
Out Youth Austin, education and support group for gays, lesbians and bisexuals age 22 and younger, 708-1234; youth help line 477-HELP
Parents, Families and Friends of Lesbians and Gays (P-FLAG), 302-FLAG

BOOKSELLERS

B. Dalton Booksellers
1202 Highland Mall, 512-452-5739
Northcross Mall, Burnet Road & Anderson Lane, Austin, TX 78757, 512/454-5125

Barnes & Noble Booksellers
10000 Research Blvd., 512/418-8985
701 Capital of TX Hwy. South, West lake Hills, 512/328-3155
2246 Guadalupe (opening summer 1997)

Book People
603 North Lamar, 512/472-5050

Booksource
13729 Research Blvd., 512/258-1313
4543 South Lamar, 512/891-9588

Bookstop
Crossroads Shopping Center, 9070 Research Blvd., 451-5798
Lincoln Village Shopping Center, 6406 North Interregional Hwy., 512/453-7297
Sunset Valley Market Fair, 5400 Brodie Lane, 892-1580
4001 North Lamar, 452-9541

Borders Books & Music
10225 Research Rd., 512/795-9553

Congress Avenue Booksellers
716 Congress Ave., 512/478-1157

Just For Us
9616 North Lamar Blvd., 512/451-3631

Paradigm Books & Lecture Notes
407 West 24th St., 512/472-7986

Waldenbooks
Barton Creek Square, 2901 Capitol of Texas Hwy., 512/327-1668

INDEX

Accommodations, 27-49;
Downtown Austin, 27-31;
North Austin, 31-38;
Northwest Austin, 38-41;
Southwest Austin, 41;
South Austin, 41-47; East
Austin, 47-49
Airports, 22-25; Robert
Mueller Airport, 22-23;
Austin-Bergstrom
International Airport, 23-24
Amusement parks, 115
Antiques, 144, 145
Arboretum, the, 100, 153
Austin City Limits, 190
Austin Convention Center, 5, 10, 77
Austin History Center, 77-78, 120
Austin Museum of Art at Laguna Gloria, 116-117
Austin Museum of Art Downtown, 117
Austin Music Network, 193
Austin Nature and Science Center, 100, 105
Austin Public Library, 78
Austin Rangers, 21
Austin Steam Train, 92
Austin, Stephen F., 2, 12
Austin Writer's League Creative Writing Camp, 103
Austin Zoo, 102
Austin's Bat Colony, 78, 102
Austin Children's Museum, 105, 107

Babysitting, 115, 206-207
Barnes and Noble, 110, 207
Barton Creek Greenbelt, 90, 138, 156, 159
Barton Springs Pool, 16, 90, 102
Basketball, 170
Bed and Breakfasts, 31, 37-38, 46-47, 49
Beer, 93, 195-197
Biking, 21-22, 155-156
Blues, 186-187

Boating, 156-158
Bookpeople, 110, 207
Borders (bookstore), 110, 207
Bowling, 158-159
Bus service (regional/national), 17, 19, 25

Calendar of Events, 10-11
Camp Mabry National Guard, 88, 96, 107-108
Camping/backpacking, 41, 47, 49, 159
Canoeing, 159
Capitol Complex Visitors Center, 78, 120
Car rental, 206
Celebration Station, 114
Celis Brewery, 93
Center for American History at the University of Texas, 83, 120
City Tours, 99, 206
Clarksville Pottery and Galleries, 126
Comedy clubs, 172, 197
Concert venues, 135, 180, 187, 197-198
Congress Avenue, 3, 5, 14, 16
Congress Avenue Bridge, 4, 8, 17
Country and Western, 193-195

Dallas, 15
Dallas Cowboys, 161, 170
Dance, 179-180
Dance clubs, 185
Day trips, 199-205
'Dillo bus, the, 17, 19, 78
Discovery Zone Fun Center, 114
Drag, the, 83, 144-147
Driskill Hotel, 4, 27, 29, 43

Elisabet Ney Museum, 5, 83, 117, 128
Emma Long Metropolitan Park, 41, 129-130, 158

Festivals, 107, 172, 179
Fire Island Hot Glass Studio, 126
Fireworks, 136
Fishing, 161-163
Fitness clubs, 163
Flatbed Press and Gallery, 126-127
Football, 161, 165, 169, 170
Frank Erwin Center, 180
Free-tailed bats, 7, 8, 78, 102
French Legation Museum, the, 16, 93, 120-121, 124

Galleries, 119, 124-128
Garage sales, 147
Gardens, 139-140
George Washington Carver Museum, 121
German Free School, 78, 80
Gethsemane Lutheran Church, 80
golf, 161, 163-165
Governor's Mansion, 80
Greenbelts, 82, 90, 139-140, 155-156, 161

Harry Ransom Humanities Research Center, 117
Henry G. Madison Cabin, 95
High-tech industry, 5, 6, 7-8, 10
Hiking, 108, 110, 159-160
Hill Country Flyer, 92
Historic districts, 16, 99
History, 2-6, 80, 95, 99, 121
Hockey, 170
Horse Racing, 169-170
Horseback Riding, 165-166
Houston, 15
Huntington Art Gallery, 119
Huston-Tillotson College, 1, 9

Ice cream, 112
Images of Austin and the Southwest, 128
Inner Space Cavern, 102

Jazz, 185-186
Jogging, 166
John Henry Faulk Central

Library, 112
Jourdan-Bachman Pioneer Farm, 103, 114
Just Imagine, 114

Kids, 100-115, 126, 132
Kidssports Family Fun and Fitness Center, 115

Lake Austin Spa Resort, 37, 39
Lamar, Mirabeau B., 2, 4, 80
Libraries, 4, 78, 80-81, 85, 86, 108, 111-112, 121, 123
Littlefield Fountain, 85, 97
Lone Star Riverboat, 80, 103
Lorenzo de Zavala State Archives and Library, 80-81, 121, 123
Los Dias de los Muertos, 119
Lyndon Baines Johnson Presidential Library, 85, 86, 98, 108, 121

MacGregor Park (Hippie Hollow), 81
Malibu Grand Prix, 115
Mayfield Park, 88
Mexic-Arte Museum, 119, 175
Mount Bonnell, 88
Movie houses, 198
Museums, 83, 85, 93, 105, 107, 108, 116-124; art museums, 116-120; science and history museums, 120-124
Music clubs, 185-195

National Wildflower Research Center, 88, 90, 103, 139
Neill-Cochran Museum House, 85, 123
Nightlife, 183-198
non-smoking, 57

O. Henry, 2, 5, 81
O. Henry Home and Museum, 81, 123
Oasis Cantina del Lago, 67, 70
Ol' Cactus Jack, 103
Old Bakery and

Emporium, 81
Opera, 172, 176-179, 181
Outlet malls, 154

Paramount Theatre, 5, 81, 180
Parks, 129-136
Pseudo Rock, 115
Public Art, 95-99; Downtown Austin, 95-97; North Austin, 97; Northwest Austin, 98; South Austin, 98-99; East Austin, 99
Public Transportation, 17-20, 158
Pubs and bars, 195-197

Republic of Texas Museum, 108, 123
Restaurants, 50-77; Downtown Austin, 52-59; North Austin, 61-64; Northwest Austin, 64-67; Southwest Austin, 69-70; South Austin, 70-74; East Austin, 74-77
Rock, 187-190

San Antonio, 15
Santa Rita No. 1, 86
Scenic Overlook, 90
Scenic View, 90
Schools, 8-9
Senior Activity Center, 86
Senior citizens, 19, 85, 90
Shoal Creek Greenbelt, 86, 138, 160
Shopping, 141-154; West End, 141-144; The Drag, 144-147; Kerbey Lane, 147-148; South Congress Avenue, 148-151; West Lynn, 151
Sixth Street, 81, 93
Skating, ice, roller, in-line, 167-168
Soccer, 170
South Austin Senior Activity Center, 90, 93
South by Southwest Music and Media Conference, 195
State Capitol, 81-82, 108
State Cemetery, 95
Swimming, 168-169
Symphony Square, 82

Taxi service, 19-20
Tennis, 169
Tex-Mex, 63
Texas barbecue, 69
Texas Memorial Museum, 108, 124
Theater, 171-176
Tickets, 174, 182
Tom Miller Dam, 5, 16, 90, 163
Town Lake Greenbelt, 82, 138, 155-156, 160
Town Lake Metropolitan Park, 133, 135
Town Lake, 3, 15, 16
Toy stores, 112, 113
Train services, 25
Treaty Oak, 82

Umlauf, Charles, 97, 120
Umlauf Sculpture Garden and Museum, 119-120
University of Texas at Austin, 3, 4, 6, 9, 86, 88
University of Texas Tower, 5, 88

Valley Creek Stables, 103
Veloway, 156, 168
Visitor Information, 206
Visitor Information Center, 82-83

Waller Creek Walkway, 83, 160
Weather, 11-13
West End, 83
Wild Basin Wilderness Preserve, 90, 108, 110, 160-161
Women and their Work, 128

Zachary Scott Theatre, 110-111, 176
Zilker Botanical Garden, 103, 105, 124, 135, 140
Zilker Dinosaur Trackways, 105
Zilker Park, 16, 93, 136
Zilker Park Canoe Rentals, 105, 159
Zilker Railroad, 105

Titles from John Muir Publications

Rick Steves' Books

Asia Through the Back Door, 400 pp., $17.95
Europe 101: History and Art for the Traveler, 352 pp., $17.95
Mona Winks: Self-Guided Tours of Europe's Top Museums, 432 pp., $18.95
Rick Steves' Baltics & Russia, 160 pp., $9.95
Rick Steves' Europe, 560 pp., $18.95
Rick Steves' France, Belgium & the Netherlands, 304 pp., $15.95
Rick Steves' Germany, Austria & Switzerland, 272 pp., $14.95
Rick Steves' Great Britain & Ireland, 320 pp., $15.95
Rick Steves' Italy, 224 pp., $13.95
Rick Steves' Scandinavia, 192 pp., $13.95
Rick Steves' Spain & Portugal, 240 pp., $13.95
Rick Steves' Europe Through the Back Door, 512 pp., $19.95
Rick Steves' French Phrase Book, 192 pp., $5.95
Rick Steves' German Phrase Book, 192 pp., $5.95
Rick Steves' Italian Phrase Book, 192 pp., $5.95
Rick Steves' Spanish & Portuguese Phrase Book, 336 pp., $7.95
Rick Steves' French/German/Italian Phrase Book, 320 pp., $7.95

Adventures in Nature Series

Belize: Adventures in Nature, 400 pp., $18.95
Guatemala: Adventures in Nature, 400 pp., $18.95

City•Smart™ Guidebooks

City•Smart Guidebook: Austin, 224 pp., $12.95
City•Smart Guidebook: Cleveland, 208 pp., $14.95
City•Smart Guidebook: Denver, 256 pp., $14.95
City•Smart Guidebook: Indianapolis, 224 pp., $12.95
City•Smart Guidebook: Kansas City, 248 pp., $12.95
City•Smart Guidebook: Memphis, 224 pp., $12.95
City•Smart Guidebook: Milwaukee, 224 pp., $12.95
City•Smart Guidebook: Minneapolis/St. Paul, 232 pp., $14.95
City•Smart Guidebook: Nashville, 256 pp., $14.95
City•Smart Guidebook: Portland, 232 pp., $14.95
City•Smart Guidebook: Tampa/St. Petersburg, 256 pp., $14.95

Travel+Smart™ Trip Planners

American Southwest Travel+Smart Trip Planner, 256 pp., $14.95
Colorado Travel+Smart Trip Planner, 248 pp., $14.95
Eastern Canada Travel+Smart Trip Planner, 272 pp., $15.95
Florida Gulf Coast Travel+Smart Trip Planner, 224 pp., $14.95
Hawaii Travel+Smart Trip Planner, 256 pp., $14.95
Kentucky/Tennessee Travel+Smart Trip Planner, 248 pp., $14.95
Michigan Travel+Smart Trip Planner, 232 pp., $14.95
Minnesota/Wisconsin Travel+Smart Trip Planner, 232 pp., $14.95
New England Travel+Smart Trip Planner, 256 pp., $14.95
New York State Travel+Smart Trip Planner, 256 pp., $15.95
Northern California Travel+Smart Trip Planner, 272 pp., $15.95
Pacific Northwest Travel+Smart Trip Planner, 240 pp., $14.95
Southern California Travel+Smart Trip Planner, 232 pp., $14.95
South Florida & The Keys Travel+Smart Trip Planner, 232 pp., $14.95

Other Terrific Travel Titles

The 100 Best Small Art Towns in America, 256 pp., $15.95
The Big Book of Adventure Travel, 400 pp., $17.95
The Birder's Guide to Bed and Breakfasts, 416 pp., $17.95
Costa Rica: A Natural Destination, 416 pp., $18.95
Indian America, 480 pp., $18.95
The People's Guide to Mexico, 608 pp., $19.95
Ranch Vacations, 632 pp., $22.95
Understanding Europeans, 272 pp., $14.95
Watch It Made in the U.S.A., 400 pp., $17.95
The World Awaits, 280 pp., $16.95

Automotive Titles

The Greaseless Guide to Car Care, 272 pp., $19.95
How to Keep Your Subaru Alive, 480 pp., $21.95
How to Keep Your Toyota Pick-Up Alive, 392 pp., $21.95
How to Keep Your VW Alive, 464 pp., $25.00

Ordering Information

Please check your local bookstore for our books, or call **1-800-888-7504** to order direct and to receive a complete catalog. A shipping charge will be added to your order total.

Send all inquiries to:
**John Muir Publications
P.O. Box 613
Santa Fe, NM 87504**

El Arroyo
1624 W. 5th Street, Austin, TX 78703
512-474-1222

$7 value!

Expires 9/15/99

Buy one enchilada dinner and receive second enchilada dinner free. Dine-in only between 1:30 p.m. and 6:30 p.m. Not valid with other discounts or daily specials.

CITY·SMART GUIDEBOOK — Austin

Mongolian BBQ
117 San Jacinto, Austin, TX 78701
512-476-3938

50% off!

Expires 9/15/99

Buy one dinner and receive second dinner at half price.
Valid only after 5 p.m.

CITY·SMART GUIDEBOOK — Austin

Frontera @ Hyde Park Theatre
511 W. 43rd Street, Austin, TX 78751
1-512-454-TIXS (reservations)

20% off!

Expires 9/15/99

20% off general admission; good for up to 4 people per coupon. Not valid with other discount offers. Must reserve seat prior to performance.

CITY·SMART GUIDEBOOK — Austin

Jourdan-Bachman Pioneer Farm
11418 Sprinkle Cut-Off Road
Austin, TX 78754   512-837-1215

$3 value!

Expires 9/15/99

Buy one adult admission ticket and receive the second ticket free.
Special events not included.

CITY·SMART GUIDEBOOK — Austin

CiTY·SMaRT™ GUIDEBOOK
Austin

John Muir Publications • Santa Fe, New Mexico

CiTY·SMaRT™ GUIDEBOOK
Austin

John Muir Publications • Santa Fe, New Mexico

CiTY·SMaRT™ GUIDEBOOK
Austin

John Muir Publications • Santa Fe, New Mexico

CiTY·SMaRT™ GUIDEBOOK
Austin

John Muir Publications • Santa Fe, New Mexico

Celebration Station
4525 S. I-35, Austin, TX 78744
512-448-3533

$4 value!

Expires 9/15/99

Buy one round of golf and receive one free.
Not valid with other discount offers.

CiTY-SMaRT GUIDEBOOK **Austin**

Just Imagine
Brodie Oaks Shopping Center
Loop 360 & S. Lamar
Austin, TX 78704   512-444-8898

$5 value!

Expires 9/15/99

Buy one general admission and receive second general admission free or
$5.00 off kid's night out admission price. Not valid with other discount offers.

CiTY-SMaRT GUIDEBOOK **Austin**

KidsSports Family Fun & Fitness Center
8015 Shoal Creek Blvd., #115
Austin, TX 78757   512-452-8775

up to $4.95 value!

Expires 9/15/99

Buy one children's general admission and receive second children's general
admission free. Must have adult attendance. Not valid with other discount offers.

CiTY-SMaRT GUIDEBOOK **Austin**

Live Oak Theatre
719 Congress Avenue, Austin, TX 78701
512-472-5143 (reservations)

$8 value!

Expires 9/15/99

$2.00 off full-price admission; good for up to 4 people per coupon.
Not valid with other discount offers. Valid Sept–June.

CiTY-SMaRT GUIDEBOOK **Austin**

CiTY·SMaRT™ GUIDEBOOK
Austin

John Muir Publications • Santa Fe, New Mexico

CiTY·SMaRT™ GUIDEBOOK
Austin

John Muir Publications • Santa Fe, New Mexico

CiTY·SMaRT™ GUIDEBOOK
Austin

John Muir Publications • Santa Fe, New Mexico

CiTY·SMaRT™ GUIDEBOOK
Austin

John Muir Publications • Santa Fe, New Mexico

Vortex Repertory Company at Planet Theatre

2307 Manor Road, Austin, TX 78722
512-478-LAVA (reservations)

two FOR THE PRICE OF one!

Expires 9/15/99

Valid for one complimentary full-price seat when second full-price seat of equal or greater value is purchased. Not valid for sold-out performances or guest artists.

CiTY·SMART GUIDEBOOK **Austin**

Austin Lyric Opera

Bass Concert Hall, UT Campus
512-472-5992 (reservations)
1-800-31-OPERA

10% off!

Expires 9/15/99

10% off Monday evening performances only. Up to 4 tickets per person. Not valid with other discounts. Mention coupon at time of reservation.

CiTY·SMART GUIDEBOOK **Austin**

Tapestry Dance Company

507 Pressler Street, Suite B
Austin, TX 78703   512-4-Rhythm

up to $14 value!

Expires 9/15/99

One free trial class for new students. Includes children and adults, beginning through professional levels. Not valid with other discount offers

CiTY·SMART GUIDEBOOK **Austin**

National Wildflower Research Center

4801 La Crosse Avenue, Austin, TX 78739
512-292-4100

$3.50 value!

Expires 9/15/99

Buy one regular adult admission ticket and receive a second ticket free.
Not valid with other discount offers.

CiTY·SMART GUIDEBOOK **Austin**

CiTY·SMaRT™ GUIDEBOOK
Austin

John Muir Publications • Santa Fe, New Mexico

CiTY·SMaRT™ GUIDEBOOK
Austin

John Muir Publications • Santa Fe, New Mexico

CiTY·SMaRT™ GUIDEBOOK
Austin

John Muir Publications • Santa Fe, New Mexico

CiTY·SMaRT™ GUIDEBOOK
Austin

John Muir Publications • Santa Fe, New Mexico

Austin Children's Museum
Second and Colorado Streets
Austin, TX 78703   512-472-2499

two FOR THE PRICE OF one!

Expires 9/15/99

Buy one full-price adult admission and receive one child admission free. One coupon per family. Not valid with other offers or during special events.

CiTY·SMaRT™ GUIDEBOOK   Austin

Umlauf Sculpture Garden & Museum
605 Robert E. Lee Road, Austin, TX 78704
512-445-5582

$3 value!

Expires 9/15/99

Valid for one complimentary admission when a second full-price admission of equal or greater value is purchased. Valid during regular museum hours only.

CiTY·SMaRT™ GUIDEBOOK   Austin

The French Legation Museum
802 San Marcos Street, Austin, TX 78702
512-472-8180

$3 value!

Expires 9/15/99

Buy one regular adult admission ticket and receive a second ticket free. Not valid with other discount offers.

CiTY·SMaRT™ GUIDEBOOK   Austin

Lazy Oak Inn
211 West Live Oak, Austin, TX 78704
512-447-8873

$10 off!

Expires 9/15/99

$10 off per night per two. Not valid UT football weekends, South by Southwest music festival and other holiday weekends. Mention coupon during reservation.

CiTY·SMaRT™ GUIDEBOOK   Austin

CiTY·SMaRT™ GUIDEBOOK
Austin

John Muir Publications • Santa Fe, New Mexico

CiTY·SMaRT™ GUIDEBOOK
Austin

John Muir Publications • Santa Fe, New Mexico

CiTY·SMaRT™ GUIDEBOOK
Austin

John Muir Publications • Santa Fe, New Mexico

CiTY·SMaRT™ GUIDEBOOK
Austin

John Muir Publications • Santa Fe, New Mexico